I N   A C T I O N

Measuring ROI
in the
Public Sector

TEN

CASE STUDIES

FROM THE

REAL WORLD

OF TRAINING

*Linking People,
Learning & Performance*

JACK J. PHILLIPS
SERIES EDITOR

PATRICIA PULLIAM PHILLIPS
EDITOR

ASTD Press is an internationally renowned source of insightful and practical information on workplace learning and performance topics, including training basics, evaluation and return-on-investment (ROI), instructional systems development (ISD), e-learning, leadership, and career development.

Ordering information: Books published by ASTD Press can be purchased by visiting our Website at store.astd.org or by calling 800.628.2783 or 703.683.8100.

Library of Congress Catalog Card Number: 2002103042

ISBN: 1-56286-325-8

Table of Contents

Introduction to the
In Action Series

Professionals involved in performance improvement are eager to see practical applications of models, techniques, theories, strategies, and issues relevant to their field. In recent years, practitioners have developed an intense desire to learn about the firsthand experiences of organizations implementing programs and solutions. To fill this critical void, the Publishing Review Committee of the American Society for Training & Development established the *In Action* casebook series. Covering a variety of topics, the series significantly adds to the current literature in the field.

The *In Action* series objectives are:

- *To provide real-world examples of program application and implementation.* Each case describes significant issues, events, actions, and activities. When possible, actual names of organizations and individuals are used. Where names are disguised, the events are factual.

- *To focus on challenging and difficult issues confronting professions in the field.* These cases explore areas where it is difficult to find information or where processes or techniques are not standardized or fully developed. Emerging issues critical to success are also explored.

- *To recognize the work of professionals by presenting best practices.* Each casebook represents the most effective examples available. Issue editors are experienced professionals, and topics are carefully selected to ensure that they represent important and timely issues.

- *To serve as a self-teaching tool.* As a stand-alone reference, each volume is a practical learning tool that fully explores numerous topics and issues.

- *To present a medium for teaching groups about the practical aspects of performance improvement.* Each book is a useful supplement to general and specialized textbooks and serves as a discussion guide to enhance learning in formal and informal settings.

These cases will challenge and motivate you. The new insights you gain will serve as an impetus for positive change in your organization.

If you have a case that might serve the same purpose for other professionals, please contact me. New casebooks are being developed. If you have suggestions on ways to improve the *In Action* series, your input is welcomed.

Jack J. Phillips
Series Editor
Box 380637
Birmingham, AL 35238-0637

Preface

Since the publication of *Measuring Return on Investment,* volume 1, the interest in measuring the return on investment (ROI) in training and performance improvement continues to grow. Volume 1 filled an important void in the training literature. Published in 1994, it remains one of ASTD's all-time bestsellers. Volume 2, published in 1997, demonstrated further progress with measuring the return on investment in a variety of programs. Volume 3, published in 2001, has also proven to be successful in that it provides evidence of even greater success in implementing ROI.

Measuring ROI in the Public Sector will add a new dimension to the *Measuring Return on Investment* volumes. There is a movement in the public sector to increase accountability of all processes—not only training programs within the organization environment, but education programs in academic settings as well as community development programs. Accountability is not isolated to one sector, one industry, or one type of program. Its importance proliferates organizations and programs of all types. But the actual implementation of accountability processes is still in its infancy in many sectors, industries, organizations, and programs. The public sector is one area in which accountability, more specifically ROI, is just beginning to grow—but it is growing rapidly.

Measuring ROI in the Public Sector is a first attempt to publish case studies exclusively from the public sector. It incorporates case studies from a variety of organizations. The authors of these case studies are diligently pursuing accountability in their areas of expertise. Through their writing, they share their experiences with a process that continues to be at the forefront of measurement and evaluation.

Target Audience

The book should interest anyone interested in building accountability into various specific programs, including training, education, human resources, and community development initiatives. The primary audience is practitioners who are struggling to determine the value of programs. They are the ones who request more real-word examples. This same group also expresses concern that there are too many models, methods, strategies, and theories, and too few examples to show if any of them has really made a difference. This publication should satisfy practitioners' needs, by providing successful examples of the implementation of comprehensive evaluation processes.

The second audience comprises instructors and professors. Whether they choose this book for students in university classes or public seminars on program evaluation, the casebook will be a valuable reference. This book can also serve to supplement textbooks on program evaluation, training and education in the public sector, and human resources programs. The combination of text and casebooks offers the technical details of the measurement and evaluation process along with examples of practical applications, which together show participants that the measurement and evaluation process makes a difference.

A third audience is composed of the researchers and consultants who are seeking ways to document results from programs. This book provides additional insight into how to satisfy the client with impressive results. It shows the application of a wide range of models and techniques, some of which are based on sound theory and logical assumptions and others of which may not fare well under close examination. Unfortunately, a prescribed set of standards and techniques for measuring the ROI of public sector programs does not exist. But the case studies in this volume represent many steps and methodologies that are becoming routine practices in private sector organizations as well as a few public sector organizations.

The last audience is made up of managers who must work on a peripheral basis—managers who are participants in many of various training and education programs to develop their own management skills, managers who send other employees to participate in the various programs, and managers who occasionally lead or conduct many of the programs themselves. In these roles, managers must understand the process and appreciate the value such programs bring to an organization. This casebook should provide evidence of this value.

Each audience should find the casebook entertaining and engaging reading. Questions are placed at the end of each case to stimulate additional thought and discussion. One of the most effective ways to maximize the usefulness of this book is through group discussions, using the questions to develop and dissect the issues, techniques, methodologies, and results.

The Cases

The most difficult part of developing this book was to identify case authors who were implementing a credible and practical process to measure the ROI of public sector programs and were willing to share their experience. In partnership with the International Personnel Management Association (IPMA), approximately 5,000 letters were sent to its members along with as many members of ASTD. In order to tap the global market, about 1,500 of these letters were sent internationally. We were pleased with the number of responses and have selected 10 case studies to be presented in this volume.

The authors of the case studies we selected attempted to meet very specific guidelines. The guidelines required that each case study include data that was converted to a monetary value so that ROI could be calculated. This fifth level of Donald Kirkpatrick's four-level evaluation framework, created by Jack Phillips, aligns the return on the program investment with that of other operational investments in organizations. (A description of Kirkpatrick's evaluation framework appears in his book *Evaluating Training Programs,* published in 1998. Further information on the fifth level is available in Phillips' article "The Search for Best Practices" in the February 1996 issue of *Training & Development.*) The selected case studies were also required to provide a method of isolating the effects of the program. The isolation step is imperative in showing the true value of a program. Through our attempt to ensure that all ROI studies met the specific criteria, we found that many public sector organizations are still grappling with both the data conversion and isolation issues. While these issues are imperative for a credible ROI, those case studies in which these steps were omitted still provide some indication of program success as well as efforts to bring accountability to the programs.

Although there was some attempt to structure cases similarly, they are not identical in style and content. It is important for the reader to experience the programs as they were developed and identify the issues pertinent to each particular setting and situation. The result is a variety of presentations with a variety of styles. Some cases are brief and to the point, outlining precisely what happened and what was achieved. Others provide more detailed background information, including how the need for the program was determined, the personalities involved, and how their backgrounds and biases created a unique situation.

In some cases, the name of the organization is identified, as are the individuals who were involved. In others, the organization's name is disguised at the request of either the organization or the case author. In today's competitive world and in situations where there is an attempt to explore new territory, it is understandable that an organization might choose not to be identified. Identification should not be a critical issue, however. Though some cases are lightly modified, they are based on real-world situations faced by real people.

Case Authors

It would be difficult to find a more impressive group of contributors than those for this casebook. For such a difficult topic, we expected to find the best, and we were not disappointed. If we had to describe the group, we would say they are experienced, professional, knowledgeable, and on the leading edge of their chosen fields. Collectively, they represent practitioners, consultants, researchers, and professors.

Best Practices?

In our search for cases, we contacted well-known public sector organizations, leading experts in the field, and prominent authors and researchers. We were seeking examples that represent best practices in measurement and evaluation in the public sector. Whether they have been delivered, we will never know. What we do know is that if these are not best practices, no other publication can claim to have them either.

Suggestions

We would like to hear from you and understand how you are doing with ROI implementation. If you are working on a project and would like to share your thoughts, please contact us. If you have ideas or recommendations regarding presentation, selection, or quality of the case studies in this casebook, please send them to me. You can contact me with your comments and suggestions at The Chelsea Group, Box 380637, Birmingham, AL 35238-0637, or email me at thechelseagroup@aol.com.

Acknowledgments

Although this casebook is a collective work of many individuals, the first acknowledgment must go to all the case authors. They are appreciated not only for their commitment to developing their case studies, but also for their interest in furthering the development and implementation of ROI evaluation in their organization. We also want to acknowledge the organizations that have allowed us to use their names and programs for publication. We realize this action is not without risk. We trust the final product has portrayed them as progressive organizations interested in results and willing to try new processes and techniques.

I would also like to thank two key individuals in making this publication a success. Neil Reichenberg, executive director of IPMA, immediately liked the idea of partnering with us on this project. This provided us the impetus needed to pursue the topic further. Also, Judith Brown, director of HR research for IPMA, diligently worked to promote our efforts to gather case studies and make this publication a success.

Thanks also go to two invaluable resource individuals who try to keep everything on track. First to Joyce Alff, our director of publishing and editor extraordinaire. Alff ensured that case authors received appropriate assistance and feedback in developing their case studies. She also worked to ensure deadlines were met and coordinated our efforts with ASTD. Thanks also go to Francine Hawkins, who handles all the "stuff" and is a greatly appreciated asset.

Many thanks go to Ruth Stadius, ASTD's director of publications. Ruth is always supportive and willing to help to ensure the success of each casebook. Ruth has a sincere desire to develop quality publications for the ASTD membership. She is a great supporter, and I appreciate her many efforts.

Finally, thanks go to my number one supporter—my husband, Jack Phillips. Jack is always supportive and encouraging and is the one person who can lighten my load even in the most stressful of situations. He has a real passion for his work and has given me the opportunity to add my "two cents" to a process he developed many years ago. His support and input during the development of this casebook are greatly appreciated, as they are in all of our endeavors!

Patricia Pulliam Phillips
Birmingham, Alabama
April 2002

The American Society for Training & Development would like to recognize the International Personnel Management Association for contributing its support and resources to this significant research effort, without which this publication would not be possible.

How to Use This Casebook

These cases present a variety of approaches to evaluating training, performance improvement, human resources, and other types of programs and solutions. Most of the cases focus on evaluation at the ultimate level—return on investment (ROI). Collectively, the cases offer a wide range of settings, methods, techniques, strategies, and approaches and represent all levels of governmental organizations. Target groups for the programs vary from all employees to managers to specialists. As a group, these cases represent a rich source of information about the strategies of some of the best practitioners, consultants, and researchers in the field.

Each case does not necessarily represent the ideal approach for the specific situation. In every case it is possible to identify areas that could benefit from refinement and improvement. That is part of the learning process—to build on the work of other people. Although the implementation processes are contextual, the methods and techniques can be used in other organizations.

Table 1 represents basic descriptions of the cases in the order in which they appear in the book. This table can serve as a quick reference for readers who want to examine the implementation approach for a particular type of program, audience, or level of government.

Using the Cases

There are several ways to use this book. It will be helpful to anyone who wants to see real-life examples of the return on investment. Specifically, four uses are recommended:

1. This book will be useful to professionals as a basic reference of practical applications of measurement and evaluation. A reader can analyze and dissect each of the cases to develop an understanding of the issues, approaches, and, most of all, possible refinements or improvements.

2. This book will be useful in group discussions in which interested individuals can react to the material, offer different perspectives, and draw conclusions about approaches and techniques. The questions at

Table 1. Overview of case studies.

Case	Industry	Focus of Case	Key Participants
Department of Veterans Affairs Sunshine Health Care Network	Veterans health administration	Develop future leaders for the organization.	Education program designers, VA employee educators, program facilitators, and evaluators
The Commonwealth of Massachusetts	State legislature	Create legislation requiring the insurance industry to invest in community development projects and calculate the ROI of this program.	State legislators, insurance companies staff, community development groups
U.S. Immigration and Naturalization Service	Federal agency	Implement and evaluate a competency-based promotional assessment system for managers and supervisors.	INS top management, INS R&D Branch, subject matter experts, HRD professionals
New York State Governor's Office of Employee Relations	State government	Initiate a pilot study to determine how ROI could be used to evaluate training.	Labor management committee, program trainers, subject matter experts, focus group participants
The University of Arkansas	State university	Implement process mapping to plan and analyze the redesign of the procurement process.	University's department of finance and administration, business affairs manager, state purchasing office, external consultants, and trainers
The Royal New Zealand Navy	Department of the Navy	Calculate the ROI of a retention bonus plan.	Retention committee, finance department, budget advisors, marine engineers, and their managers

Federal Information Agency	Government agency	Evaluate a graduate program to improve agency employee retention and technical skills.	Program administrators, implementation and evaluation teams, agency employees, teaching staff
Silicon Valley Private Industry Council	Industry council	Assess the economic impact of workforce development programs.	Industry council, public policy management consultants
Australian Capital Territory Community Care	Government health-care agency	Implement and evaluate a client relationship management system.	Key stakeholders, management, staff, external consulting group
Metro Transit Authority	Metropolitan transit	Implement and evaluate an absenteeism reduction program.	Bus drivers and their supervisors, managers, HRD department

the end of each case can serve as a beginning point for lively and entertaining discussions.

3. This book will serve as a supplement to other references or textbooks. It provides the extra dimensions of real-life cases that show the outcomes of performance improvement.

4. Finally, this book will be extremely valuable for managers who do not have primary performance improvement responsibility. These managers provide support and assistance, and it is helpful for them to understand the results that programs can yield.

It is important to remember that each organization and its program implementation are unique. What works well for one may not work for another, even if both are in similar settings. The book offers a variety of approaches and provides an arsenal of tools from which to choose in the evaluation process.

Follow-Up

Space limitations necessitated that some cases be shorter than the author and editor would have liked. Some information concerning background, assumptions, strategies, and results had to be omitted. If additional information on a case is needed, the lead author can be contacted directly. The lead author's addresses are listed at the end of each case.

The Public Sector Challenge: Developing a Credible ROI Process

Patricia Pulliam Phillips and Jack J. Phillips

Introduction

Consider the following scenarios:

- The U.S. Veterans Administration is using a return-on-investment (ROI) process to measure the success and impact of dozens of training and educational programs. (This process, developed by Jack J. Phillips, is a registered trademark of the Franklin Covey Company—all rights reserved.)
- A human resources manager in a medium-size southern U.S. city is using an ROI process to show the impact of a variety of human resources programs.
- A U.S. federal government agency is measuring the ROI of a master's degree program conducted on site by a prestigious major university.
- The county board of education for a large eastern U.S. metropolitan area is requiring a projected ROI before in-service teacher training is conducted.
- A large western U.S. city is using an ROI process to measure the impact of an absenteeism reduction program for city bus drivers.
- The Italian Postal Service is using an ROI process to increase the efficiency and contribution of services as it competes with other postal services within the European Union and with private sector package carriers, such as DHL Worldwide.

And the list goes on.

Those examples did not exist 10 years ago. Measuring the return on investment of human resources, training, and performance improvement programs is commonplace around the globe. Initially, the trend was most evident in the private sector. Now the public sector faces new challenges. Not only is there increased emphasis on understanding the public sector's inefficiencies, but also a new emphasis on building accountability into its processes.

Measuring ROI in the Public Sector shows how all types of public sector organizations are using ROI evaluation as a way to meet these challenges. The settings for ROI applications range from small local governments to state governments, from major cities to national and federal programs. The types of programs suitable for ROI evaluation vary significantly. Table 1 presents a sample list of programs appropriate for this type of comprehensive evaluation.

Although the interest in return on investment has heightened and much progress is being made in understanding and calculating ROI, it is still an issue that challenges even the most sophisticated public sector organizations. Some professionals argue that it is not possible to calculate the ROI for any type of program. Others quietly and deliberately proceed to develop meaningful measures and ROI calculations. Regardless of the position taken on an issue, the reasons for taking the ROI approach to evaluation are clear. Almost all training and performance improvement professionals share the belief that they must eventually show a return on investment. If an ROI is not shown, funding may be reduced, or the function may not be able to maintain or enhance its present status and influence in the organization.

The dilemma surrounding ROI evaluation is a source of frustration for many senior staff members and executives. Executives believe that most services are necessary to meet competitive and economic challenges. New programs and initiatives are important during restructuring and rapid change when employees must learn new skills and often juggle multiple projects. Executives intuitively feel that there

Table 1. ROI is appropriate for all types of programs and solutions.

- Performance improvement programs
- Training and learning solutions
- Education programs
- Organization development initiatives
- HR programs
- Change initiatives
- Technology implementation

is value in implementing these various programs. They logically conclude that programs and solutions will pay off in important business measures such as productivity improvements, quality enhancements, cost reductions, and time savings. They also believe that solutions enhance taxpayer satisfaction, improve morale, and build teamwork. Yet the frustration comes from the lack of tangible evidence of results. Although the payoffs are assumed, more evidence is needed to build credibility and secure funding for future programs.

The ROI process, developed by Jack J. Phillips and described in his book *Measuring Return on Investment in Training and Performance Improvement Programs* (1997), represents a comprehensive, balanced approach to measuring the success of any type of solution. As shown in table 2, the process develops a scorecard reporting six types of data, representing one of the most comprehensive methods to measure public sector programs.

Public Sector ROI Dilemma
Drivers for Increased Accountability

The public sector's activities are so complex that it is difficult to determine its expenditures. Regardless, increased accountability appears to be surfacing at federal, state, and local levels in a variety of programs and activities. While there are dozens of reasons for increased accountability, 10 specific drivers are influencing significantly the public sector's need to measure the ROI of programs, solutions, or services:

Table 2. ROI definition: A balanced approach.

A comprehensive and systematic performance-based process that generates six types of measures:

- Reaction and satisfaction
- Learning
- Application and implementation
- Business impact
- Return on investment
- Intangible measures

This balanced approach to measurement includes a technique to isolate the effect of the program or solution.

1. **Pressure from taxpayers to show how government funds are being used.** During the past 50 years, public expenditures in the United States have increased significantly. As a rate of gross domestic product (GDP), expenditures have risen from 10 percent in 1940 to 31 percent in 1997 (Stiglitz, 2000). While in countries such as Australia, Germany, Italy, and the United Kingdom, the total expenditures are higher, taxpayer concern that government services are not adding enough value (in all countries) is driving the accountability issue. An ROI can show the contribution for government expenditures.

2. **Government regulation requiring accountability.** In the United States, the Government Performance and Results Act of 1993 (GPRA) is an attempt to bring accountability for expenditures to public sector programs and initiatives. The purpose of this act is to establish strategic planning and performance measurement in the U.S. federal government. Consequently, this act is forcing many government organizations to plan for accountability in the beginning and show the results generated from expenditures on programs and initiatives.

3. **Privatization of government sector.** Under this arrangement, a government function or organization is sold to the private sector and operates on a for-profit basis. Consequently, these government entities have to be streamlined and made more efficient prior to the sale. In other cases, the new "for-profit agency" must be efficient to compete with the private sector. In either case, ROI is being used to help streamline programs and solutions, making them more efficient and effective.

4. **A consistent lack of results or alignment.** With many public sector programs and solutions, the results have been unclear—sometimes nonexistent—forcing more focus on business impact and ROI. Also, in many situations, there has been a serious lack of alignment with business needs as the public sector program fails to be linked to impact measures.

5. **A new breed of government managers with a business mindset.** New government executives are managing agencies the same way as executives in the private sector—they're requiring ROI information on new programs and initiatives. They bring a business mindset and are demanding accountability up to and including ROI.

6. **Increased cost for many programs and initiatives.** New programs and processes are expensive—particularly those involving human resources and technology—creating more focus on accountability. A larger expenditure becomes a bigger target for criticism, scrutiny, and attention. That demands a higher level of accountability, including ROI.

7. **Government agencies are learning from business organizations.** Through benchmarking and best practice exploration, agencies are learning the ways of the private sector. Because of the successes enjoyed in the private sector, many government agencies are attempting to apply the same principles in the government sector. ROI is one of the benchmarked processes being transferred from the private to the public sector.

8. **Previous evaluation methods for government programs have been inadequate.** Traditional program evaluation methods have left many agencies seeking new and different approaches. Even a cost benefit analysis using traditional program evaluation hasn't always provided a full array of data needed to provide a complete picture of the impact of a new program or solution. In addition, the effects of other influences are often ignored in these types of evaluations. A more comprehensive, balanced, yet credible process is needed as offered with ROI, consisting of six types of data and a method to isolate the effects of the program.

9. **Overall trend of accountability for all types of processes.** The public sector is reacting to the trend of increased accountability for all processes, functions, and programs. This persistent trend is a global phenomenon where the focus is on efficiencies, costs, and productivity. The monetary contribution of programs must be developed, including ROI.

10. **Lack of management support for programs and solutions.** Managers will not support a process unless they see the value added in terms they understand, such as ROI. The ROI process is an excellent way to build support for new initiatives.

Collectively, these drivers for increased accountability bring a renewed focus on measurement and evaluation in the public sector, including measuring return on investment.

Paradigm Shift in Public Sector Programming

In recent years, the programs and solutions implemented in public sector organizations have shifted from an activity-based process to a results-based profile. Previously, the activity-driven paradigm was based on the desire to have an abundance of programs—with many activities—consuming all available resources. Even the reporting of results was based on the number of programs, hours, participants, costs, and content. (These indicators are input-focused instead of output-focused.) Now public sector programming is moving to a results-based paradigm. Programs are only initiated when specific business needs are identified and a variety of processes are used to ensure a linkage to business alignment, success, and results in every phase of the program—up to and including reporting the results based on the actual contribution of the program. Table 3 provides more detail about the paradigm shift involving eight specific programming phases that are fast becoming a results-based profile.

Special Issues for the Public Sector

Public sector organizations implementing ROI must confront several issues unique to the setting. While issues require special attention, they are sometimes mystical barriers that should not necessarily impede implementation. Five specific issues follow:

1. **Absence of revenues and profits.** Most government agencies don't generate profits for their organizations, particularly those connected with social and military programs. Sometimes there's a perception that an ROI value can only be developed when there are profits and revenues. In reality, this is far from the truth. When examining the ROI formula, presented later in this chapter, the numerator in the equation represents net benefits derived from either the profit margin or

Table 3. Paradigm shift.

Activity Based	Results Based
No business need for the program/initiative/solution	Program solution linked to specific business needs
No assessment of performance issues	Assessment of performance effectiveness
No specific measurable objectives	Specific objectives for implementation and impact
No effort to prepare program participants to achieve results	Results expectations communicated to participants
No effort to prepare the work environment to support transfer	Environment prepared to support transfer/application
No efforts to build partnerships with key managers	Partnerships established with key managers and sponsors
No measurement of results or benefit cost analysis	Measurement of results and benefit cost analysis
Planning and reporting on programs/solutions is input-focused	Planning and reporting on programs/solutions is output-focused

a cost savings. In practice, the vast majority of case studies, even in the private sector, develop monetary benefits based on cost savings. When productivity is improved, quality is enhanced, and cycle times are reduced; the result is a cost savings—a direct, bottom-line contribution. Thus, in the public sector, while revenues and profits may not exist, there are many other opportunities to develop successful ROI studies based on productivity, quality, and time improvement as well as direct cost savings through efficiency enhancements. Based on our direct involvement with 400 ROI impact studies, less than 15 percent of those have profit margins as a driver for the ROI, stemming directly from revenue improvements. An impressive 85 percent or more have ROI payoffs based on cost savings.

2. **Absence of hard data.** Sometimes the perception is that hard data is not available in government agencies—only intangible, soft data. That is not necessarily the case. Even in the simplest government unit, there is output, quality, cost, and time—the four major categories of hard data illustrated in table 4. For example, in an agency charged with processing forms (such as applications for work visas), all four types of hard data elements come into play. Productivity (number of applications processed per day), quality (number of errors per 100 applications processed), time (the average time to complete an application), and cost (the cost per approved application) are all potential measures linked to training or HR programs. Thus, a particular program aimed at improving productivity, quality, or time will have a direct payoff on cost savings. Table 4 shows a sample of the types of hard data available in government units, illustrating the vast array of possibility when capturing hard data.

3. **Multiple constituencies must be served.** Additional constituencies must be served with a government agency, exceeding the number usually found in the private sector. For example, in a typical ROI impact study, six major groups would always be interested in the outcome: employees, who are the participants in the programs; the immediate managers of participants who support the program; the sponsor who initiates or approves the program; the top administrators who manage the agency; the lawmakers, who create laws and regulations about the accountability of programs; and taxpayers, who are concerned about the use of tax dollars. This scenario is a little more complex than private sector groups, where the senior executives, managers, and participants are the primary targets for communicating results.

4. **Government services are essential and, therefore, shouldn't have this level of evaluation.** Many government services *are* essential and

Table 4. Examples of hard data.

Output	Quality	Costs	Time
Services provided	Waste	Budget variances	Cycle time
Taxpayers served	Rejects	Unit costs	Response time for complaint
Applications processed	Defects	Cost by individual	Equipment downtime
Forms processed	Error rates	Variable costs	Overtime
Applications approved	Rework	Fixed costs	Average delay time
Inventory turnover	Shortages	Overhead costs	Time to project completion
Patients visited	Deviation from standard	Operating costs	Processing time
Students graduated	Service failures	Delay costs	Supervisory time
Tasks completed	Inventory adjustments	Penalties/fines	Training time
Work unit productivity	Percentage of tasks	Project cost savings	Meeting time
Work backlog	completed properly	Accident costs	Efficiency (time-based)
Requests honored	Number of accidents	Program costs	Order response time
	Customer complaints	Administrative costs	Late reporting
		Average cost reduction	Lost time days

must be provided, regardless of the accountability or contribution. That is not always the case in the private sector where many programs can be altered, changed, or replaced if they're not working properly. Many critical government support services can be changed very little and, thus, often create the illusion that they should not be evaluated. In reality, they should be subjected to detailed evaluation, at least for some major programs because the efficiency and effectiveness of the program can be changed, even if the program itself cannot be altered dramatically.

5. **Restricted range of options to correct problems.** In the public sector, when a program has major problems, a full range of options is available to correct those problems, including discontinuing the program. A full range of options may not be available in the government sector because, in many cases, making radical changes or altering a program may not be the best course of action. On the positive side, many options are often available to improve the program in terms of efficiency, effectiveness, and its connection to the desired results.

At times, these five issues are considered impediments to measurement at the ROI level, rather than realistic barriers. They are often myths that must be dispelled for public sector units to make progress in this important area.

Status of Measurement and ROI
Global Trends

Before examining the specific status of ROI, a few global trends—about measurement in both private and public sector organizations—should be examined. The following general accountability trends have been identified in our research and are evolving slowly across organizations and cultures in more than 35 countries. Collectively, these 10 important trends have significant impact on the way accountability is addressed in the public sector:

1. Evaluation is an integral part of the design, development, delivery, and implementation of the solutions.
2. There is a shift from a reactive approach to a more proactive approach with evaluation planned early in the cycle.
3. Measurement and evaluation processes are systematic and methodical, often built into the cycle.
4. Technology is enhancing significantly the measurement and evaluation process.
5. Evaluation planning is becoming a critical part of the measurement and evaluation cycle.

6. Implementing a comprehensive measurement and evaluation process usually leads to increased emphasis on the front-end analysis.

7. Organizations without comprehensive measurement and evaluation have reduced or eliminated their budgets.

8. Organizations with comprehensive measurement and evaluation have enhanced their program budgets.

9. Many successful examples of comprehensive measurement and evaluation applications are available.

10. A comprehensive measurement and evaluation process can be implemented for about 4 percent or 5 percent of the direct program budget.

Progression of ROI Application

The ROI process described throughout this book had its beginnings in the 1970s as it was applied to the development of a return on investment for a supervisory training program. Since then it has been developed, modified, and refined to represent the process reported here and expanded in all types of situations, applications, and sectors. Figure 1 shows how the process is progressing from sector to sector. Applications began in the manufacturing sector, where the process is easily developed. Applications migrated to the service sector, as many major service firms such as banks and telecommunications companies used ROI to show the value of various programs. Applications evolved into the health-care arena as the industry sought ways to improve educational services, human resources, quality, risk management, and case management. Applications in nonprofit organizations began to emerge as these organizations were seeking ways to reduce costs and generate efficiencies. Finally, applications in the public sector began to appear in a variety of types of government organizations. Public sector implementation has intensified in recent years. An outgrowth of public sector applications is the use of the process in the educational field where it is now being applied to different educational settings. It becomes clear that implementation is spreading and that the public sector and educational settings are now enjoying application of the ROI process.

ROI Status

With the expansion of the ROI process, its status has grown significantly and the rate of implementation has been phenomenal. The number of organizations and individuals involved with the process underscores the magnitude of ROI implementation:

Figure 1. Progression of ROI implementation.

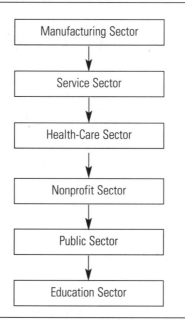

- The ROI process has been refined over a 20-year period.
- Thousands of studies have been developed using the ROI process.
- At least 100 case studies are published on the ROI process.
- Almost 1,000 individuals are certified to implement the ROI process in their organizations.
- Organizations in 33 countries have implemented the ROI process.
- Twelve books have been developed to support the process.
- A 400-member professional network has been formed to share information.
- The ROI process has been adopted by hundreds of organizations in manufacturing, service, nonprofit, and government settings.

With this much evidence of the growing interest, ROI is now becoming a standard tool for program evaluation.

Typical Applications

The specific types of program applications and solution implementations vary significantly. Table 5 shows a full range of current applications representing programs and solutions from training and development to education, human resources, change, and technology.

Table 5. ROI applications.

- Executive education
- Global leadership
- Diversity programs
- Wellness/fitness initiatives
- Total quality management
- Self-directed teams
- Skill-based/knowledge-based compensation
- Organizational development
- Safety and health programs

- Competency systems
- Career development programs
- Recruiting strategies
- Orientation systems
- Associate relations programs
- Gain sharing programs
- Technology implementation
- Web-based training

Building a Credible ROI Process
Concerns with ROI

Although progress is evident, the ROI process is not without its share of problems and concerns. The mere presence of the process creates a dilemma for many public sector organizations. When an organization embraces the concept and implements the process, the management team is usually anxiously waiting for results, only to be disappointed when they are not quantifiable. For an ROI process to be useful, it must balance many issues such as feasibility, simplicity, credibility, and soundness. More specifically, three major audiences must be pleased with a specific ROI process to accept and use it—practitioners; senior managers, sponsors, and clients; and researchers.

For years, practitioners have assumed that ROI could not be measured. When they examined a typical process, they found long formulas, complicated equations, and complex models that made the ROI process appear confusing. With this perceived complexity, administrators could visualize the tremendous efforts required for data collection and analysis, and more important, the increased cost necessary to make the process work. Because of these concerns, practitioners are seeking an ROI process that is simple and easy to understand so they can easily implement the steps and strategies. Also, they need a process that will not take an excessive amount of time to implement and will not consume too much precious staff time. Finally, practitioners need a process that is not too expensive. With competition for financial resources, they need a process that will not command a significant portion of the budget. In summary, the ROI process, from the perspective of the practitioner, must be user friendly, efficient, and cost-effective.

Senior managers, sponsors, and administrators who must approve budgets, request programs or solutions, or live with the results, have a strong interest in developing ROI. They want an ROI process that provides quantifiable results using a method similar to the ROI formula applied to other types of investments. Senior managers have a never-ending desire to have it all come down to an ROI calculation reflected as a percentage. And, like practitioners, they want a process that is simple and easy to understand. The assumptions made in the calculations and the methodology used in the process should reflect their point of reference, backgrounds, and level of understanding. They do not want, or need, a string of formulas, charts, and complicated models. Instead, they need a process that they can explain to others, if necessary. More important, they need a process with which they can identify, one that is sound and realistic enough to earn their confidence.

Finally, researchers will only support a process that measures up to their scrutiny. Researchers usually insist that models, formulas, assumptions, and theories are sound and based on commonly accepted practices. Also, they want a process that produces accurate values and consistent outcomes. If estimates are necessary, researchers want a process that provides the most accuracy within the constraints of the situation, recognizing that adjustments need to be made when there is uncertainty in the process. The challenge is to develop acceptable requirements for an ROI process that will satisfy researchers and, at the same time, please practitioners and senior managers. Sound impossible? Maybe not.

Criteria for an Effective ROI Process

To satisfy the needs of these three critical groups, the ROI process must meet several specific requirements. Eleven essential criteria for an effective ROI process are outlined below:

1. The ROI process must be *simple,* void of complex formulas, lengthy equations, and complicated methodologies. Most ROI models have failed to satisfy that requirement. In an attempt to obtain statistical perfection and use too many theories, several ROI models and processes have become too complex to understand and use.

2. The ROI process must be *economical* and able to be implemented easily. The process should have the capability to become routine without requiring significant additional resources. Sampling for ROI calculations and early planning for ROI are often necessary to make progress with this concept without adding new staff.

3. The assumptions, methodology, and techniques must be *credible.* For an ROI process to earn the respect of practitioners and senior

managers, it must have logical, methodical steps. That requires a very practical approach for the process.

4. From a research perspective, the ROI process must be *theoretically sound* and based on generally accepted practices. Unfortunately, this requirement can lead to an extensive, complicated process. Ideally, the process must strike a balance between maintaining a practical and sensible approach and having a theoretical basis for the process. This is perhaps one of the greatest challenges to those who have developed models for the ROI process.

5. An ROI process must *account for other factors* that have influenced output variables. Isolating the influence of the program or solution, one of the most often overlooked issues, is necessary to build credibility and accuracy within the process. The ROI process should pinpoint the contribution of the program when other factors have influenced the business measures.

6. The ROI process must be appropriate for use with a *variety of programs.* Some models apply to only a small number of programs, such as team leader training. Ideally, the process must be applicable to all types of training and HR programs, such as career development, organization development, and major performance improvement change initiatives, including technology.

7. The ROI process must have the *flexibility* to be applied on a preprogram as well as a postprogram basis. In some situations, an estimate of the ROI is required before the actual program is developed. Ideally, the ROI process should be able to adjust to a range of potential timeframes for collecting data.

8. The ROI process must be *applicable with all types of data,* including hard data (typically represented as output, quality, costs, and time) and soft data (job satisfaction, grievances, and complaints).

9. The ROI process must *include the costs* of the program. The ultimate level of evaluation is a comparison of benefits with costs. Although the term ROI has been loosely used to express any benefit of a solution, an acceptable ROI formula must include costs. Omitting or underestimating costs will only destroy the credibility of ROI values.

10. The actual calculation must use an *acceptable ROI formula.* That is often the benefits/cost ratio (BCR) or the ROI calculation, expressed as a percent. These formulas compare the actual expenditure for the program with the monetary benefits driven from the program. While other financial terms can be substituted, it is important to use a standard, acceptable financial calculation in the ROI process.

11. Finally, the ROI process must have a successful *track record* in a variety of applications. In far too many situations, models are created

but never successfully applied. An effective ROI process should withstand the wear and tear of implementation and should obtain the expected results.

Because these criteria are considered essential, an ROI process should meet most, if not all, of these criteria.

When to Pursue ROI

Not every public sector organization is ready for ROI, nor does every organization need it. Several important issues should be explored before launching the process. The quiz in figure 2 provides a brief assessment of several critical issues. Any public sector executive considering the application of ROI should examine these issues by taking this quiz. A score in the 40 to 50 range indicates the timing is urgent and the need for ROI is immediate. Scoring in the 30 to 40 range indicates that, while the urgency is not as great, it is time to begin the process, recognizing that implementing ROI takes several months—even years—to fully accomplish. The need for ROI is not a concern on the immediate horizon if the score falls in the 20 to 30 range, but it would be helpful to build more formal structure into accountability to prepare for a potential shift in the future. A score below 20 indicates little need for this level of accountability in the foreseeable future, and may perhaps be completely unnecessary. A more detailed assessment is available in other publications (Phillips, Stone, and Phillips, 2001).

Several key issues are underscored in this brief examination. The ROI process is used by organizations reflecting certain characteristics. Typically, the larger the organization, the more likely the agency focuses on ROI. High-profile agencies demand accountability because of their presence and visibility. The size of the budget for the functional unit being examined for ROI can sometimes be a factor. Large, growing budgets are often targets for increased accountability. The internal drivers for accountability are another concern. Examining the specific influences for increased measurement often cause these organizations to migrate to the ROI process. Finally, organizations are more successful where there has been a focus on measurements, particularly through a quality improvement process, reengineering, or Six Sigma implementation. These types of initiatives often require many other parts of the organization to measure the success as well.

The symptoms for the need for ROI implementation are often readily apparent. Pressure from senior administrators within the agency is one of the greatest motivators to pursue this type of process. A historically low investment in measurement and evaluation is another signal that

Figure 2. Readiness quiz for ROI implementation.

Is your public sector organizational unit ready for additional measurement and evaluation?

Check the most appropriate level of agreement for each statement:
1 = Strongly Disagree; 5 = Strongly Agree

	Disagree			Agree	
	1	**2**	**3**	**4**	**5**
1. Our organization is undergoing significant change.	☐	☐	☐	☐	☐
2. There is pressure from senior administrators to measure results of solutions.	☐	☐	☐	☐	☐
3. Our organization has a culture of measurement and has established a variety of measures including some for solutions.	☐	☐	☐	☐	☐
4. Our function currently has a very low investment in measurement and evaluation.	☐	☐	☐	☐	☐
5. Our organizational unit has experienced more than one disaster in the past.	☐	☐	☐	☐	☐
6. Our team would like to be the leaders in accountability.	☐	☐	☐	☐	☐
7. The image of our function is less than satisfactory.	☐	☐	☐	☐	☐
8. Our sponsors/clients are demanding that solutions show results.	☐	☐	☐	☐	☐
9. Our function competes with other functions for resources.	☐	☐	☐	☐	☐
10. There is increased emphasis on linking solutions to the strategic direction of the organization.	☐	☐	☐	☐	☐

more emphasis is needed. One or more disasters in a particular function (such as human resources or training) can translate into an increased need for accountability to avoid a repeat in the future. A new leader of the function will sometimes initiate additional accountability. That new leader is usually not attached to any previous programs—emotionally or fiscally—and, therefore, a review of what works and doesn't work is a logical step. Often, the image of the agency, or a function within the agency, calls for more accountability. An agency frequently under fire or a particular function that's notorious for wasting money creates the need for more accountability.

The motivation for individuals pursuing ROI varies considerably. As shown in figure 3, sometimes the implementation is a reactive process— responding to an executive's request for measurement or justifying budgets. Still others see the need for more accountability in the future to protect the budgets or function. Others are pursuing this process to show the accountability of funds. A few others are merely experimenting and want to explore new techniques to measure the success of their processes. While the overwhelming majority of previous implementations have been in a reactive mode—and less in the proactive—we see a trend shifting to more of the proactive approach. This is the good news! Agencies are recognizing that accountability to the taxpayer, which includes developing the ROI for specific programs, is not only in the best interest of the taxpayer, but the agency as well.

The ROI Methodology
Elements of the ROI Process

Building a comprehensive measurement and evaluation process is much more than implementing a statistical process. It includes significant components and is best represented as a puzzle where the pieces are developed and put in place over time. Figure 4 depicts this puzzle and the individual pieces. The first piece is the selection of an evaluation framework, which is a categorization of data.

The recommended framework for the process modifies Kirkpatrick's four levels to include a fifth: return on investment (Kirkpatrick, 1998). The concept of different levels of evaluation is both helpful and instructive in understanding how ROI is calculated. Table 6 shows a modified version of Kirkpatrick's four-level framework with the fifth level added to include cost-benefit comparison.

Figure 3. Rationale for individuals pursuing ROI.

30%	☐	Top executives are requiring ROI. I have to pursue this!	**Reactive**
30%	☐	I have pressure to justify any T&D budget. I need this!	
25%	☐	I know I will need to demonstrate more accountability in the future.	
10%	☐	I want to show increased accountability for T&D expenditures.	
5%	☐	I want to experiment with, and explore, new techniques to measure training success.	**Proactive**

Figure 4. ROI: The pieces of the puzzle.

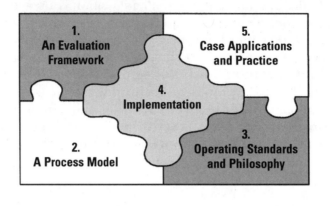

Next, an ROI process model must be developed showing how data is collected, processed, analyzed, and reported to various target audiences. This process model ensures that appropriate techniques and procedures are consistently used to address almost any measurement issue. Also, there must be consistency as the process is implemented. The ROI process model is described in more detail later.

The third piece of the puzzle is developing operating standards, which provide rules for processing data. These standards help ensure that the results of the study do not overly influence it. Replication

Table 6. Five levels of evaluation.

	Level	Measurement Focus
1	Reaction, satisfaction, and planned action	Measures participants' reaction to, and satisfaction with, the program and captures planned actions.
2	Learning	Measures changes in knowledge, skills, and attitudes.
3	Application and implementation	Measures changes in on-the-job behavior and progress with planned actions.
4	Business impact	Measures changes in business impact variables.
5	Return on investment	Compares program monetary benefits to the costs of the program.

is critical for the credibility of an evaluation process, and operating standards in the form of guiding principles allow for this. The following guiding principles have a conservative approach:

- When an evaluation is planned for a higher level, the previous level does not have to be comprehensive.
- When a higher-level evaluation is conducted, data must be collected at lower levels.
- When collecting and analyzing data, use the most credible sources.
- When analyzing data, choose the most conservative approach among alternatives.
- At least one method must be used to isolate the effects of the program.
- If no improvement data is available for a population or from a specific source, it is assumed that little or no improvement has occurred.
- Estimates of improvement should be adjusted for the potential error of the estimate.
- Extreme data items and unsupported claims should not be used in ROI calculations.
- The first year of benefits (annual) should be used in the ROI analysis of short-term programs.
- Program costs should be fully loaded for ROI analysis.

Next, appropriate attention must be given to implementation issues as the ROI process becomes a routine part of the training, HR, and performance improvement functions. Several issues must be addressed involving skills, communication, roles, responsibilities, plans, and strategies. An earlier *In Action* casebook focused specifically on this issue (Phillips, 1998).

Finally, there must be successful case studies that describe the implementation of the process within the organization, the value that a comprehensive measurement and evaluation process brings to the organization, and the impact specific programs evaluated have on the organization. While it is helpful to refer to case studies developed by other organizations, such as those found in this casebook, it is more useful and convincing to have a collection of studies developed within the organization.

The ROI process model, shown in figure 5, provides a systematic approach to ROI calculations. It shows the steps involved in calculating the return on investment of a solution. A step-by-step approach helps keep the process manageable so that practitioners can address one issue at a time. Application of the model provides a consistent methodology from one ROI calculation to the next. Following is a brief description of each step of the model.

Figure 5. The ROI process model.

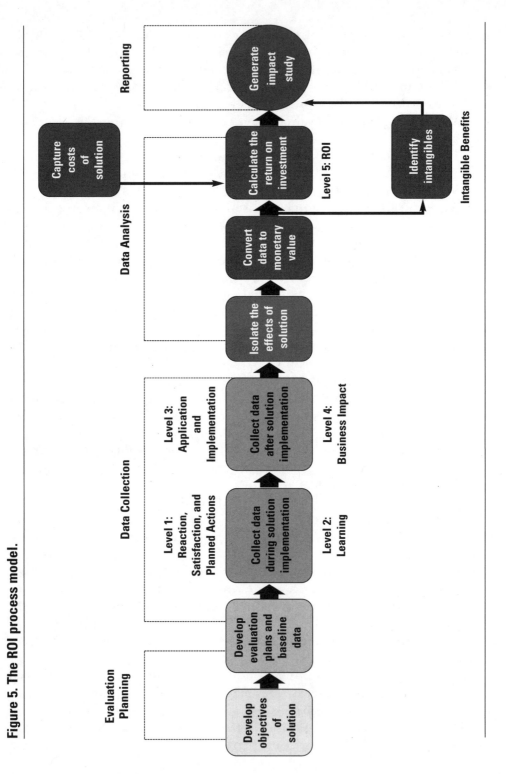

Planning the Evaluation

One of the most important and cost-savings issues in the ROI process is planning the evaluation. A first step in the planning process is to develop specific objectives at different levels, sometimes including all five levels described in table 6. Application, impact, and ROI objectives are necessary to generate the business contribution of programs and solutions.

Data collection is necessary for a comprehensive evaluation, and a data collection plan outlines, in detail, the steps involved. When selecting the data collection methods and developing the plan, four elements should be considered—evaluation purposes, instruments, levels, and timing. Typical items in a plan include the following:

- Broad areas for objectives are initially identified; more specific program objectives are developed later.
- Specific measures or data descriptions are indicated when they are necessary to explain the measures linked to the objectives.
- Specific data collection methodologies for each objective are listed.
- Sources of data such as participants, team leaders, and organization records are identified.
- The timeframe in which to collect the data is noted for each data collection method.
- Responsibility for collecting data is assigned.

The ROI analysis plan is a continuation of the data collection plan. This planning document captures information on several key issues necessary to develop the actual ROI calculation. The key issues include the following:

- significant data items, usually Level 4 (business impact measures), but in some cases could include Level 3 data
- the method for isolating the effects of the program
- the method for converting data to monetary values
- the cost categories, noting how certain costs should be prorated
- the anticipated intangible benefits
- the communication targets—those who will receive the information
- other issues or events that might influence program implementation.

These two planning documents are necessary to successfully implement and manage the ROI process.

Collecting Data

Following the planning process, implementation begins. Data collection is central to the ROI process. Both hard data (output, quality, costs, time) and soft data (work habits, work climate, attitudes) are collected. Data is usually collected at two timeframes: During the process for Level 1 and Level 2 and following the program for Level 3 and Level 4. A variety of methods are available for collecting the postprogram data used in the ROI evaluation. Figure 6 lists these data collection techniques.

The challenge is to match the data collection method or methods with the setting and the specific program, within the time and budget constraints of the public sector organizational unit.

Isolating the Effects of the Program

The most critical step in the evaluation process is one that is often overlooked: isolate the effects of the program or solution. In this step of the ROI process, specific strategies are explored that determine the amount of performance that is directly related to the program or solution. The result is increased accuracy and credibility of the ROI calculation. The following techniques have been used to address this important issue:

- use of a control group arrangement
- trend line analysis of performance data
- use of forecasting methods of performance data
- participant's estimate of program impact (percent)
- supervisor's estimate of program impact (percent)
- management's estimate of program impact (percent)
- use of previous studies
- calculating or estimating the impact of other factors
- use of customer/client input.

Collectively, these techniques provide a comprehensive set of tools to isolate the effects of training and performance improvement programs.

Figure 6. Postprogram data collection techniques.

	Level 3	Level 4
• Follow-up surveys	✔	
• Follow-up questionnaire	✔	✔
• Observation on the job	✔	
• Interview with participants	✔	
• Follow-up focus groups	✔	
• Program assignments	✔	✔
• Action planning	✔	✔
• Performance contracting	✔	✔
• Program follow-up sessions	✔	✔

Converting Data to Monetary Values

To calculate the return on investment, impact data collected at Level 4 is converted to monetary values to compare with program costs. This step requires a value to be placed on each unit of data connected with the program. Ten approaches are available to convert data to monetary values where the specific technique selected usually depends on the type of data and the situation. These approaches are

1. converting output to contribution—standard value
2. converting the cost of quality—standard value
3. converting employee's time
4. using historical costs
5. using internal and external experts
6. using data from external databases
7. linking with other measures
8. using participants' estimates
9. using supervisors' and managers' estimates
10. using staff estimates.

The preceding step is absolutely necessary for determining the monetary benefits from training and performance improvement programs. While challenging (particularly with soft data), this step can be methodically accomplished using one or more of the above techniques.

Tabulating Program Costs

The next step in the process is tabulating the costs of the program. Tabulating the costs involves monitoring or developing all of the related costs of the program targeted for the ROI calculation. Among the cost components that should be included are the following:

- the cost to design and develop the program, possibly prorated over the expected life of the program
- the cost of all program materials provided to each participant
- the cost of the facilitator, including preparation times as well as delivery time
- the cost of the facilities for the program
- travel, lodging, and meal costs for the participants, if applicable
- salaries plus employee benefits of the participants for the time they attend the program
- administrative and overhead costs of the training and performance improvement function allocated in some convenient way to the program.

In addition, specific costs related to the front-end analysis and evaluation should be included, if appropriate. The conservative approach is to include all of these costs so that the total is fully loaded.

Calculating the ROI

The ROI is calculated using the program benefits and costs. The benefit-cost ratio is the program benefits divided by cost. In formula form it is:

$$BCR = \frac{Program\ Benefits}{Program\ Costs}$$

The ROI uses the net benefits divided by program costs. The net benefits are the program benefits minus the costs. In formula form, the ROI becomes:

$$ROI\ (\%) = \frac{Net\ Program\ Benefits}{Benefits} \times 100$$

This is the same basic formula used in evaluating other investments where the ROI is traditionally reported as earnings divided by investment. The ROI from some programs may be high. For example, in supervisory, leadership, and managerial training, the ROI is frequently over 100 percent, while the ROI value for HR, change, and technology may be lower.

The specific value for the ROI calculation has meaning only in relationship to what was expected. It is important to develop expectations, and, in some situations, the actual ROI value as an objective for the project. Four specific strategies have been used to establish the expectation:

1. **Set the value the same as with other investments (for example, 15 percent).** When an agency constructs a new building, an expected annual rate of return is established for that building. That value is developed internally and is usually a function of the cost of capital, if the agency had to raise the capital externally. For most countries in North America, Western Europe, and Asia Pacific, the value is in the 15 to 20 percent range. Consequently, when this strategy to set the expected return for a program or solution is set at that same value, it is treated no differently from other investments.

2. **Establish the value slightly above other investments (for example, 25 percent).** With this strategy, the acceptable return is set above what would be expected for the ROI for other investments. Because this concept is new to the public sector, this strategy may be preferred as it sets the program or solution accountability at a higher standard, when compared with other investments.

3. **Establish the percent at break even (0 percent).** Use of this strategy underscores the fact that many of the functions, solutions, and

programs within an agency were not designed to make a profit, but merely represent a payoff that would at least equal the expenditures. When the payback in monetary terms equals the expenditures, it is a 0 percent ROI.

4. **Determine a specific acceptable amount from the sponsors of the program or solution.** As a new solution is implemented, the sponsors (client) indicate the acceptable ROI from the project for a specified timeframe. This brings the focus on client expectations into the public sector situation.

Together, these four strategies provide an ample range of possibilities to establish the actual ROI value for a public sector unit.

Identifying Intangible Benefits

In addition to tangible, monetary benefits, most programs or solutions have intangible, nonmonetary benefits. Data items not converted to monetary values are considered intangible benefits. While many of these items can be converted to monetary values, they often are not because the process used for conversion is too subjective and the resulting value loses credibility through the process. These intangible benefits are the sixth measure reported in the definition of the ROI process and may include:

- increased job satisfaction
- increased organizational commitment
- improved teamwork
- improved service
- reduced complaints
- reduced conflicts.

For some programs, these intangible, nonmonetary benefits are extremely valuable, often carrying as much influence as the hard data items.

The Payoff for the ROI Process

The ROI process produces some important payoffs, both for the long and short term. Based on the experience of public sector organizations implementing the ROI process, payoffs fall into five categories:

1. **Show the business contribution of selected programs and solutions.** The ROI process is the most credible way to show the actual impact, in business terms, for a solution within the public sector.

2. **Earn the respect and support of senior management and administrators.** Agency heads will support programs and initiatives when they see value added. Other managers in the agency will support a process they believe is benefiting the agency and helping them meet their particular objectives in the agency.

3. **Improve processes.** Because this is an evaluation method, an important part of the process is to determine what can be changed, altered, or modified to improve the program or solution. These improvements often translate into efficiency, effectiveness, and actions.

4. **Identify ineffective programs or solutions that need to be redesigned or eliminated.** Often, a program needs to be altered to make it more effective to increase the value. In some cases, it may need to be eliminated. When necessary, this process is the most rational approach to provide convincing data to discontinue the program.

5. **Identify successful programs or solutions that can be expanded to other areas.** On the positive side, the ROI process will provide convincing evidence to expand a program or solution when it's adding value and another area, division, or agency needs the same program.

Collectively, these major payoffs from this process make it a very useful, convincing, and necessary tool for the public servant.

Implementing the ROI Process

Successfully implementing ROI takes time and a concerted effort to integrate all the pieces of the evaluation puzzle (figure 4) into the training and performance improvement function. The ROI process is not a quick fix to proving a program's worth. It is a comprehensive process that, when implemented to its fullest, can help position the training, HR, and performance improvement function as a strategic player in the organization. Initial strategies that will assist in ensuring successful implementation of the ROI process include:

- *Planning and discipline.* A great deal of planning and a disciplined approach will keep the process on track. Implementation schedules, evaluation targets, data collection plans, measurement and evaluation policies, and follow-up schedules are required.

- *Establish goals and targets.* An important part of implementation is to decide specifically how many programs are evaluated at specified levels. The issue is particularly important when considering those programs for business impact (Level 4) and ROI (Level 5) calculations. The approach involves two decisions: establishing target percentages and applying selection criteria. Table 7 shows the recommended percentages for a full array of possible solutions. In the training area, for instance, where a large agency may have 100 programs, these percentages are recommended as annual targets. For example, 30 percent of the programs will be destined for a Level 3 evaluation, but not necessarily every session of the program.

Table 7. Percentage of programs evaluated at each level.

Level of Evaluation	Percent of Programs Evaluated at This Level
1. Reaction and satisfaction	100%
2. Learning	60%
3. Application and implementation	30%
4. Business impact	10-20%
5. ROI	5-10%

Consequently, sampling is occurring in two ways: selecting the individual program or solution to evaluate and selecting the particular sessions or groups within that program.

This approach leaves the overall percentage for Level 4 and 5 quite low. At Level 5, a percentage of 5 to 10 is common and probably all that is necessary for most public sector environments. These low percentages for Levels 3, 4, and 5 are needed to ensure that the ROI process is feasible in terms of budgets, time, and disruption. Greater percentages may cost too much, be too disruptive, and would be overwhelming for the staff to accomplish.

A second part of this decision is to determine which specific programs would be subjected to business impact and ROI evaluation. Table 8 shows the typical criteria used to select programs for this level of analysis. Only those programs or solutions that are considered to be strategic, visible, expensive, or designed to deliver business impact are targeted for business impact and ROI evaluation.

Table 8. Criteria for selecting solutions/programs for business impact and ROI analysis.

- Life cycle of the solution
- Linkage of solution to operational goals and issues
- Importance of solution to strategic objectives
- Top executive interest in the evaluation
- Cost of the solution
- Visibility of the solution
- Size of the target audience
- Investment of time required

- **Assigning responsibilities.** There are two key areas of responsibilities. The entire program or solutions staff, regardless of their individually assigned responsibilities, are responsible for measurement and evaluation. These responsibilities include ensuring that perceived needs include business impact measures, developing appropriate program objectives to include Level 3 (application) and Level 4 (business impact) objectives, focusing content to relate to the desired objectives, designing appropriate data collection instruments, and communicating processes and evaluation results. The second area of responsibility is assigned to the group specifically involved with measurement and evaluation. Responsibilities for this group include designing data collection instruments, providing assistance for developing an evaluation strategy, analyzing data, interpreting results, developing the evaluation report or case study, and providing technical assistance with the ROI process.
- **Developing staff skills.** Many staff members neither understand ROI nor have the basic skills necessary to apply the process within their scope of responsibilities. The typical program does not focus on business results—it focuses more on learning outcomes. Consequently, staff skills must be developed to use the results-based approach of the ROI methodology.
- **Improving front-end analysis.** The ROI process is often undertaken to improve the evaluation of existing programs. That process often uncovers inadequate front-end analysis, revealing that programs are not needed or are improperly aligned with business needs. Consequently, the processes used in the initial analysis are often improved.
- **Implementing cost-savings approaches.** The ROI process can quickly become an expensive and time-consuming process unless it's managed and organized correctly. Table 9 shows a variety of cost-savings approaches or strategies available to minimize the actual cost of this process. It is essential to undertake most of these approaches to conserve resources, including money and time, and keep the amount of disruption to a minimum. Using these cost-savings approaches can enable a comprehensive process to be implemented for less than 4 percent of the total direct functional budget (for example, training or HR). Additional information on cost savings approaches can be found in other publications (Phillips and Burkett, 2001).
- **Communicating progress.** It is important to communicate progress on efforts and address needs of appropriate audiences for evaluation data. It is also important to show the impact the programs have on an organization, usually through routine reports and meetings. Consequently, a communication plan must be developed and implemented.

Table 9. Cost-savings approaches to ROI.

- Plan for evaluation early in the process.
- Build evaluation into the process.
- Share the responsibilities for evaluation.
- Require participants to conduct major steps.
- Use short-cut methods for major steps.
- Use sampling to select the most appropriate programs for ROI analysis.
- Use estimates in the collection and analysis of data.
- Develop internal capability to implement the ROI process.
- Streamline the reporting process.
- Use Web-based software to reduce time.

The ROI Challenge

The challenge for public sector organization units is to determine if this process is needed now. Several key questions should be addressed about implementing a measurement and evaluation process, including ROI:

- What will happen if nothing is done?
- Will the budget be reduced or not increased as desired or needed?
- Will the influence of our function be reduced in some way?
- Will the support we enjoy for our programs be diminished?

These and other questions are critical in deciding if this process is appropriate for the organizational unit. Some issues are clear, while others need further analysis.

ROI Reality

The reality is that ROI is here to stay—it is not a passing fad. It is a process that has been used for centuries to show accountability for expenditures. More important, ROI has now moved to the public sector and is being endorsed, supported, and implemented by many organizations. Several issues underscore the reality of ROI in the public sector:

- Executives, administrators, and sponsors of programs and solutions desire ROI information. Resistance to a request for information in this area may be an uncomfortable path.
- The ROI process provides a balanced, credible approach with six types of data. It meets the requirements of practitioners, administrators, and researchers.

- All types of organizations are routinely using the ROI process. Almost all levels of the public sector agencies are embracing the concept.
- The ROI process can be implemented without draining resources. It is estimated that a comprehensive process can be implemented for 4 to 5 percent of the direct functional budget.
- The ROI process is a long-term goal for many organizations as they pursue the journey of increased accountability. Many organizations have collected different types of data and now see the need for the addition of a business impact and ROI measure as part of the mix.
- The ROI process takes time to implement. It is not a quick fix and will take months for it to be implemented effectively.

With these issues, there is no time like the present to begin the process.

A Rational Approach to ROI

As the process is implemented, it is important to keep seven points in mind when selecting and supporting an ROI process:

1. **Keep the process as simple as possible.** Complexity only adds to the confusion.
2. **Use sampling for ROI calculation.** There's no need to tackle every ROI for even the majority of programs or solutions.
3. **Always account for the influence of other factors.** Other influences always exist. Failure to include them in the analysis may invalidate the study. Ignoring the issue is even worse.
4. **Involve management in the process.** Managers and administrators need to understand the ROI concept. Increased understanding will ensure that managers ask for the ROI process appropriately, interpret and use the data wisely, and understand their role in making the process work.
5. **Communicate results carefully.** The communication of results needs to be planned and delivered to each audience in the right spirit and with appropriate content. This is a critical issue that's often overlooked.
6. **Give credit to participants and managers.** After all, the results of other individuals are being reported in the impact study. Be sure to always make that connection.
7. **Plan for ROI calculations.** Planning will save time, effort, and resources and can avoid confusion and concerns along the way. Excellent planning can sometimes make the difference between success and failure for a study.

Those issues make the process adaptable to any organization. It is rational, logical, and feasible.

Next Steps

The next steps for an organization vary considerably, depending on the current status and desired objectives. Also, other factors will influence the timing, such as the amount of pressure the agency is under to make change, the capability of the staff, and the existence of adequate data collection systems. Table 10 shows some recommended next steps if an agency or organizational unit within an agency is interested in exploring the ROI process in more detail. The process should be regarded as a major change effort to bring accountability to the organizational unit. It will require changing approaches, practices, policies, guidelines, and, more important, mindsets, attitudes, and perceptions.

Conclusion

This opening chapter has attempted to outline the basic strategies and techniques concerned with bringing increased accountability to public sector organizations, including measuring the actual ROI. This introductory material sets the stage for reading and understanding the various key studies that follow.

ROI calculations are being developed by hundreds of public sector organizations to meet the demands of influential stakeholders. The ROI process described in this chapter is the most validated process used to bring balance and credibility to program measurement and evaluation. The trend to develop a comprehensive measurement process is likely to continue as public sector units become more streamlined, yet have greater reach. Through careful planning, methodical procedures, and logical and practical analysis, ROI calculations can be developed

Table 10. Typical next steps.

Action items to implement a comprehensive ROI process:

• Develop a policy and philosophy statement	• Establish a management support system
• Communicate results to selective audiences	• Enhance management commitment and support
• Assess your progress and readiness	
• Clarify roles	• Move from simple to complex project
• Develop a transition plan	• Achieve short-term results
• Set targets for evaluation levels	• Organize a task force/network
• Develop procedures and guidelines	• Teach the process to others
• Build staff skills	• Establish a quality review process

reliably and accurately for any type of program or solution, in any public sector organization, in any part of the world. Examples of the successful application of ROI evaluation are found throughout this book.

References

Kirkpatrick, Donald L. (1998). *Evaluating Training Programs* (2d edition). San Francisco: Berrett-Koehler Publishers, Inc.

Phillips, Jack J., editor. (1998). *Implementing Evaluation Systems and Processes.* Alexandria, VA: ASTD.

Phillips, Jack J. (1997). *Measuring Return on Investment in Training and Performance Improvement Programs.* Woburn, MA: Butterworth-Heinemann.

Phillips, Jack J., Ron D. Stone, Patricia P. Phillips. (2001). *The Human Resources Scorecard.* Woburn, MA: Butterworth-Heinemann.

Phillips, Patricia P., and Holly Burkett. (2001). *ROI on a Shoestring.* Alexandria, VA: ASTD.

Stiglitz, Joseph E. (2000). *Economics of the Public Sector* (2d edition). New York: W. W. Norton & Company, Inc.

Competency Development for Leaders in the 21st Century

Department of Veterans Affairs
Sunshine Health Care Network

Victoria Clark and Debra Peeples
in collaboration with Timothy Bothell

Given the incredible and volatile challenges of the future, organizations must groom internally identified high performers in order to provide a continuous pool of leaders who can step up to the leadership plate already outfitted with the necessary leadership competencies. In this case study, the Veterans Health Administration's Veterans Integrated Service Network #8 (VISN 8) recognized the need to develop a pool of future leaders who could potentially succeed its current leaders. Using blended learning, VISN 8 program developers presented a 10-day leadership development program over a period of six months to build leadership competencies in eight core areas. They also conducted an analysis process to measure the program's organizational impact and return on investment. That analysis process yielded positive results.

Background

The Veterans Affairs Sunshine Health Care Network, also known as the Veterans Integrated Services Network #8 (VISN 8), is one of 22 veterans health-care networks throughout the nation under the Veterans Health Administration (VHA). The VISN 8 service area covers South Georgia, the entire state of Florida, Puerto Rico, and the U.S. Virgin Islands.

VISN 8 offers a full range of medical, surgical, and mental health services in inpatient, outpatient, nursing home, and home care settings. It provides primary, preventive, and specialty health-care services to 1.7 million men and women veterans who now reside within

This case was prepared to serve as a basis for discussion rather than to illustrate either effective or ineffective administrative and management practices.

its service area through an integrated system of seven Veterans Affairs Medical Centers (VAMCs), 10 multispecialty outpatient clinics, and 26 primary care community-based outpatient clinics.

The Network's mission is to provide a full continuum of high quality, patient-focused health care to veterans. Its vision is to become the health-care provider of choice for veterans in South Georgia, Florida, Puerto Rico, and the U.S. Virgin Islands. Commitment, excellence, trust, respect, compassion, innovation, and collaboration are the core values that guide the Network's decision-making process and behavior when interacting with its internal and external customers. The 13,258 full-time equivalent employees, 60 percent of whom are clinical care providers and clinical support staff, give life and meaning to the mission, vision, and values of the Network (Veterans Affairs Sunshine Health Care Network, 2000).

Continuous leadership development is necessary for VISN 8 to remain healthy and able to face the incredible and volatile challenges of the future. By internally identifying and subsequently grooming high performers, the Network will have a pool of leaders ready to step up to the leadership plate already outfitted with the necessary competencies for the job. VISN 8's senior leaders have recognized the importance of a pool of future leaders who could potentially succeed its current leaders. The need for vigorous succession planning stems from the fact that 75 percent of all Veterans Health Administration employees in leadership positions are eligible for retirement within five years (VA Learning University, 2000). Because succession planning is one of VISN 8's top priorities, Network leaders developed and implemented a VISN-wide leadership development program in fiscal year 2000. The program is called Competency Development for Leaders in the 21st Century.

Needs Assessment

Developers of the leadership program curriculum used a variety of needs assessment sources. They analyzed local medical center educational surveys to determine educational concerns of current and future leaders. They reviewed the VHA and VISN strategic plans as well as data reflecting the number and ages of employees now and the predicted number in the future. They also carefully reviewed Level 2 and 3 behaviors of the eight core competencies (see table 1) in relationship to requested needs of employees and to educational experiences already available in VISN. Lastly, they looked at current educational programs within VISN designed for leaders. Upon completion of their comprehensive review, curriculum developers discussed their findings with the VISN director to clearly understand his concerns about developing future leaders and to ascertain the issues he thought needed to be addressed. Developers also held this discussion with the executive leadership at each medical center.

As a result of their analysis, program developers determined that leaders needed skills in all areas of the eight core competencies, particularly in the areas of organizational stewardship, systems thinking, interpersonal skills, and creativity. They also found that leaders were not familiar with new roles such as coaching and the skills required to fulfill these roles. Based on their assessment of the needs in VISN 8, the developers formulated a curriculum that would meet the following criteria: It would influence Level 2 and 3 behaviors of the VHA eight core competencies; it would consist of modules spread out over time to allow application of knowledge and skills; it would organize workgroups to work virtually across the network on applying skills learned to a particular "real work" problem; and it would use a variety of interactive strategies including self-assessment, role play, and learning maps. The plan involved presenting the eight modules at paired sites, using local facilitators and videoconferencing in order to reduce travel costs. The overall goals of the curriculum were to provide knowledge and skills that would potentially save time, reduce costs, promote organizational commitment, reduce turnover, and improve quality customer service and employee satisfaction. Primarily, the curriculum helped address VISN's need to identify employees who could be groomed to move into leadership positions.

Program Design, Development, and Implementation

In designing the leadership development program, representatives from VISN 8 and the VA Employee Education System (EES) created a 10-day leadership curriculum presented in one-day modules spread over six months. They used the VHA's High Performance Development Model (HPDM) as a framework for eliciting the maximum potential from VA employees. The eight-module HPDM program focused on developing leadership behaviors in eight core competencies: personal mastery, technical skills, interpersonal effectiveness, customer service, flexibility/adaptability, creative thinking, systems thinking, and organizational stewardship.

The leadership program designers based learning objectives for each module on behavioral expectations of the eight core competencies for first-line supervisors (Level 2 behaviors) and service chiefs (Level 3 behaviors), sequentially arranging the modules to ensure the orderly building of foundational competencies, such as personal

Table 1. Behavioral expectations of the VHA's eight core competencies.

Level 1 Nonsupervisory Employees	Level 2 Immediate Supervisors	Level 3 Second Level Supervisors, Assistant Chiefs, Management Officials	Level 4 Service Chiefs or Equivalent
Personal Mastery	**Personal Mastery**	**Personal Mastery**	**Personal Mastery**
• Takes time to plan each day's work. • Participates in training and other self-development activities. • Demonstrates improvement in behavior and skills needed. • Participates in evaluations of self, others, and the organization. • Invests in personal development and growth.	• Has a sense of own career options and preferences. • Provides feedback and coaches employees on their development. • Seeks feedback on supervisory/coaching skills from supervisees and peers. • Encourages and supports the efforts of employees to develop and grow.	• Sets aside time each week to reflect on personal/professional development. • Provides employees with time resources and opportunities to pursue self-development, which will contribute to work effectiveness. • Models effective management of time and physical/emotional health.	• Inspires and demonstrates passion for excellence in every aspect of work. • Creates a climate where continuous learning and self-development are valued. • Seeks continuous feedback about impact on others, through both formal and informal mechanisms.
Interpersonal Effectiveness	**Interpersonal Effectiveness**	**Interpersonal Effectiveness**	**Interpersonal Effectiveness**
• Keeps commitments • Treats all employees with respect regardless of their level, personality, culture, or background. • Gives courteous, accurate, and complete responses. • Expresses thoughts, ideas, and concerns clearly. • Listens attentively to others without interruption. • Seeks accurate information (avoids jumping to conclusions).	• Encourages employees to express their opinions, ideas, and concerns and listens emphatically. • Effectively involves team members in building consensus. • Shares information readily. • Uses negotiation skills to settle conflicts in the work group. • Expresses ideas clearly in writing.	• Confronts issues that block achievement of goals and mission. • Encourages shared decision making. • Regularly coaches staff on their contribution to agency mission and their performance development. • Exhibits the negotiation skills required to achieve cooperation among service line managers, chiefs, or team leaders.	• Gives authority and responsibility to others. • Breaks down barriers to effective communication. • Exhibits clear, candid, and open communication in meetings, town halls, and other interactions. • Conducts credible and prudent briefing sessions for Congress or the national media. • Develops collaborative relationships across the Network.

Customer Service
- Is highly responsive to requests for help, information, and services.
- Seeks to go beyond what the customer requests and does something extra to be helpful.
- Recognizes coworkers as customers and responds to them accordingly.
- Courteous in all interactions with patients, visitors, and coworkers.
- Listens to concerns of customers and resolves complaints and concerns effectively and promptly.
- Assists customers in making informed decisions.

Flexibility/Adaptability
- Is willing to learn new procedures and technology.
- Is open to ideas different from one's own.
- Looks for better alternatives to "the way we've always done it."

Customer Service
- Recognizes employees who provide good customer service.
- Establishes mechanisms for ongoing customer feedback.
- Effectively addresses episodes of poor customer service.

Flexibility/Adaptability
- Handles multiple projects and duties simultaneously, prioritizing as needed.
- Adapts supervisory style to individual needs of employees.
- Respects and deals effectively with others' fears of change.
- Fosters flexibility through cross-training and developmental work assignments.

Customer Service
- Empowers staff to resolve problems and complaints independently at the lowest level.
- Rewards creativity in the pursuit of excellent customer service.
- Searches for and recognizes "best practices" in customer service.
- Uses customer feedback data to continuously plan, provide, and improve products and services.
- Is highly visible and accessible to all customers, including staff.

Flexibility/Adaptability
- Understands and applies change management principles.
- Applies leadership and management skills to newly assigned positions and duties.
- Responds to decreases in staffing or increases in workload by involving all parties in restructuring the work.

Customer Service
- Bases strategic planning on customer feedback and projected needs.
- Establishes a customer-oriented culture and promotes hiring of persons who fit that culture.
- Shares resources across VA in order to serve customers effectively and efficiently ("One VA").
- Breaks barriers that impede good service delivery.

Flexibility/Adaptability
- Responds to changing priorities and resources with optimism, encouraging staff to respond positively and proactively.
- Stays abreast of, and educates staff about, changing conditions in the health care market.
- Teaches application of change management principles.

(continued on page 38)

Table 1. Behavioral expectations of the VHA's eight core competencies (continued).

Level 1 Nonsupervisory Employees	Level 2 Immediate Supervisors	Level 3 Second Level Supervisors, Assistant Chiefs, Management Officials	Level 4 Service Chiefs or Equivalent
Creative Thinking	**Creative Thinking**	**Creative Thinking**	**Creative Thinking**
• Generates new ideas. • Suggests ways to improve quality and efficiency. • Demonstrates the willingness and capacity to resourcefully meet internal or external customer needs on the spot. • Tries different ways of accomplishing a task. • Suggests ways to improve quality and efficiency.	• Responds to changing priorities and resources with optimism, encouraging staff to respond positively and proactively. • Effectively conducts brainstorming sessions with a team. • Fosters acceptance of creative ideas by others. • Challenges assumptions and the "way we've always done it." • Encourages risk-taking and entrepreneurial behavior.	• Conducts benchmark studies and applies them within the organization. • Reframes problems as opportunities. • Fosters creativity in others, by example and through use of creative-thinking strategies and tools. • Finds ways to change the system so new and creative ideas can be implemented. • Is receptive to challenges to "the way we've always done it." • Recognizes and rewards creative thinking.	• Encourages demonstration projects, pilots, and other experimental approaches. • Champions new ideas and approaches. • Creates new functional processes that lead to the development of revenue streams or other gains in organizational outcomes. • Encourages and rewards risk-taking and entrepreneurial behavior. • Looks beyond current reality to prepare organization for alternative futures.
Systems Thinking	**Systems Thinking**	**Systems Thinking**	**Systems Thinking**
• Is able to explain how one's work contributes to the organization's mission. • Understands the roles and responsibilities of others in one's work group.	• Helps staff to understand the context of their work and how it relates to others. • Considers the impact on others before making changes to a work process.	• Helps staff understand how their function or department relates, and complements, the overall mission of the organization. • Actively communicates with others about how planned changes may affect their work.	• Shares the "big picture" with staff, including the consequences of not thinking holistically. • Breaks down barriers and silos in the workplace in favor of high performance work systems.

- Acknowledges that sacrifices may need to be made in some areas in order to improve overall performance.

Organizational Stewardship

- Builds an atmosphere of trust by being trustworthy.
- Understands the mission, vision, and values of the organization and acts accordingly.
- Speaks favorably of the organization and its people, both at work and in the community.
- Provides support to fellow employees in accomplishing mission.
- Takes initiative to seek and suggest improvements in how work is done.

- Creates a climate of collaboration rather than competition.

Organizational Stewardship

- Stays abreast of changes in VA goals, objectives, and initiatives.
- Teaches and practices the mission, vision, and values of the organization.
- Takes responsibility for the physical and human resources of the work team.
- Leads team-based process improvement activities.
- Encourages diversity of opinions, experiences, and cultures.

- Rewards collaborative initiatives in pursuit of organizational goals.

Organizational Stewardship

- Helps staff understand how their function or department relates to, and complements, the overall mission of the organization.
- Manages toward organizational outcomes within limited budget and staff.
- Demonstrates leadership by providing support and resources to staff to enable them to carry out the organizational mission.
- Goes the extra mile to ensure that all open positions are filled with the best candidates.
- Develops organizational depth by developing individuals.

- Understands the needs and complexities of the Network health-care delivery system components.
- Recognizes and accepts global consequences of every decision.

Organizational Stewardship

- Provides a clear vision of the future and leads organization through necessary changes.
- Demonstrates commitment to the Network's business and strategic plan.
- Encourages an atmosphere of trust and empowerment by example.
- Demonstrates commitment and accountability to the "One VA" concept.
- Models behavior, attitudes, and actions expected of all staff.

(continued on page 40)

Table 1. Behavioral expectations of the VHA's eight core competencies (continued).

Technical Skills	Technical Skills	Technical Skills	Technical Skills
• performs accurate work in a timely and efficient manner. • Maintains knowledge and skills through continuing education, journals, and practice. • Takes responsibility for safety and high quality in the work place.	• Explores environment for best practices and works to implement them. • Supports and encourages employees in maintaining and upgrading skills and knowledge related to assignments. • Involves staff in seeking to constantly improve work processes and outcomes. • Seeks out learning opportunities in areas of professional interest.	• Is actively involved in one or more professional organizations. • Provides employees with time, resources, and opportunities to master new material. • Is acknowledged as a subject matter expert in one's professional area, through publication, invited lectures, or requests for advice or consultations. • Natures innovations that are recognized as best practices or models.	• Uses technical or professional skill in creating new approaches to the field. • Is nationally recognized as a consultant or advisor on current topics. • Fosters and rewards high standards for accuracy, safety, and constant improvement in all areas of the organization.

mastery and technical skills. Table 2 shows the eight modules, the key concepts covered in each module, delivery methods used, and the length of each module.

During its implementation, the program accommodated 73 participants from all VISN 8 facilities. Four VISN medical center sites simultaneously presented the program through local facilitation, video-conferencing, and face-to-face presentations. The highly interactive, application-based training used blended learning activities designed to meet the outcome objectives. By providing job-related assignments, each module allowed participants the opportunity to apply knowledge and skills learned during the program. Discussion pertaining to lessons learned from each assignment occurred at the beginning of each subsequent module.

The program also required each participant to work with cohorts from other sites in resolving a VISN issue or project. The program leaders assigned participants to virtual teams, and encouraged team members to apply the steps of the problem-solving process, demonstrate effective interpersonal skills, think creatively, and recognize the complexity of the VISN ecosystem.

Participation in the program was competitive in that potential participants had to meet eligibility requirements and submit an application packet with a written note of support from their supervisor. The application packet included a questionnaire that required, among other things, that each potential applicant state his or her leadership goals and reasons for wanting to take part. The packet also required that the applicants cite specific examples of leadership activities both within and outside of the VA. Upon review, a committee selected participants based on specific eligibility and selection criteria, and the program site coordinator gave them the Four Roles of Leadership 360-degree assessment tool to complete and distribute to their supervisors, direct reports, and peers for feedback. The 360-degree assessment, given about one month prior to starting the program, provided baseline data regarding each participant's skills in four leadership roles: pathfinding, aligning, empowering, and role modeling. It also served as a prework activity to help participants start thinking about their own leadership behaviors.

Purpose of Evaluation

The need to measure the program's organizational impact was critical because of the program's comprehensive nature, its strategic importance to the organization's future, and its large commitment of time and dollars. Program developers used an impact analysis process

Table 2. Leadership program modules.

Competency Development for Leaders in the 21st Century (FY 2000 curriculum)

Module	Key Concepts Covered	Delivery Method	Length
Module 1: Personal Mastery and Technical Skills	Overview of program High performance development model Four roles of leadership 360-degree assessment Individual development planning Learning in the workplace	Facilitator-led, videoconferencing	1 day
Module 2: Interpersonal Effectiveness	Communication skills Consensus building Coaching	Facilitator-led, use of video-based program	1 day
Module 3: Systems Thinking	VHA and VISN mission, vision, and strategic priorities VISN projects	Face-to-face meeting with all VISN participants	2 days
Module 4: Organizational Stewardship, Parts 1 and 2	Living VISN's mission and vision Building organizational trust Empowerment Team-based process improvement Managing physical, fiscal, and human resources	Facilitator-led, use of video-based program, videoconferencing	2 days
Module 5: Customer Service	VISN and local customer service FISH philosophy	Facilitator-led, use of video-based program	1 day
Module 6: Flexibility/Adaptability	Change management Leadership style	Facilitator-led, use of video-based program, videoconferencing	1 day
Module 7: Creative Thinking	Creativity Futures planning	Facilitator-led, use of video-based program	1 day
Module 8: Graduation	VISN project presentations	Face-to-face meeting with VISN participants	1 day

to measure Levels 1 to 5 outcomes. They had to know if the human and fiscal resources allocated for developing and implementing this VISN-wide program provided any tangible and intangible benefits to the organization.

Evaluation Methodology and Model

Program developers used a five-level evaluation process, based on Kirkpatrick's four levels of evaluation and Jack Phillips' return-on-investment (ROI) process (Phillips, 1997), to assess the organizational impact of this leadership development program. That process enabled them to measure participant reaction and knowledge learned (Levels 1 and 2 evaluation) at the end of each module. It also enabled them to measure job application of skills (Level 3) and business results affected by the program (Level 4). In addition, this process gave the developers a measurement tool (Level 5) to use in calculating the program's return on investment.

Data Collection Methodology

Immediately following each module, program developers administered paper-based questionnaires to collect data about the participants' reactions and key learning (Levels 1 and 2). The module-specific satisfaction surveys collected information about the participants' overall reactions to the module, the program's success in achieving module objectives, the participants' reactions to the instructors, and any other positive or negative comments or suggestions the participants had about the module.

In addition to the module-specific reaction and learning questionnaires, participants completed a paper-based questionnaire after completing all eight modules. That questionnaire collected information about the participants' overall reaction to the entire program as well as feedback about the program design and logistics, program content, their planned action items, the management support they received, and their predictions as to the monetary impact of the program on the VA.

About three months after completing the leadership training, participants filled out a follow-up questionnaire designed to collect information about skill application on the job (Level 3) and organizational results directly affected by the program (Level 4). They also responded to Likert Scale-type questions measuring their performance both before and after training to quantify their improvements in the skills and behaviors related to the program. Developers compared the baseline before-training rating to the after-training rating to demonstrate the difference in performance. To determine the extent to which the application of knowledge, skills, and behavior learned from the program positively influenced identified key business results (such as work output, work quality, response to customers, and so forth), developers asked participants to indicate whether the program: 1) had a very significant influence; 2) had moderate influence; 3) had some influence; 4) applied but had no influence; or 5) was not applicable.

Participants completed the Four Roles of Leadership 360-degree assessment one month prior to and six months after completing the program. Program developers aggregated pre- and postprogram 360-degree assessment results and compared them to show any improvement in the participants' leadership behavior in the areas of pathfinding, aligning, empowering, and role modeling as directly observed by the participants, their supervisors, direct reports, and peers.

About three months after completing the leadership program, developers gave participants a follow-up evaluation to collect Level 5 data. The ROI calculation used participants' estimates of time saved as a result of applied skills and knowledge gained in the program as they implemented planned actions. Also, the ROI calculation used participants' estimates of the monetary impact of these implemented actions.

Results

Participants reacted positively to this program. They particularly liked the one-day format and the length of time between each module. Ninety-six percent of the participants said they would highly recommend the course to other VA employees. Seventy-six percent said that 100 percent of what they learned in the course was applicable to their job, and 81 percent said that they were very likely to use the skills they learned in the course back on the job. Ninety-four percent felt that the 360-degree assessments and feedback were helpful to them. Table 3 shows selected Level 1 (reaction) evaluation data. Although most all the reactions were positive, one concern was that 53 percent of the participants reported little or no management support in preparation for the program.

Participants mentioned valuable learning (Level 2) as a direct result of the program. They frequently identified six key learnings, shown in table 4. Participants also mentioned key learnings they had hoped for but did not get. These included time management, conducting performance reviews, tools for recruitment and retention,

Table 3. Selected Level 1 (reaction) data.*

Item	Low	High	Mean
Success with Objectives	3.82	5.00	4.62
Individual Module Ratings	4.37	5.00	4.73
Overall Program Rating			4.9
Instructor Ratings	3.67	5.00	4.61

*based on a 5-point scale

Table 4. Selected Level 2 (lessons learned) data.

In an open-ended question asking participants to write out what was the most valuable* learning to them, the most frequently mentioned items were:

- Improved understanding of how to creatively think and the importance of creative thinking
- Improved self-awareness of strengths and weaknesses
- Improved understanding of the big picture—the whole VA concept
- Improved understanding of how to adapt to change—how to be flexible
- Improved understanding of how to improve communication
- Improved understanding of different leadership styles

*Most valuable learning listed in order, with the most frequently mentioned learning listed first.

and computer skills. The developers decided to address these issues during follow-up training.

Participants reported improvements in various competencies and specific behaviors targeted by the program (Level 3 application). They reported the application of those competencies in the job setting through implementing action plans. Participants also identified specific behaviors that improved the most, as well as behaviors they continued to have difficulty with after training. Figures 1 to 3 and tables 5 and 6 show selected Level 3 results.

The results of the pre- and posttraining 360-degree assessments revealed significant improvement in scores in the four roles of leadership—pathfinding, aligning, empowering, and role modeling. Table 7 shows aggregated data comparing pre- and posttraining scores in specific items related to the four roles of leadership.

Figure 4 shows Level 4 evaluation data that indicates that the leadership program had the most positive impact on the organizational results of response to customers, organizational commitment, employee

Figure 1. Selected Level 3 (application) data.

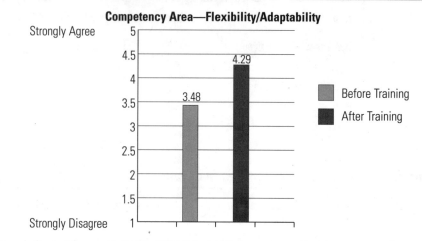

Before and after training results for Flexibility/Adaptability competency. Participants reported greatest improvement in the competency area of Flexibility/Adaptability (16% improvement).

Figure 2. Selected Level 3 (application) data.

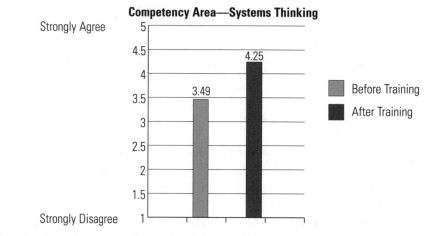

Before and after training results for Systems Thinking competency. Participants reported greatest improvement in the competency area of Systems Thinking (16% improvement).

Figure 3. Selected Level 3 (application) data.

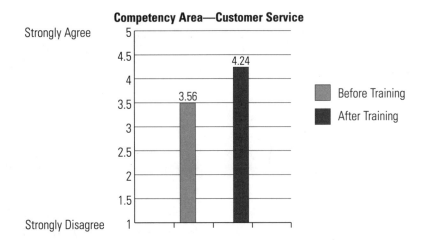

Competency Area—Customer Service

Before and after training results for Customer Service competency. Participants reported a 14% improvement in the competency area of Customer Service.

Table 5. Selected Level 3 (application) data.

Behaviors participants improved the most:

- Empowering staff members to resolve complaints independently at the lowest level of leadership possible
- Adapting their leadership style to individual needs of employees as changes occur
- Understanding and applying change management principles in their interactions with others
- Considering the impact on others before making changes to work processes

Participants reported greatest improvements in the specific behaviors listed. These behaviors were targeted in Organizational Stewardship, Flexibility/Adaptability, and Systems Thinking modules.

Table 6. Selected Level 3 (application) data.

Behaviors participants were having the most difficulty with after training:

- Acknowledging that sacrifices need to be made in some departments in order to improve the overall performance of the entire organization
- Setting aside time each week to reflect on their personal and professional development
- Being actively involved in one or more professional associations

These behaviors were selected based on the participants' ratings of their after-training performance. Items with the lowest after-training means were selected as the behaviors that participants still struggle with. These behaviors improved, yet still received a low after-training rating. These behaviors were targeted in Systems Thinking, Personal Mastery, and Technical Skills modules and relate to time management and interdependent work habits.

Table 7. Comparative 360-degree assessment aggregate data.

	Item Areas	Total Others' Scores	Total Self Scores	Evaluation Timing
2	Mission	84	78	Before Training
		93	90	After Training
3	Values	84	78	Before Training
		93	90	After Training
11	Rewards	84	81	Before Training
		92	88	After Training
16	Competence	84	81	Before Training
		92	93	After Training
15	Character	83	78	Before Training
		92	93	After Training
5	Strategy	82	76	Before Training
		92	87	After Training
8	People	82	69	Before Training
		92	93	After Training
9	Information	82	74	Before Training
		91	88	After Training
10	Decisions	82	74	Before Training
		91	87	After Training
12	Ecosystems	82	78	Before Training
		91	89	After Training
14	Win-Win Agreements	82	72	Before Training
		91	90	After Training
1	Stakeholders	81	76	Before Training
		91	92	After Training
4	Vision	80	78	Before Training
		90	90	After Training
6	Process	77	78	Before Training
		88	91	After Training
7	Structure	77	74	Before Training
		88	89	After Training
13	Leadership Style	76	68	Before Training
		87	85	After Training

Figure 4. Level 4 (evaluation) data.

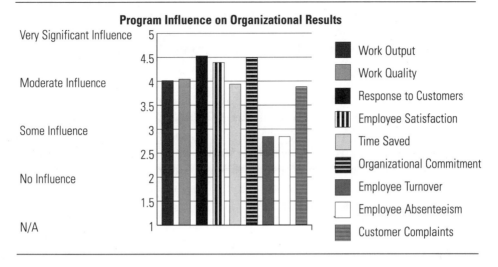

satisfaction, time savings, work quality, work output, and customer complaints. Participants reported an average of four hours a week saved or gained due to the training they received. They reported that the training had no influence on the organizational results of turnover and absenteeism.

Isolation Methodology

A paper-based survey conducted three months after completion of the training isolated the effects of the training. In that survey, participants identified key performance areas affected directly by the training. The developers then asked participants to estimate the percentage of the identified change that was directly due to their participation in the program. Because the use of a control group was not feasible, they used the participants' estimate of the impact to isolate the effects of the training. Developers also attempted a trend line analysis using patient satisfaction survey results; however, they were unable to establish a trend.

Data Conversion Methodology

To identify key organizational results that were affected by the program, developers used the follow-up evaluation given to participants about three months after the program. The developers first asked the participants to identify key business results affected by the training. In response, the participants identified the following examples of organizational results influenced directly by the program: decreased patient wait time, time savings as a result of applied skills and knowledge gained, increased insurance capture, improved patient care, and increased billing. Developers then asked participants to estimate the monetary value of the key organizational results identified and determine their confidence level in the monetary value they assigned to the organizational results. They also asked participants how many hours a week they had saved or gained as a result of the leadership program. Furthermore, they asked participants to estimate the dollar value of their implemented planned actions. Data gathered from this survey was used to calculate the program's benefits. Table 8 shows the program's annualized benefits based on 52 participants who completed the survey.

Costs

The ROI calculation included all costs incurred by VISN in planning, developing, implementing, and evaluating the program. The program site coordinators, facilitators, clerical support personnel, and program participants outlined the costs related to the program. Because the designers only wanted to determine the return on VISN's investment, costs incurred by EES were not included in the calculation even though EES contributed a substantial amount toward developing and implementing the program. EES dollars earmarked for VISN educational activities were taken from the national EES budget, entirely separate from VISN's budget. Table 9 depicts the summary of program costs.

Intangible Benefits

The intangible benefits of the program included improved work quality, faster response to customer needs, increased employee satisfaction, improved organizational communication, decreased employee turnover, decreased employee absenteeism, and decreased customer complaints. Prior to the program's implementation, the program developers had anticipated these business results among others. About three months after completing the program, program participants verified those intangible benefits through their responses to a paper-based questionnaire, in which they identified the business measures that were positively influenced as a result of the application of knowledge, skills, and behavior learned from the program.

Table 8. Annualized program benefits.

Average time saved/gained annually	208 Hours
Annual savings per 52 people trained (based on $71,762 average annual salary and 28% for benefits)	$478,608
Participants' average estimate (based on increased means test capture, inputting all documentation into computer, decreasing patient wait time in lab draws, not adding two FTEs, increased billing, decentralized pharmacy procedures, better patient care)	$1,190,287

Table 9. Summary of program costs.

Salary costs for participants (including travel time and benefits)	$289,422
Material costs	$815
Travel costs	$42,534
Meal costs	$2,175
Developmental costs	$8,128
Presenter fees (including travel)	$58,143
Evaluation fees	$17,000
Overhead costs	$41,821
Total Costs	**$460,038**

Salary costs for participants included costs for 73 participants. Travel costs included costs for participants, coordinators, and facilitators.

ROI Calculation

Participants estimated Level 4 organizational result improvements and Level 5 financial improvements. The ROI calculation used participants' estimates of time saved as a result of applied skills and knowledge gained in the program as well as the participants' implemented planned actions and the monetary impact of those implemented actions. Table 10 shows the ROI calculations that reveal a return on investment of at least 4 percent to 159 percent, or $1.04 to $2.59 returned for every dollar spent on the training.

Table 10. Level 5 (ROI) data.

Time Savings:

Average time saved/gained per week	4 hours/week/208 hours per year
Savings per week per person trained	$177
Savings per year per person trained	$9,204
Savings per year per 52 people trained	$478,608

BCR = $478,608 ÷ $460,038 = $1.04

ROI (%) = $478,608 − $460,038 ÷ $460,038 = 4%

Participants' Estimates:

Average estimate	$1,190,287.15
Basis for monetary estimate of training's impact	Increased means test capture, increased insurance capture, inputting all documentation into computer, decreasing patient wait time in lab draws, not adding two FTEs, increased billing, decentralized pharmacy procedures, better patient care, doing the right things.

BCR = $1,190,287 ÷ $ 460,038 = $2.59

ROI (%) = $1,190,287 − $460,038 ÷ $460,038 = 159%

The ROI of the leadership program was at least 4% to 159% or $1.04 to $2.59 returned for every dollar spent on the training. The value is based on time savings and participants' estimates of the monetary value of the training.

Communication Process

Timothy Bothell, Ph.D., director of impact analysis of the Jack Phillips Center for Research and Assessment, in collaboration with the VISN 8 leadership program development and implementation team, communicated the results of the ROI study because the impact analysis process was conducted cooperatively by these two groups. Bothell was the primary researcher for this study and had collaborated with VISN 8 educators and leadership staff before VISN initiated several ROI studies. He had already established a relationship not only with members of the curriculum development team but also with executive leadership within VISN. Victoria Clark, who has established relationships with the educators from VISN 8, was the VISN coordinator for the study. Writers of a draft of the final written report first presented it through email to Clark and to the development group for comments and revisions.

Bothell and the program developers then presented the final report face-to-face to key stakeholders in VISN—the VISN director, VISN education liaison, curriculum developers and facilitators, the High

Performance Development Model workgroup, and EES representatives. Bothell and the developers also gave stakeholders a complete written report as well as a PowerPoint™ presentation. Furthermore, they provided stakeholders with an opportunity to ask questions and make comments during the presentation. The network director subsequently communicated the report to medical center directors during the executive leadership board meeting. Through both formal and informal means, VISN 8 developers shared the findings with the graduates of the leadership program. They also made copies of the report and the PowerPoint™ presentation available to all key workgroups in VISN and EES.

Developers of the leadership program believe it was important to communicate to the VISN director because he communicates the mission and vision to the rest of the medical centers. Executive and midlevel management in each facility are important supporters of the curriculum and are responsible for identifying candidates for the curriculum. These leaders are also responsible for allocating human and fiscal resources to the hospitals. Educators from each hospital and from the EES are responsible for the overall curriculum development, implementation, and evaluation of educational programs.

All communications contained the same basic information included in the executive summary report. The executive summary report covered an overview of the program and the ROI study, survey demographics, the methodology used to gather Levels 1 to 5 data, how the effects were isolated, evaluation results, the costs and benefits of the program, the ROI calculation, conclusions, and recommendations.

Lessons Learned

Upon completion of each module, the developers and facilitators used feedback from the participants to evaluate the module and determine strategies needed to improve the completed module as well as future modules. Twelve lessons learned included the following:

1. Participants initially disliked the videoconferencing sessions. They found those sessions to be less engaging and too long because of the facilitators' attempt to "talk" to each site. Based on that feedback, the VISN 8 developers planned for future videoconferencing sessions to be one hour in length and tried to schedule that hour in the morning. In order to improve the faculty's presentation skills, the program developers provided training on distance learning techniques. In addition, they designed slides and handouts more compatible with distance learning. After determining that VISN 8's current classroom configuration was not conducive to distance learning,

the Network has made initial plans to change the rooms and add extra cameras and a chromakey. Financial restraints may prove to be a barrier to this change. Changes made thus far have increased the participant satisfaction with the use of videoconferencing.

2. The initial sessions did not allow time for participants to get to know each other. Time for networking was scant because each session was packed with content. Developers added an orientation session to the curriculum the following year to give participants time to get to know each other as well as to introduce the HPDM and expectations of the course.

3. Local site presenters tended to alter the content of the modules based on local issues, thereby threatening the developers' goal of maintaining consistency and quality throughout the Network. The developers, in an effort to ensure consistency and still allow local specificity, added extra facilitator training sessions and identified some critical content areas that could be delivered simultaneously to all sites by videoconferencing so that all participants would hear the same message.

4. The selection committee identified participants primarily based upon actual or potential leadership skills. Employees did not have to be in a management position to be accepted into the program as long as they met eligibility requirements. Consequently, participants had very diverse management experience. At some sites, this huge disparity in experience limited the learning that usually occurs through discussion. On the other hand, developers also learned that participants with limited leadership background benefited from the program and have perhaps grown more than some of the other participants. For the subsequent program implementation, the selection committees may obtain a better mix of experienced and nonexperienced participants through performance-based interviewing.

5. Facilitators presented content that someone else developed. That arrangement posed quality issues among the facilitators. Furthermore, module facilitators (who sometimes differed from module to module) were not able to integrate and connect earlier module content with the current module. Facilitators also needed more indepth training on the content and, in some cases, needed to improve their facilitation skills. The developers, in order to address that issue, decided to have the same facilitators from year to year for module content and to make the site coordinators responsible for linking prior content to the current module. They decided to train new facilitators as cofacilitators.

6.   More emphasis was needed on the process improvement methodology and its application to the work area. This, in turn, could provide more data for impact analysis.

7.   Participants needed more guidance for their VISN work projects. In the following year, the developers provided a worksheet that guided them through a problem-solving process. That provided them with more structure so they could move more quickly on their projects.

8.   Graduates need follow-up activities to continue to support their growth and development. The developers are considering using satellite programs selected especially for program graduates. In addition, they are contracting with the University of Alabama in Birmingham for a program on strategic planning. They also have invited graduates to be panel presenters to discuss how they have used the 360-degree profile. Finally, the developers are planning to use graduates as facilitators for future classes and as mentors for future participants.

9.   Facilitators need more training on action planning to be able to help the participants develop meaningful action plans.

10. The action plans need to be tracked and could be an important source of data for measuring the impact of the training.

11. All facilitators should go through the 360-degree assessment process so that they understand the tool and how it is being used as an instrument to guide Individual Development Planning for each participant and so they will be able to relate their content to this assessment.

12. Allowing one month between Module 7 and graduation for groups to finish their projects/reports/presentations was best. Allowing two weeks between modules gave time for participants to apply knowledge and skills learned.

Conclusion and Recommendations

The findings of this study were positive. The participants' reaction scores were as high as any ever seen, and participants reported improvements in the competencies of the VA's High Performance Development Model. Participants also reported that the program affected key organizational results. These improvements appear to produce a positive return on investment for the program.

The program developers, although extremely satisfied with the overall outcome, believe certain changes to the curriculum design and content would improve the outcomes of the program. The changes needed are driven by the participants' feedback that some of their expectations were not met and that they would like to see some additional content relative to work issues they were facing (such as time management, conducting performance reviews, and computer training). The participants have also identified some organizational issues serving as barriers to their full application of the knowledge and skills gained from the program. Some of the issues mentioned included the lack of management support for training, lack of upward mobility for career tracks, too much workload and too little resources, and the fact that other employees are not on common ground (understanding and vocabulary) because they have not received the training. Those barriers will need to be addressed by and with the appropriate stakeholders.

Participants also identified key business results that need improvement, such as customer service, revenue generation, communication, recruitment of the right people for the job, and community involvement. The program developers will need to address these business results by making some modifications in the program's content.

Questions for Discussion

1. Were the appropriate key measures selected for this study? Why or why not?
2. What were some reasons for this study? What other reasons might there be for the study?
3. If the VISN director isn't concerned about the ROI of a program, what other reasons would you consider conducting an ROI study?
4. Should costs incurred by EES be included in an ROI calculation?
5. What other methods could be used to isolate the effects of the program?

The Authors

Victoria Clark is an education specialist for North Florida/South Georgia Veterans Health System (NF/SG VHS) and the VA Employee Education System. She coordinates and provides staff development activities in NF/SG VHS. Clark has 22 years of clinical, leadership, and teaching experience in health care. She has a master's degree in nursing and is currently working on her doctorate in health-care education. Clark is the VISN program coordinator for the Competency Development for Leaders in the 21st Century Program. She can be reached at 4132 154th Terrace, Wellborn, FL 32094; phone: 386.755.3016, x 2611; fax: 386.758.3218; email: Victoria.clark@med.va.gov.

Debra Peeples works for the VA Employee Education System, Birmingham Center, as the education service representative for VISN 8.

Peeples has a master's degree in nursing with 28 years of extensive experience in continuing education, facilitation, and consultation in health care. She currently serves as faculty with the Bayer Institute and does training on quality improvement and customer service for large groups throughout VISN 8 and nationally. Peeples has worked with VISN 8 in the development, coordination, and teaching of the Competency Development for Leaders in the 21st Century Program.

Timothy Bothell is a consultant on return on investment for Franklin Covey's Jack Phillips Center for Research & Assessment. He provides consulting services for *Fortune* 500 companies and facilitates measurement workshops at conferences, public locations, and private locations. His expertise in measurement and evaluation is based on more than seven years of experience with educational institutions and three years experience with corporate clients of many industry types. In 1997, Bothell began work in the Franklin Covey Jack Phillips Center for Research & Assessment. He facilitates about 14 impact studies a month that provide results across all five levels of evaluation, including ROI. Bothell leads Franklin Covey's one-day private and public workshops and is involved in research and publishing that supports the knowledge and development of assessment, measurement, and evaluation.

References

Phillips, J. J. (1997). "The ROI Challenge: Developing a Credible Process." *In Action: Measuring Return on Investment,* vol. 2. Alexandria, VA.: American Society for Training & Development.

VA Learning University. (2000). "From Surviving Through Thriving—A Philosophy for Personal and Professional Growth." *High Performance Development Model* **Root***Map*™ *Packet.* Perrysburg, Ohio: Root Learning, Inc.

Veterans Affairs Sunshine Health Care Network. (2000). *Application for Quality Achievement Recognition Grant.* Bay Pines, FL: Bay Pines VA Medical Center Reproduction Service.

Tax Relief and Community Investment

The Commonwealth of Massachusetts

William Hettinger

In 1998, the Massachusetts legislature passed the first act of its kind in the United States, an act requiring that the insurance industry in Massachusetts establish two pools of investment funds for the expressed purpose of investment in community development projects throughout the state. In exchange, the insurance industry was to receive relief from certain Massachusetts taxes. This case describes the process the insurance industry, the community groups, and the legislature used to create this legislation. The case also isolates the costs and benefits of the investment program and calculates the return on investment (ROI) to Massachusetts from the creation of this program.

Introduction

In 1998, the Legislature of the Commonwealth of Massachusetts passed into law "An Act Insuring Community Investment and Equitable Taxation of Insurance Companies in Massachusetts." The passage of the act was the result of many years of lobbying efforts on the part of both the Massachusetts insurance industry and the Massachusetts community development groups. What makes the passage of this legislation significant is that it was the first legislation of this type passed in the United States.

The purpose of the act was to reduce the taxes paid by the insurance industry in Massachusetts in exchange for a pool of money being set aside for community investment. With the passage of this act, Massachusetts had agreed to give up tax revenue paid by the

This case was prepared to serve as a basis for discussion rather than to illustrate either effective or ineffective administrative and management practices.

insurance industry in exchange for an investment in its communities by the insurance industry. This was a conscious decision on the part of the legislature and was the intent of the legislation.

This case study will take the reader through the calculation of ROI to the Commonwealth of Massachusetts from the passage of this legislation.

Background

The name of the legislation, "An Act Insuring Community Investment and Equitable Taxation of Insurance Companies in Massachusetts," includes two concepts: the taxation of the insurance industry and community investment by the insurance industry. For many years, these two concepts had been independent. It was only in the years immediately prior to the passage of this act that these two areas were brought together. Initially, the insurance industry had been interested in a reduction in taxation, and the community development groups had been interested in having additional dollars available for community investment.

The interests of each group will be described, as will the process by which these interests were brought together in creating this piece of legislation.

There are two primary types of insurance companies: life insurance companies, which typically offer life and health insurance and annuities, and provide pension and retirements services; and property and casualty companies, which offer insurance for such assets as homes, automobiles, and commercial property. In the United States, the insurance industry is regulated at the state level. There is no national regulatory body. The companies are incorporated in one state and licensed to do business in many others. Massachusetts is free to regulate and tax the insurance companies doing business within its boundaries. Other states may do the same.

Massachusetts is home to more than 11 life insurance companies and more than 21 property and casualty insurance companies. There are many other companies, based in other states, which offer insurance in Massachusetts.

Throughout the 1990s, the financial services industry has been consolidating, and many insurance companies have been included in this consolidation. Several in Massachusetts have merged, been acquired, or moved out of state.

At issue for the insurance industry in Massachusetts throughout the 1990s were several taxes imposed on companies whose home office was in Massachusetts, but which were not imposed on companies that did business in Massachusetts but whose home office was elsewhere. Specifically, Massachusetts-based life insurance companies were subject to an additional tax on investment income that was not imposed on out-of-state companies doing business in Massachusetts. An insurance company receives a policyholder's premiums and invests these premiums to earn income while waiting to pay the claims on the policy. Maximizing investment income is an important part of an insurance company's operating strategy and directly affects the company's competitive position in the market. The imposition of an additional tax investment income by the state of Massachusetts was often cited as a competitive disadvantage by Massachusetts-based life insurance companies. Since the early 1990s the industry had been actively campaigning to eliminate this tax.

The Massachusetts-based property and casualty insurance companies were subject to similar tax burdens. Those companies too were subject to an investment income tax. They also were limited in their ability to deduct "retaliatory" tax payments made to other states. Retaliatory taxes are taxes imposed by one state in response to another state's taxation. In the case of the property and casualty insurance companies, other states would tax the Massachusetts-based companies in "retaliation" for Massachusetts' taxation of their companies. The problem was that the Massachusetts' companies did not get to fully deduct these payments from their taxes, and in effect were experiencing double taxation.

The tax burden was such that companies were beginning to consider location in Massachusetts as a strategic disadvantage, and they were beginning to consider other New England states as potential home bases. While this could have been considered an idle threat, Massachusetts had been recently stung when Fidelity Investments, the large mutual fund manager, had moved a significant part of its operations from the Boston area to nearby Rhode Island, partially in response to tax issues. It was beginning to appear that it was only a matter of time until legislature would be forced to remove the anticompetitive taxes and that this time was going to be sooner rather than later.

At the same time that the insurance industry was lobbying for changes to the tax structure, the community development groups began seeking additional pools of funds for community investment. With a decline in community investment dollars from other sources, notably from banks and government, these groups began looking to the insurance companies as a source of investment. The community development groups wanted the insurance companies to invest in the communities in which their insurance policyholders lived. There were two precedents for this request.

First, banks have historically had a mandatory community reinvestment requirement, mandated by the Community Reinvestment Act (CRA), which requires that they lend and invest in the communities from which they take deposits. CRA lending by banks has been an important source of capital to community development activities in Massachusetts and nationwide. The community groups wanted to extend CRA beyond banks, so that insurance companies were also included.

Second, in 1977, nine insurance companies had pooled some capital and formed Massachusetts Capital Resource Corporation (MCRC). MCRC was formed as a loan fund to provide long-term risk capital to the state's small and middle market companies and act to enhance the economic development of the state. By the mid-1990s, MCRC had established a successful investment track record and had contributed to the growth of many Massachusetts companies.

The first bill on insurance industry community investment was introduced in the Massachusetts legislature in 1991. That initial legislation did not get out of committee. Each year following this, similar bills were introduced in the legislature. None of the initial bills were passed. But the introduction of those bills did bring legislative attention to the issue, and the community groups continued to press for it. In the fall of 1996, the Massachusetts Association of Community Development Corporations (MACDC) issued a report, "The Insurance Industry and Low-Income Communities: A Failure to Invest," which was highly critical of the insurance industry's community investment activities. That report contrasted insurance industry's premium dollars from low-income communities with its lack of investment in these communities. The report was to become an effective tool for the community groups in developing legislative and community support for community investment on the part of insurance companies.

While the initial insurance industry community investment legislation had failed to get through the legislative process, by the end of 1996, the insurance industry had begun to be concerned about the passage of community investment legislation and the form of that legislation. The legislation that had been introduced now had more than 30 sponsors, and the community groups had issued a report critical of the industry.

The life insurance companies responded by convening an industry task force to study community development investments. They also hired Belden Daniels of Economic Innovation International, a Boston economic development consulting firm, as a consultant to help them sort through the many existing community development investment programs. In 1977, Daniels had been the architect of the now successful MCRC. The life insurance companies were beginning to examine how a community investment program might be structured. In the spring of 1997, the insurance industry task force issued a report to member companies on community investment programs and investment alternatives.

While this study was taking place, it was becoming apparent to the insurance industry that there could be a relationship between their requests for changes in their tax structure and the community groups' requests for community investment dollars from the insurance industry. The insurance companies were very interested in having their tax structure modified. The community groups and now the legislature were interested in obtaining community investment dollars from the insurance companies.

Once the industry task force had finished its work, insurance industry representatives began negotiating with the legislature and legislative staff on the form of insurance industry community investment legislation. While there was an initial reluctance from some parts of the industry to link the tax relief to the community investment programs, over the course of negotiations it became apparent that this approach could be of benefit to all parties.

Massachusetts State Senator Dianne Wilkerson held a unique key position in the negotiation and legislative process. As senate chair of the Joint Committee on Insurance, she would play a key role in any tax relief for the insurance companies. Additionally, her district included the Dorchester-Roxbury section of Boston, a community that stood to be a primary beneficiary of community investment dollars. Linking tax relief and community investment meant that the buy-in of Senator Wilkerson would be needed for success. Ultimately, this buy-in was received.

Negotiations continued throughout the latter part of 1997 and into early 1998. Several different structures were considered. By August 1998, agreement had been reached and the legislature passed "An Act Insuring Community Investment and Equitable Taxation of Insurance Companies in Massachusetts." (See table 1.)

Table 1. Tax relief and community investment key events.

Year	Event
1977	Insurance creates MCRC as a long-term risk capital fund for economic development lending.
1991	First insurance industry community reinvestment bill is introduced to Massachusetts legislature. This bill failed to pass.
1992-1996	Additional insurance industry community reinvestment bills are introduced to Massachusetts legislature. These bills fail to pass.
1996	MACDC issues report: "The Insurance Industry and Low-Income Communities: A Failure to Invest."
1997	Life insurance industry creates task force to study community investment. Report issued in May.
1997-1998	Insurance industry and Massachusetts legislature negotiate tax relief in exchange for community investment.
August 1998	"An Act Insuring Community Investment and Equitable Taxation of Insurance Companies in Massachusetts" is passed by legislature.
1999	Life Initiative and Property and Casualty Initiative begins.

Results of Legislation

The key provisions of the act were the repeal of the taxes the insurance industry wished to eliminate and the creation of two pools of insurance company community investment money, one from the life insurance companies and one from the property and casualty companies.

The legislation established specific hurdles for the insurance industry in exchange for the tax relief that was granted. From the tax perspective, the act removed the tax on investment income that Massachusetts-based life and property/casualty insurers had been required to pay. It also contained a provision that allowed property and casualty insurers to deduct retaliatory taxes paid to other states from their Massachusetts taxes. Massachusetts had granted the insurance companies the tax relief they sought.

From the community development perspective, the act required the insurance companies to establish two pools of investment dollars to be invested into community development projects in Massachusetts. Specifically, the life insurance companies in aggregate were to contribute up to $20 million per year for five years to a pool of funds that would be used for investment. Likewise, the property and casualty companies were also to contribute up to $20 million per year for five years to a pool of community investment funds. The contribution of each individual company is pro rata based on the share of the investment income tax they had been paying. In total, the insurance industry could contribute $40 million per year for five years, which could grow to a $200 million investment. (See table 2.)

The life insurance companies established the Life Initiative to manage their community investment programs and have housed the Life Initiative operations within the MCRC organization. The property and casualty companies have established the Property and Casualty Initiative (PCI) to manage their community investment programs. Together these entities are known as the Insurance Initiatives.

The legislation mandates that the Life Initiative and PCI exist for 24 years. The insurance companies can begin to pull out their invested capital in the 20th year, and may pull out one-fifth of their investment per year in each of years 20 through 24.

The operating strategy of the Life Initiative and PCI is similar. Their investment strategies will be tailored to match both their five-year funding period between 1999 and 2004 and their final payout period between 2018 and 2023. In between, they will make both long- and short-term investments, with the intent of investing their pool of funds five or more times.

Massachusetts uses July 1 as the beginning of its tax and fiscal year. Although the legislation was passed in August 1998, the tax relief did not become effective until July 1999, nearly a full year after the passage of the legislation. As a result, the first insurance company investment capital contributions to the Insurance Initiatives were not required until mid-1999.

Both the insurance companies and the Commonwealth of Massachusetts benefit from the creation of this legislation. The remainder of this case will be devoted to evaluating the actual results of implementing the legislation and will perform an ROI evaluation of the impact of this legislation to the Commonwealth of Massachusetts.

This ROI evaluation has been conducted to determine the impact of this legislation to community development in Massachusetts.

Table 2. Summary of legislation.

A. Investment income tax repealed for life insurance companies.

B. Investment income tax repealed for property/casualty insurance companies.

C. Property/casualty companies may deduct retaliatory tax payments.

D. Life Initiative and Property/Casualty Initiatives created to invest in community development.

E. Up to $200 million to be committed to community investment for 24 years.

Evaluation Methodology

The Insurance Initiatives began operation in 1999 and have been in operation for almost two years as this study is written, so actual operating data is available for a limited period. Overall, the Insurance Initiatives will be in operation for 24 years. This evaluation will include costs and benefits over the specific operating life of the Insurance Initiatives. The value of future benefits and costs will be discounted to obtain the net present value of these future benefits.

Costs

The primary cost of this legislation is the tax revenue that Massachusetts gives up as a result of granting tax relief to the insurance companies. The two obvious questions are how many tax dollars did the state give up and over how many years could the state expect to receive this tax revenue? On the surface, both questions are difficult to answer, but through further research, it is possible to obtain conservative estimates for these values.

Insurance companies are required to file many reports of financial condition and financial operation with the state of Massachusetts. The first place to look for the value of the tax revenue is in these public reports. Unfortunately, these reports do not break out tax payments or investment income in sufficient detail to be able to obtain an estimate of the value of these tax payments. The information on the reports is too summarized.

During the negotiation process between the insurance industry and legislature, as the provisions of this act were being created, the negotiation team assigned a value of $40 million per year to these taxes ($20 million annually from the life insurance companies, $20 million annually from the property and casualty companies). The negotiating team used this $40 million number as the basis for the insurance companies' contribution to the Insurance Initiatives. They estimated the state was going to give up $40 million per year in tax revenue and wanted the industry to contribute a similar amount to the Insurance Initiatives for community investment.

Following the negotiations, the estimates of value of the tax relief increased. On August 11, 1998, when the legislation was passed, the *Boston Globe* reported "Acting Governor Paul Cellucci signed legislation that grants $48 million a year in tax relief to Massachusetts-based insurers . . . ." The act contains specific references to $20 million life insurance company investment income tax, $20 million of property and casualty company investment income tax, and $8 million of retaliatory taxes, for a total of $48 million.

Forty-eight million is the more conservative estimate of the value of the tax relief. This value is validated in the most recent newspaper accounts of the legislation and is contained within the legislation itself. This conservative estimate of $48 million per year is used as the cost of the tax relief in calculation of the ROI from this program.

In the negotiation process, the negotiating team also assigned a five-year horizon to the tax revenue when they established a five-year pay-in period to the Insurance Initiatives. The appropriate horizon for the tax revenue is a critical part of establishing the costs for the ROI calculation. As was discussed earlier, the financial services industry is in the process of consolidation, and as this consolidation continues, Massachusetts can expect fewer and fewer insurance companies to be based within its borders. Because the taxes were only imposed on companies based in Massachusetts, they were a competitive disadvantage for companies located in the state. The threat of additional companies leaving the state was real. It is highly unlikely that Massachusetts would continue to receive the tax revenue at the current level for very long. The ROI has been calculated using a five-year horizon for the phase-out of the tax revenue, the period used by the legislature when creating the legislation.

While the cost of the tax relief is the primary cost of this legislation, there are additional costs. These are the costs incurred in negotiating and setting up the programs and the costs for the ongoing operation of the Insurance Initiatives over their 24-year life.

The negotiation of the legislation took place over a 16-month period, from the spring of 1997 through August 1998. The negotiation process involved representatives from the insurance industry, representatives from the legislature, and outside attorneys. While the negotiation period was more than a year, actual time devoted to negotiations was under a month. Out-of-pocket costs were incurred by the insurance industry for outside attorneys. Other negotiators were legislative representatives and legislative staff, and staff from the insurance companies and their trade groups. Based on the negotiation time and level of staff and representatives required, the cost of negotiation is estimated at $288,000.

The legislation resulted in the creation of two organizations, the Life Initiative and PCI. The Life Initiative has been housed within the existing MCRC organization, while a new organization was created for PCI. The Life Initiative has hired a staff of three, two professional level people and an administrative person. Likewise, PCI has also hired two professional level people and one administrative person. The Life Initiative has located its offices within MCRC, sharing existing office space in MCRC's downtown Boston offices. PCI has rented space from a nonprofit agency in the Dorchester section of Boston. Staff and office space are the primary expenses of the organizations. In addition, the organizations incur costs for travel throughout the state and for outreach to the community and community groups. Overall, the annual costs of operation for the two organizations have been estimated at $700,000 per year. This conservative estimate of operating costs has been used because the organizations have only been operating for two years, and actual operating costs have not been published. An inflation factor of 2.5 percent has been applied to operating costs for future years. Overall, it is estimated to cost more than $22 million to operate the Insurance Initiatives over their 24-year life.

The organizations are structured such that the money for operating costs comes from the income earned on the investments. The community development projects pay interest to the Insurance Initiatives for the use of their money. The interest from these investments is used to pay the operating costs of the initiatives, with the remainder being paid to the participating insurance companies. (See table 3.)

Benefits

The objective of the legislation was that the Life Initiative and PCI each be capitalized with $100 million for community investment, for a total of $200 million. The funds would have a life of 24 years. The money would be deposited to these funds over the first five years, principal capital repaid from maturing investments would be reinvested in additional community development projects through the 19th year, and the insurance companies would be able to take their capital investment back in years 20 through 24.

Investment by an insurance company is optional. A company that contributes to the Life Initiative or PCI is eligible for the associated tax relief based on the amount of its contribution. A company that does not contribute is not eligible for tax relief.

While it was expected at the time the legislation was passed that a total of $200 million would be invested, the November 2000 report, "Insuring the Future of Our Communities: The First Progress Report on the Massachusetts Insurance Industry Investment Initiatives" prepared by the Massachusetts Association of Community Development Corporations, estimates that the total investment will equal $181 million, $19 million short of the expected investment amount. This short fall is due primarily to property and casualty insurance companies not investing in PCI at the level anticipated. Table 4 shows the investment by year.

Table 3. Costs.

Year	Cost of Tax Relief	Initial Fund Cost	Cost of Fund Operation	Total Annual Cost
1	$48,000,000	$288,000	$700,000	$48,988,000
2	48,000,000		717,500	48,717,500
3	48,000,000		735,438	48,735,438
4	48,000,000		753,823	48,753,823
5	48,000,000		772,669	48,772,669
6			791,986	791,986
7			811,785	811,785
8			832,080	832,080
9			852,882	852,882
10			874,204	874,204
11			896,059	896,059
12			918,461	918,461
13			941,422	941,422
14			964,958	964,958
15			989,082	989,082
16			1,013,809	1,013,809
17			1,039,154	1,039,154
18			1,065,133	1,065,133
19			1,091,761	1,091,761
20			1,119,055	1,119,055
21			1,147,032	1,147,032
22			1,175,707	1,175,707
23			1,205,100	1,205,100
24			1,235,227	1,235,227
Total	**$240,000,000**	**$288,000**	**$22,644,327**	**$262,932,327**

Before the value of the Insurance Initiatives can be calculated, the money available for investment must be adjusted for credit losses. That is, the pool of funds must be adjusted for money that is invested but is not repaid. For the ROI calculation, a credit loss factor of 10 percent over the life of the Initiatives has been assumed. This means that over time, 10 percent of the principal invested will not be repaid. Ten percent represents a conservative estimate of the credit loss factor. Other community investment organizations and financial intermediaries that lend money in a manner similar to the Insurance Initiatives

Table 4. Investment into insurance initiatives.

Year	Life Company Investment	Property/Casualty Company Investment	Total Investment
1999	$19,900,000	$16,348,800	$36,248,800
2000	19,900,000	16,348,800	36,248,800
2001	19,968,800	16,348,800	36,317,600
2002	20,000,000	16,348,800	36,348,800
2003	20,000,000	16,348,800	36,348,800
Total	**$99,768,800**	**$81,744,000**	**$181,512,800**

have credit loss factors ranging from 2.5 percent to 10 percent, with most being below 5 percent over time.

A key benefit to community development activities in Massachusetts from the Insurance Initiatives is that principal capital repaid from maturing investments will be reinvested into additional community development projects throughout the life of the Initiatives. The Insurance Initiatives are making short-term, intermediate-term, and long-term investments. Short-term investments are under three years. Intermediate-term investments are between three and seven years, and long-term investments are beyond seven years. Because the insurance companies cannot begin to pull their capital out until the beginning of the 19th year, the capital in the funds can be reinvested. As the shorter-term investments mature, the investment capital is returned to the Initiatives, and then reinvested in additional community development projects. Rufus Phillips, vice president of PCI, estimates that PCI will attempt to turn over the investment funds four or five times during the 24-year life. The Life Initiative is expected do the same. That means that the $181 million could be used to generate $724 million of community investments, assuming a turnover rate of four times.

The November 2000 report by the Massachusetts Association of Community Development Corporations provides a more conservative estimate. The Life Initiative, based on its first two years of investments (approximately $40 million), estimates $5 million of repayments available for reinvestment in year six. Translated over the entire $100 million Life Initiative investment pool, this would be $12.5 million of repayment available for reinvestment in year six. This translates to

12.5 percent of the capital being available for reinvestment in each year, from which a 2.6 times turnover rate can be calculated. With a turnover rate of 2.6 times, the $181 million would generate $470 million of community development investment over 20 years. The more conservative 2.6 times turnover rate for the investment funds has been used in the calculation of benefits for the ROI calculation. Table 5 provides a summary of funds available for investment. Table 6 shows the calculation of the turnover rate.

Table 5. Benefits.

Funds for Investment in Community Development

Year	Insurance Co. Contributions	Credit Loss	Return of Principal	Available for Investment
1	$36,248,800	$0		$36,248,800
2	36,248,800	−195,381	$0	36,053,419
3	36,317,600	−389,709	0	35,927,891
4	36,348,800	−583,360	0	35,765,440
5	36,348,800	−776,136	0	35,572,664
6	0	−967,873	22,446,027	21,478,154
7	0	−962,656	22,325,043	21,362,387
8	0	−957,467	22,204,711	21,247,244
9	0	−952,306	22,085,027	21,132,721
10	0	−947,173	21,965,989	21,018,816
11	0	−942,068	21,847,592	20,905,524
12	0	−936,990	21,729,834	20,792,843
13	0	−931,940	21,612,710	20,680,770
14	0	−926,917	21,496,217	20,569,301
15	0	−921,921	21,380,353	20,458,432
16	0	−916,952	21,265,113	20,348,161
17	0	−912,009	21,150,494	20,238,484
18	0	−907,094	21,036,493	20,129,399
19	0	−902,204	20,923,106	20,020,902
20	0	−897,341	40,723,319	0
21	0	−892,505	40,728,156	0
22	0	−668,169	40,952,491	0
23	0	−443,834	41,176,827	0
24	0	−219,499	41,401,162	0
Total	$181,512,800	−$18,151,504	$508,450,664	$469,951,352

Table 6. Investment turnover rate.

Total amount invested over 20 years	$469,951,352
Initial insurance company contributions	$181,512,800
Turnover rate $=$	$\dfrac{\text{Total Invested}}{\text{Initial Contributions}}$
Turnover rate $=$	$\dfrac{\$469{,}951{,}352}{\$181{,}512{,}800}$
Turnover rate $=$	2.59

ROI Calculation

Once the costs and benefits have been determined, the next step is the calculation of the net present value (NPV) of the costs and benefits. The annual benefit and cost amounts have been determined as described above. Benefits include the initial investment into the Insurance Initiatives by the insurance companies and the reinvestment of principal from matured investments, net of estimated credit losses. Costs include the value of the tax relief granted the insurance companies and the annual costs of operating the Insurance Initiatives.

The costs and benefits have been discounted using a 7.5 percent discount rate. The investments from the Insurance Initiatives are expected to yield between 6.0 percent and 7.5 percent. Seven-and-a-half percent represents the highest rate, which is most conservative, and hence has been used as the discount rate.

The NPV of the program costs is $204.0 million. The NPV of the program benefits is $268.8 million. Table 7 shows the NPV calculation for the program benefits and costs.

Once the net value of the program costs and programs benefits are known, the benefit-cost ratio (BCR) and return on investment are calculated. (See table 8.)

The ROI to the Commonwealth of Massachusetts from the passage of this legislation is 31.77 percent. This ROI calculation was performed using conservative estimates of both benefits and costs.

It appears that the full benefits anticipated by the legislature when they passed this legislation will not be realized. Instead, benefits will

Table 7. Net present value of costs and benefits.

Year	Total Annual Cost	NPV of Annual Cost at 7.5%	Funds Available for Investment	NPV of Available Funds at 7.5%
1	$48,988,000	$45,570,233	$36,248,800	$33,719,814
2	48,717,500	42,156,842	36,053,419	31,198,199
3	48,735,438	39,230,106	35,927,891	28,920,536
4	48,753,823	36,506,889	35,765,440	26,781,180
5	48,772,669	33,973,024	35,572,664	24,778,446
6	791,986	513,176	21,478,154	13,917,017
7	811,785	489,308	21,362,387	12,876,283
8	832,080	466,549	21,247,244	11,913,377
9	852,882	444,849	21,132,721	11,022,478
10	874,204	424,159	21,018,816	10,198,202
11	896,059	404,430	20,905,524	9,435,566
12	918,461	385,620	20,792,843	8,729,961
13	941,422	367,684	20,680,770	8,077,122
14	964,958	350,582	20,569,301	7,473,104
15	989,082	334,276	20,458,432	6,914,255
16	1,013,809	318,728	20,348,161	6,397,197
17	1,039,154	303,904	20,238,484	5,918,806
18	1,065,133	289,769	20,129,399	5,476,189
19	1,091,761	276,291	20,020,902	5,066,672
20	1,119,055	263,440	0	0
21	1,147,032	251,187	0	0
22	1,175,707	239,504	0	0
23	1,205,100	228,364	0	0
24	1,235,227	217,743	0	0
	NPV =	$204,006,657	NPV =	$268,814,404

be a smaller amount. This smaller program amount has been used in the ROI calculation.

Likewise, a conservative estimate of program costs has been used. First, there were several estimates of costs of the tax relief to state. Program costs have been calculated using the higher of these estimates. Second, because the insurance industry has not invested in PCI at the anticipated levels, the tax relief will not be as costly to the state as originally anticipated, however, program costs continue to include the costs estimates for tax relief. (See table 9.)

Table 8. Benefit-cost (BCR) ratio.

Program Benefits	$268,814,404
Program Costs	$204,006,657

$$BCR = \frac{\text{Program Benefits}}{\text{Program Costs}}$$

$$BCR = \frac{\$268,814,404}{\$204,006,657}$$

$$BCR = 1.32$$

Table 9. Return on investment (ROI).

Program Benefits	$268,814,404
Program Costs	$204,006,657
Net Program Benefits	$64,807,747

$$ROI\,(\%) = \frac{\text{Net Program Benefits}}{\text{Program Costs}}$$

$$ROI\,(\%) = \frac{\$64,807,747}{\$204,006,657}$$

$$ROI\,(\%) = 31.77\%$$

Intangible Benefits

In addition to the financial benefits described above, the passage of this community investment act by the Massachusetts legislature has generated some benefits that could not be quantified and included in the ROI calculation. These are known as intangible benefits.

The first intangible benefit is improved relations between the insurance industry and the community development groups. During most of the 1990s the relationship between these groups was characterized by a degree of distrust. In spite of the success of MCRC, the insurance industry was not actively and consistently investing in community development in Massachusetts. The insurance companies had the impression that community development projects were bad investments. The community development groups felt that the insurance companies were happy to take premium dollars from a community, but that they wanted no part of investing in those communities.

The creation of the Insurance Initiatives and the process by which these initiatives were created has changed that. The life insurance companies formed a task force to study community development and community development organizations. One of the outcomes of this task force was an understanding of community development organizations on the part of the insurance companies and an understanding that community development investments did not have to be bad investments. Sound community development investments could be made, and in fact were routinely made by many of the community development lending institutions.

The process of negotiating the legislation also improved the relationship between the groups. In order to get to consensus, each group—the legislature, the community groups, and the insurance companies—had to understand the particular issues affecting the other groups. With this understanding came an improved relationship.

A second intangible benefit was that additional funds were available for community development investment in Massachusetts. One of the financing gaps identified by the life insurance company investment task force was the lack of funds for longer-term loans. A part of the investments from the Insurance Initiatives are for longer-term loans. Additionally, the Insurance Initiatives have invested some of their funds into the loan funds of Massachusetts-based community development lending institutions. That has served to provide additional loan capital to these institutions, strengthening their financial position, and has improved the relationship between these institutions and the insurance industry.

Finally, with this legislation, Massachusetts has provided a model for effective community investment on the part of insurance companies.

Communication Process

This is the first-of-its-kind legislation in the United States. As a result, it has received considerable attention and press coverage. The local Boston press provided extensive coverage of the legislation as it was being negotiated with the legislature and as it became law. The press has continued to cover the Insurance Initiatives over the first years of their existence. This legislation has also been discussed in two articles in journals published by Federal Home Loan Bank of Boston. These journals target banking and investment professionals and are distributed nationally. The articles are also available online.

Additionally, the Insurance Initiatives have held outreach and information meetings throughout the state, and they are required to distribute their investments geographically throughout Massachusetts. One of the criticisms of MCRC had been the concentration of its investments in the Boston area. The purpose of these meetings is to ensure that information regarding the legislation and the Insurance Initiatives is given to community development groups throughout the state.

The Massachusetts Association of Community Development Corporations has written by far the most comprehensive reports on the insurance industry and community investment. Their 1996 report, "The Insurance Industry and Low-Income Communities: A Failure to Invest," was widely distributed among legislators and community groups, and started the wave of industry criticism and community support that ultimately led to the passage of the legislation. Their 2000 report, "Insuring the Future of Our Communities: The First Progress Report on the Massachusetts Insurance Industry Investment Initiatives," describes the progress to-date in implementing the Insurance Initiatives and the benefits from the legislation.

Lessons Learned

The Massachusetts experience in granting tax relief for community investment has been a complicated process. What lessons can we take away from this process?

The primary lesson from this process is the importance of consensus and need for effective negotiation to arrive at consensus. This program provides a positive ROI for the state of Massachusetts, provides significant benefits for the insurance industry, and provides significant benefits for the community development community. The key to structuring this win-win situation is consensus. The insurance industry had been seeking tax relief throughout the 1990s, but had failed to receive it. The community development groups had been looking to the insurance industry for community development dollars since 1991. These efforts too had failed. The relationships between the insurance industry, community development groups, and the legislature included tension and distrust.

These relationships began to change in 1997 when the life insurance companies convened the community development investment task force and continued throughout the negotiation process and through the passage of the legislation in 1998. The linking of community development investment and tax relief was a critical step in creating a win-win situation.

The initial insurance industry community investment bills proposed to the legislature were copies of the bank community investment legislation. The insurance industry felt that these bills did not accurately reflect their unique investment practices, nor did the bills fit within the legal and regulatory structure of an insurance company. The insurance industry had always felt that the community investment provisions were not appropriate as presented. Through the negotiation process, the insurance companies were able to craft legislation that accommodated their investment and regulatory structure. The community development groups received representation on the boards of the Life Initiative and PCI. The process of creating the legislation included representatives from each constituency. The legislation that was ultimately passed reflected this consensus.

The consensus process is what ultimately allowed the program to be structured and was critical in getting the program structured to match the requirements of each party. Had the negotiation and consensus process been started sooner, years of wasted effort could have been avoided.

The other lesson learned from determining the ROI of this program is that it is difficult to determine the appropriate costs and benefits when a longtime horizon is involved. In this case, the program has a 24-year life expectancy. Costs and benefits do not all occur in the same time period. Initial costs are incurred to achieve long-term benefits. In order to calculate the ROI, the program costs and benefits must all be brought back to the present period. This requires that assumptions be made. Care must be taken when making these assumptions, or incorrect or overstated program costs and benefits could be determined. In this case, the program costs and benefits have been brought back to the present period using a net present value calculation, which is a standard method for this purpose. Costs and benefits have been analyzed several different ways, and the most conservative results have been used in the ROI calculation. The process to determine these conservative results requires a complete analysis of the data under differing scenarios. Thoroughness in data analysis is critical to the ROI process.

Questions for Discussion

1. Discuss the NPV assumptions. Would you change any of the NPV assumptions? Which ones? Why?
2. The costs and benefits of this program have been analyzed over the 24-year life. Is this appropriate? If not, what time horizon would you use?
3. Because the Property/Casualty Initiative is not expected to be fully funded and the full tax benefits are not expected to be received by the property/casualty insurance companies, is it still appropriate to include

the full cost of tax relief in the calculation of program costs, or should a different number be used? Discuss.

4. What would the ROI be if the cost of tax relief were based on the amount actually contributed to the Insurance Initiatives rather than the full $200 million expected contribution?

5. How important was the linking of community investment and insurance industry tax relief? Could this program have been effectively implemented without this link?

6. Discuss the importance of the negotiation and consensus building process in creating the Insurance Initiatives.

7. Is the model for community development investment developed here applicable in other states? Why? Does tax relief have to be part of the model, or would the model be transportable without tax relief?

The Author

William Hettinger is president and founder of The Wyndham Financial Group, Ltd., an economic development and community development consulting organization. He is an experienced community and economic development professional with more than 20 years' diverse experience in the for-profit and nonprofit sectors. He has extensive experience in real estate, affordable housing development, and community development programs. Prior to Wyndham Financial, he held senior positions with Aetna Inc., Coopers & Lybrand, The MassMutual Financial Group, and Co-op Initiatives, Inc. During the development of the Life Initiative, he served as a member of the life insurance company investment task force. He can be contacted at The Wyndham Financial Group, 274 Ballamahack Road, Windham, CT 06280; email: billhettinger@earthlink.net.

Further Resources

Browning, Lynnley. (1998). "Wait Is Over for In-State Insurers." *The Boston Globe*, August 11.

Callahan, Thomas. (1997). "Now is the Time for Insurance Companies to Invest in Poor Communities." *The Boston Globe,* February 13.

Commonwealth of Massachusetts. (1998). Chapter 259 of the Acts of 1998, "An Act Insuring Community Investment and the Equitable Taxation of Insurance Companies in Massachusetts." Boston, MA.

Economic Innovation International, Inc. (May 1997). "Community Investment Preliminary Market Assessment and Range of Investment Options." Report to the Life Insurance Association of Massachusetts and the Life Insurance Companies of Massachusetts. Boston, MA.

Luquetta, Andrea C. (Winter 2001). "Productive Partnerships: A Progress Report on Insurance Industry Investors." *Communities and Banking.*

Massachusetts Association of Community Development Corporations. (October 1996). "The Insurance Industry and Low-Income Communities: A Failure to Invest." Boston, MA.

Massachusetts Association of Community Development Corporations. (November 2000). "Insuring the Future of Our Communities: The First Progress Report on the Massachusetts Insurance Industry Investment Initiatives." Boston, MA.

Wilmsen, Steven. "Agreement Clears Way for Passage of Tax Cut for Insurance Companies." *The Boston Globe,* August 1.

Competency-Based Assessment of Managers and Supervisors

U.S. Immigration and Naturalization Service

Ilene F. Gast

Facing the challenges presented by unprecedented growth and the unparalleled complexity of its mission, the U.S. Immigration and Naturalization Service (INS) implemented a competency-based promotional assessment system for selecting its supervisory and managerial officer corps personnel. The new system was a critical component in the agency's efforts to develop, retain, and promote the best-qualified candidates. A return-on-investment study was performed to evaluate the cost-effectiveness and acceptance of the new selection system. This study, which examined the costs, the selection utility, and customer satisfaction with the new selection system, demonstrated its cost-effectiveness and provided input for enhancing its acceptance by candidates and selecting managers.

About the U.S. Immigration and Naturalization Service

The U.S. Immigration and Naturalization Service (INS), an agency of the Department of Justice, is responsible for enforcing the laws regulating the admission of foreign-born persons (aliens) to the United States and for administering various immigration benefits, including the naturalization of qualified applicants for U.S. citizenship. Headquartered in Washington, D.C., INS employs more than 30,000 individuals nationwide who fulfill its complex mission.

The operational and management functions of INS are administered in 33 district offices and 21 Border Patrol sectors throughout the United States and in three district offices and 39 area offices

This case was prepared to serve as a basis for discussion rather than to illustrate either effective or ineffective administrative and management practices.

outside U.S. territory. INS field offices provide direct service to applicants for benefits under the Immigration and Nationality Act and implement INS policies to carry out statutory enforcement responsibilities in their respective geographical areas. In addition, overseas offices facilitate the exchange of information between INS and U.S. Foreign Service officers and foreign government officials abroad.

Background: The Need to Improve Selection at the INS

Under a congressional mandate to strengthen its enforcement and benefit-providing capabilities, the INS workforce has grown by 60 percent since 1995. During this time of unprecedented growth, INS could have easily set its sights on meeting the stringent hiring goals while compromising on hiring standards or ignoring the need for employee development. Rather than cutting corners, INS identified increasing the professionalism of the INS workforce to be a key goal, and the INS dedicated the requisite resources to improving employee selection and development. To accomplish this, INS constructed and validated state-of-the-science objective, competency-based assessments to ensure that new employees were selected based on the key competencies required for outstanding performance and then were trained on those same competencies.

With the dramatic increase in the number of new, entry-level employees came a corresponding need for well-qualified supervisors and managers. Consequently, INS revamped both its entry-level selection and promotional systems. This study describes the initial implementation and evaluation of a competency-based promotional assessment system within one of the INS's major programs, the U.S. Border Patrol. Based on the successful implementation within the U.S. Border Patrol, the system has since been expanded to cover promotions in all of INS's officer corps occupations.

A New Approach to Promoting Supervisors and Managers: The Competency-Based Promotional Assessment System
The Need for a New Promotional System

For years, INS had relied on a system of rating and ranking candidates' qualifications to select the supervisors and managers in its officer corps occupations. Candidates for supervisory and managerial positions submitted written statements of their qualifications in several key areas along with a standard federal government resume form. For each vacancy, the Office of Human Resources and Development (HRD) convened a panel of job incumbents who rated and ranked all candidates who met the minimum qualifications.

Candidates expressed concern about the objectivity of this selection process and about the lack of feedback regarding the reasons they were not selected for a given position. Unless candidates were among the top few who were called by the hiring manager for an interview, they were unlikely to receive feedback about why they were not selected for the position.

Recognizing a clear need to modernize and streamline the process for selecting supervisors and managers, INS's top management looked to its Research and Development Branch (R&D) to design, develop, and implement a state-of-the-science promotional assessment system. (The R&D Branch is a group of 16 psychologists and five support personnel who are located at INS's Office of Human Resources and Development.)

Developing a New Competency-Based Promotional Assessment System

Before developing the new system, the R&D Branch conducted a comprehensive job analysis that defined the tasks comprising supervisory and managerial U.S. Border Patrol agent jobs and identified the competencies most critical for successful performance in these jobs. R&D psychologists visited several U.S. Border Patrol installations where they held a series of subject matter expert (SME) panels. From the SMEs, R&D psychologists collected information about job duties of supervisory and managerial Border Patrol agents and the competencies required to perform these jobs effectively. That information enabled the R&D Branch to prepare a survey that was mailed to a sample of job incumbents. Once analyzed, this data profiled typical job activities and outlined the competencies required for effective job performance.

Armed with information about the important components of supervisory and managerial jobs, the R&D Branch specified the kinds of assessments that would comprise the new promotional system. To be included, an assessment had to replicate key job activities and had to provide accurate measurement of the competencies required for successful performance. In addition, assessments could not be burdensome to implement in INS's decentralized field structure.

Working extensively with SMEs, the R&D Branch developed four objectively scored assessments for the new selection system: the Past Achievement Record, the Decision-Making Situational Assessment, the In-Basket Job Simulation, and the Managerial Writing Skills Exercise. Development of these assessments relied heavily on critical incidents, documents, and other job-related materials that SMEs had provided to the assessment development team. In addition, SMEs participated in the review, refinement, and documentation of the validity of the assessments. As a result, these assessments provided realistic yet balanced coverage of the critical competency areas.

The Competency-Based Assessments

The Past Achievement Record solicited candidates' written descriptions of their optimal achievements in a number of job-related competencies including technical skills and personal attributes such as flexibility and leadership. These written descriptions were scored against standardized benchmarks by a panel of trained R&D psychologists.

Participants completed the Past Achievement Record before scheduling themselves for three multiple-choice assessments. One of these, the Decision-Making Situational Assessment addressed important thinking skills of reasoning, decision making, and problem solving. Candidates evaluated information that they would be expected to encounter frequently on the job. The second, the In-Basket Job Simulation, simulated the administrative portion of the job. It addressed administrative skills such as planning and evaluating, managing and organizing information, and self-management. Finally, the Managerial Writing Skills Exercise evaluated participants' job-related writing skills.

The Assessment Process

The process begins when a candidate submits an application to complete the assessments. HRD screens all applications to ensure that candidates meet the minimum job qualifications. If applicants meet the minimum qualifications, they are scheduled for an assessment session during which they complete the three multiple-choice assessments.

Before the assessment session, HRD sends candidates detailed information about the assessments. These materials explain how the assessments were developed, which competencies are measured, and how assessment scores will be used. Candidates also receive practice exercises and tips for performing optimally on the assessments. Finally, candidates receive the Past Achievement Record, which should be completed and returned prior to the assessment. (As a result of the present study, the Past Achievement Record was replaced with a new Job Experience Measure. The basic application and assessment procedure has remained the same.)

After completing the assessments, candidates receive their score and become eligible to compete for job vacancies. Candidates also receive competency-linked diagnostic feedback and developmental recommendations to enhance areas of strength and to improve on areas of weakness.

Implementation of the Competency-Based Promotional Assessments in the Border Patrol

The first application of the competency-based promotional assessment system was developed for filling supervisory, managerial, and staff officer vacancies in the U.S. Border Patrol. The new competency-based system was implemented in January 1997. Subsequently, assessments have been administered nationwide in January, May, and September of each year.

The Target Population

The U.S. Border Patrol is the mobile, uniformed branch of the Immigration and Naturalization Service. The Border Patrol's mission is to detect and prevent the smuggling and illegal entry of aliens into the United States. Border Patrol agents work primarily along, and in the vicinity of, the 8,000 miles of United States boundaries. Agents patrol by means of automobile, boat, aircraft, horseback, snowmobile, motorcycle, bicycle, and on foot. Currently about 10,000 individuals work in the U.S. Border Patrol. About 1,500 hold supervisory, managerial, and staff officer positions.

INS uses its competency-based promotional assessment system for selecting the full range of supervisory, managerial, and staff officer positions in the U.S. Border Patrol. For example, the system covers the first-line supervisors who are directly responsible for the day-to-day supervision of Border Patrol agents; Field Operations Supervisors, who supervise the first-line supervisors in the larger stations; and Chief Patrol Agents and their deputies who manage U.S. Border Patrol stations. The system also applies to staff officers who are responsible for U.S. Border Patrol program coordination at the regional and headquarters level. Since its implementation in 1997, more than 4,600 individuals have participated in the Border Patrol competency-based promotional assessment process.

Evaluating INS's Return on its Investment in Improved Selection
The Return-on-Investment Model

To be able to evaluate the benefits of the competency-based assessment process for the U.S. Border Patrol, the R&D Branch conducted a return-on-investment (ROI) study. As a first step, the R&D Branch developed a generic ROI model to guide this and all future ROI studies. This model, presented in figure 1, addresses the costs and returns—monetary and nonmonetary—that accrue from use of valid personnel assessment systems.

Figure 1. Return-on-investment model.

Investment	Return on Investment
Costs	**Monetary Returns**
• Basic research and design	• Utility
• Assessment development	• Organizational economies
• Implementation	
• Program administration	**Intangibles**
• Evaluation	• Impact on direct customers
	• Impact on indirect customers

Costs

The ROI model specifies broad categories of costs incurred in producing a new assessment system. Costs include the basic research and design of the assessment system, the development of the specific assessments, the implementation of the new system, program administration, and evaluation.

Monetary Returns

The ROI model also outlines potential payoffs of a new assessment system. One form of payoff is expressed in dollars. Dollar-valued returns can be expressed as selection utility, or the monetary value of improved performance attained through test use. Dollar-valued returns can also be expressed as organizational economies, which derive from the increased efficiency of the new assessment system. For example, a new, more highly automated selection system might decrease staff time and associated costs involved in processing candidates' applications for promotion.

Intangibles

Equally important are the costs and benefits that are not easily expressed in dollars. Many new assessment systems fail even though they produce dramatic cost savings through improved selection. Failure may result from insufficient attention to candidates' concerns, lack of acceptance by decision makers, or poor public perception of the program. Therefore, the model addresses the perceptions of direct customers (test takers and selecting officials) and indirect customers (prospective coworkers and members of the public).

The Return-on-Investment Study for the Competency-Based Promotional Assessment System

Based on its ROI model, the R&D Branch developed a plan to measure the return-on-investment study of the Competency-Based Promotional Assessment System that was implemented for the U.S. Border Patrol. The ROI study had three distinct phases. During the first phase the tangible costs of the new system and its predecessor were measured.

The second phase examined the monetary returns from the new selection system. A utility study estimated the dollar-valued increase in productivity attributable to the new selection procedure. During this phase, the R&D Branch also intended to determine whether the INS realized cost savings from a reduction in the number of requests for assessment-related information under the Freedom of Information Act (FOIA). R&D psychologists had devised a plan to monitor FOIA requests received by one of INS's regional offices. However, operational concerns prevented data collection.

In the final phase, the R&D Branch analyzed the intangible costs and benefits of the new program. Data came from two customer satisfaction surveys, interviews with hiring managers, and town hall–type meetings with candidates.

Phase 1: Analysis of Tangible Program Costs
The Cost of the Competency-Based Promotional Assessment System

Table 1 summarizes the estimated costs for designing, developing, implementing, operating, and evaluating the new selection system. Costs were estimated for personnel, resources, and project-related travel.

Table 1. Annualized investment costs for the competency-based promotional system in the U.S. Border Patrol.

Cost Category	Staff Costs	Travel	Resources	Total
Basic research and design	$17,220	$1,000	$740	$18,960
Development	$172,200	$5,000	$1,200	$178,400
Project administration	$23,200	$10,000	$500	$33,700
Implementation	$224,350	$10,000	$285,500	$519,850
Evaluation	$33,200	$5,000	$1,350	$39,550
Total Costs	$470,170	$31,000	$289,290	$790,460

Project staff members provided detailed estimates of the time spent working on each aspect of the new promotional system. Personnel costs were then calculated based on the average staff salary and benefits for the year in which the work was performed. Financial records provided the actual costs of purchases, contracts with other organizations, and project-related travel. Unless otherwise indicated, design, development, and evaluation costs were amortized over two years, which is the length of the typical assessment development cycle. Implementation and administration costs were annualized to yield an average yearly cost for operating the selection system.

Basic research and design included the costs for laying the groundwork for the new selection system. Staff activities included a review of relevant literature and best practices, the job analysis, and the development of the assessment plan. Costs were amortized over five years because this groundwork was expected to hold firm for five years. Development, a more substantial cost, covered producing all the materials, systems, and procedures required by the new system. Included were staff costs, site visits, and software purchased to support the design and operation of the candidate database. Project administration costs covered the time spent by R&D's managers in directing and overseeing R&D staff activities. Project management activities included conducting briefings, developing new policies, and monitoring contractor performance.

Implementation was by far the greatest cost involved in the new system. It included the costs of running the application process (dissemination, screening, and processing), administering and scoring assessments, disseminating assessment results to candidates, and preparing lists of eligible candidates, which were forwarded to hiring managers. By contrast, the costs of evaluation were relatively small, including the cost of conducting the cost-benefit analysis, the utility study, and the customer satisfaction survey and interviews.

The total estimated annualized cost of the new system was $790,460. The estimated cost of filling a vacancy is $2,744, and the cost of assessing a single candidate is about $284. (See table 2.)

The Cost of the Prior Promotional Assessment System

To estimate the cost of filling a vacancy under the preexisting selection system, the R&D Branch worked closely with HRD and the Office of Finance. The resulting estimate included the salary, travel expenses, and per diem of the three senior job incumbents who rated and ranked applicants for a typical vacancy. The estimate also included the salary of a personnel specialist who set up and managed the panel. Table 2

Table 2. Costs of selection under the competency-based promotional assessment system and the preexisting selection system.

Costs	Preexisting Selection System For supervisors	For managers	Competency-Based Assessments For supervisors or managers
—Per applicant	$172	$532	$284
—Per vacancy	$1,597	$5,810	$2,744
Program cost per year	$733,781		$790,460

Note: Cost figures are based on annualized estimates for evaluating 2,781 applicants (2,073 supervisory applicants and 708 managerial applicants) to fill 288 vacancies (223 supervisory vacancies and 65 managerial vacancies).

provides the costs under the prior system for assessing an applicant, filling a vacancy, and operating the system for one year.

Comparing the Two Promotional Assessment Systems

The competency-based promotional assessment system relies on standardized assessments for filling all vacancies. Therefore, costs remain constant across all vacancies ($2,744), regardless of the level of the position. This was not true for the preexisting selection system. Filling managerial vacancies cost substantially more ($5,810) than filling supervisory vacancies ($1,597). Salary and travel costs explain this difference. Supervisory job incumbents are plentiful in all but the smallest U.S. Border Patrol sectors. They are readily available to serve on rating panels, so raters did not typically incur travel and per diem costs. The higher-graded, managerial incumbents are fewer in number and more dispersed geographically. Panel members' salary, travel expenses, and extended per diem expenses drove up the cost of filling managerial vacancies.

Nevertheless, the annualized cost for filling vacancies under the prior system was slightly less than that of the competency-based system. (See table 2.) This advantage is illusory, however; the cost analysis fails to take into account the increased productivity that can be realized from increasing the accuracy of predicting supervisory and managerial performance.

Phase 2: The Utility Analysis
What is Utility Analysis?

Utility analysis builds on cost analysis by assigning a dollar value to the gain in productivity that comes from using a more effective selection instrument. One determination of a selection instrument is its validity (r_{xy}), or the relationship between the selection instrument and an indicator of job performance. The validity coefficient provides an index of the accuracy of a selection instrument to predict performance. When an organization uses valid selection instruments to select employees and chooses the high scorers rather than the low scorers, then the new employees perform better and are more productive than employees chosen by a less accurate selection procedure. Assessments with higher validity produce proportionally higher gains in productivity. Utility analysis provides a means of translating this gain in productivity into economic terms.

Utility also depends on the variability in job performance (SD_y). If employees did not vary in their job performance, an employer could hire anyone and it would not matter. However, employees do vary in their productivity, and productivity can be translated into economic terms. For decades, the process for translating variability in performance into dollar terms eluded personnel selection experts. Then in 1979, two such experts, Frank Schmidt and John Hunter, developed a procedure for assigning a dollar value to variability in job performance (Schmidt, Hunter, McKenzie, and Muldrow, 1979). Their procedure enabled personnel selection experts to assign a dollar figure to the increase in productivity that could be expected as the organization used more accurate selection procedures.

Schmidt and Hunter asked SMEs, usually individuals who are supervising the job, to establish the worth of performance at various levels. First, these researchers asked SMEs to examine the range of possible job performance. Next, the SMEs estimated the dollar value of an average employee (one who performs at the 50th percentile). SMEs also placed a dollar value of a superior employee (one who performs at the 84th percentile or 1 standard deviation above the mean). Finally, SMEs established the worth of a poor performer (one whose performance is at the 16th percentile or 1 standard deviation below the mean).

After conducting several studies, Schmidt and Hunter (1983) found that SMEs consistently described poor performers as worth about 40 percent of the valuation of an average performer. SMEs also consistently described superior performers as worth at least 40 percent more than average performers. For example, if the value of an average employee is estimated at $40,000 per year, the value of a superior performer would add 40 percent more ($16,000) to total $56,000. Thus, by using Schmidt and Hunter's method, it is relatively easy to estimate the dollar value of job performance based on a job incumbents' salary and benefits package.

The utility of a selection procedure also depends on applicant quality. A good indicator of an applicant's quality is how well he or she performed on the selection procedure. Therefore, the utility calculation incorporates the average standardized test score ($\bar{Z}$) of those who were selected. To a great extent, the labor market will dictate applicant quality. In a tight labor market, an organization may need to hire everyone who applies for a job; a valid selection procedure will have less practical value than when labor is more plentiful. In these times, the organization may have the luxury of hiring the top 1 percent of applicants, and it can realize large gains from using a valid selection procedure.

These three factors: validity, variability in job performance, and applicant quality comprise the basic utility model. The basic utility model is expressed in the following equation:

$$) = r_{xy} SD_y \bar{Z}$$

The basic model calculates the dollar-valued increase in productivity for one employee for one year, assuming that no prior selection procedure existed. But the basic model is flexible and can be tailored to meet the needs of a specific study.

The current study used a variation of the basic model that incorporated the costs and validities of the present and preexisting systems into the analysis (Schmidt, Mack, and Hunter, 1984). This model, shown in figure 2, adjusts "gains in productivity" for the number of employees selected per year and for their average tenure. Benefits continue to accrue to the organization for as long as an employee remains in the job. This model uses the validity of the existing system as a baseline and computes the net gain (or decrement) in validity attributable to a new selection system.

The expanded model also subtracts the net difference in the cost of the two programs from the "gains in productivity." If the new program costs less than the one it replaces, the organization realizes additional gains. This difference in cost is divided by the selection ratio, which is the average number of applicants for each job opening. Assuming that the selection ratio is .1, an organization must pay the cost of assessing 10 applicants to select one. In this case, dividing the selection ratio of .1 appropriately multiplies the cost figure by a factor of 10.

Figure 2. The utility analysis formula and terms used in the current study.

$$)U = \frac{\text{Gains in Productivity}}{[TN_s\,(r_1 - r_2)\,SD_y\,\bar{z}]} \quad - \quad \frac{\text{Program Costs}}{[N_s\,(C_1 - C_2)\,/\,p]}$$

Term	Definition	Term	Definition
$)U$	The gain in productivity in $ during tenure of employee	N_s	The number selected per year
T	Tenure in years of the average selectee	C_1	The cost of the competency-based promotional system
N_s	Number selected per year	C_2	The cost of the preexisting selection procedure
r_1	Validity of the competency-based promotional system		
r_2	Validity of the preexisting selection procedure	p	The selection ratio
SD_y	The dollar value of performance		
$\bar{z}$	The mean score of those who were selected		

The Predictive Validity of the Competency-Based Promotional Assessment System

A validity coefficient, the numerical index of how well the assessment predicts future performance, is a prerequisite for determining the utility of a selection procedure. At the time the ROI study was conducted, the R&D Branch did not have the data necessary to calculate an INS-specific estimate of predictive validity. A job analysis had established the assessment battery's content validity, or correspondence to important job tasks, and its construct validity, or coverage of critical competencies (Pollack, Gast, Beatty, Kimball, and Malik, 1997). Therefore, to obtain the requisite estimate of predictive validity, R&D psychologists relied on cumulated research evidence, or metanalysis (Schmidt, Hunter, and Jackson, 1982).

Several researchers had conducted metanalytic studies that cumulated validity evidence on assessments similar to those in INS's promotional battery. In one such metanalytic study, McDaniel, Schmidt, and Hunter (1988a) cumulated the validity evidence for behavioral consistency-based assessments similar to the Past Achievement Record and estimated their validity to be .32. Trattner (1988) metanalyzed the validities of cognitive ability tests and verbal ability tests for selecting managers. His research provided the validity estimates for the Decision-Making Situational Assessment and Managerial Writing

Skills Exercise, which were .39 and .58 respectively. A metanalytic study conducted by Doverspike, Winter, Healy, and Barrett (1996) provided the validity estimate for the In-Basket Job Simulation ($r = .52$). Finally, another metanalysis done by McDaniel, Schmidt, and Hunter (1988b) provided an estimate for the validity of the preexisting selection system ($r = .14$). Table 3 displays these estimates of validity.

R&D psychologists combined these estimates to yield an overall validity estimate for the promotional assessment battery. (Individual validity estimates were combined using the formula for differentially weighted composite scores and an outside criterion variable presented in Ghiselli, Campbell, and Zedeck, 1981.) Because the assessments received different weights in the supervisory and managerial batteries, separate validity coefficients were calculated for each battery. Table 4 displays the weights assigned to the assessments included in these batteries and the resulting validity estimates. These estimated validities (.56 for the supervisory battery and .64 for the managerial battery) enabled R&D psychologists to complete the utility analyses.

The Utility of the Competency-Based Promotional Assessment System

Figure 3 shows each value entered into the utility model. After examining retention data, R&D psychologists estimated tenure to be five years. The data suggested that once individuals are promoted into the supervisory ranks they remain with the U.S. Border Patrol for at least five years. At the time the R&D Branch conducted this study, the annualized selection rate (N) was 223 supervisors and 65 managers per year. The U.S. Border Patrol averaged 10 applicants for each managerial and supervisory vacancy, making the selection ratio (p) .10.

Table 3. Validity estimates for the competency-based promotional assessment system and the preexisting selection system.

Assessment	Validity Estimate	
	Mean r	**Corrected r***
Past Achievement Record	.25	.32
Decision-Making Situational Assessment	.30	.39
Managerial Writing Skills Exercise	.45	.58
In-Basket Job Simulation	.40	.52
Preexisting Training and Experience Evaluation System	.11	.14

Note: The analysis used validities that were corrected for criterion unreliability.

Table 4. The estimated validity of the supervisory and managerial batteries.

Assessment	Supervisory Battery		Managerial Battery	
	r	Weight	r	Weight
Past Achievement Record	.32	30	.32	20
Decision-Making Situational Assessment	.39	50	.39	30
Managerial Writing Skills Exercise	.58	20	.58	20
In-Basket Job Simulation	.52	N/A	.52	30
Estimated Battery Validity	.56		.64	

The battery validities were estimated based on the previously described metanalytic studies. Program costs were calculated as described in the cost analysis. The dollar value of performance (SD_y), was estimated to be 40 percent of an average supervisor's or manager's salary (see Schmidt & Hunter 1998).

Table 5 provides the results of the utility analysis. For the average U.S. Border Patrol supervisor, who makes about $86,000 per year in salary and benefits, the $10,030 utility figure translates into about six weeks worth of additional productivity from each supervisor per year. For managers, who earn about $105,000 per year in salary and benefits, the $15,251 utility figure translates into nearly two months

Figure 3. The values of variables included in the utility analysis.

$$)U = \quad \frac{\text{Gains in Productivity}}{[TN_s \, (r_1 - r_2) \, SD_y \, \bar{z}]} \quad - \quad \frac{\text{Program Costs}}{[N_s \, (C_1 - C_2) / p]}$$

Term	Value		Term	Value
T	5 years		C_1	$289 per applicant
N_s	223 supervisors 65 managers		C_2	$172 per applicant for supervisors $532 per applicant for managers
r_1	.56 for supervisors .64 for managers		p	.10
r_2	.14			
SD_y	40% of salary $37,028 for supervisors $42,037 for managers			
$\bar{z}$	.66 for supervisors .61 for managers			

Table 5. The results of the utility analysis.

Tenure	Supervisors (N = 223)		Managers (N = 65)	
	1 year	5 years	1 year	5 years
Overall utility	$2,236,726	$11,183,630	$991,334	$4,324,867
Utility per selectee	$10,030	$50,151	$ 15,251	$66,536
Total Annualized Utility	$3,228,060			

Note: Some minor discrepancies in calculations are due to rounding error.

of additional productivity. The organizational utility value of these assessments has been conservatively estimated at $3.2 million per annum.

Phase 3: Analysis of Intangibles

The R&D Branch used a range of qualitative information to evaluate the intangible costs and benefits of the new promotional system. The data sources included a brief exit survey administered after candidates had completed the assessments, a more comprehensive customer satisfaction survey that was mailed to candidates, proceedings from town hall–type meetings with candidates, and interviews with managers at several U.S. Border Patrol facilities.

An exit survey conducted immediately after candidates completed the written assessments produced a cursory view of candidates' attitudes toward the new promotional system. Of the 1,453 candidates who completed the assessments at that time, only about 11 percent returned the survey. These candidates were relatively satisfied with the administration process and the quality of the assessment instruments. However, communication between Border Patrol managers and R&D management suggested that the R&D Branch needed to take a closer look at other aspects of implementation.

Consequently, the R&D Branch mailed a more extensive customer satisfaction survey to all 1,453 candidates who had thus far completed the assessment process. The expanded survey addressed candidates' opinions about the assessment process, the personnel who conducted the assessments, the assessment sites, the preassessment materials, the assessments themselves, and the postassessment feedback reports. This more comprehensive survey provided additional insight into candidates' reactions and their opinions of the assessment process. This time, 475 candidates (33 percent) returned their surveys, 383 of whom elected to provide written comments. The results of the customer satisfaction were tabulated and summarized. Written comments were content analyzed into logical categories.

In addition to conducting the survey, R&D psychologists visited six strategically selected U.S. Border Patrol facilities. During these visits, R&D psychologists conducted individual meetings with senior managers and town hall–type meetings open to anyone who wished to attend. In these meetings, R&D psychologists took detailed notes that were content analyzed and combined with the results of the two customer satisfaction surveys.

The results of the second customer satisfaction survey proved consistent with the results of the earlier survey. The majority of candidates were satisfied with the delivery of the assessments, assessment administrators were viewed as professional, and candidates were generally pleased with the quality of the assessment sites. The vast majority of respondents indicated that they had sufficient time to complete the assessments. In addition, candidates were well satisfied with the customer service provided by the R&D personnel in handling questions about the assessment process.

In their written comments and in their meetings with the R&D psychologists, candidates indicated that the assessment system as a whole did not give adequate weight to their specialized job knowledge and experience. The Past Achievement Record frustrated many candidates because its format prevented them from providing adequate depth and breadth in their descriptions. Candidates also wanted more specific feedback about their performance on the assessments so that they could target their efforts to improve. Finally, candidates requested that the assessments be administered more frequently.

During their discussions with the R&D psychologists, the hiring managers expressed satisfaction with the quality of the candidates referred to them for job openings and the timeliness of these referrals. But managers were dissatisfied with the number of candidates referred. In many cases, the new system provided them with the names of the three best-qualified candidates. Under the previous system, hiring managers typically received eight to 12 names, which gave them a greater amount of discretion over the selection process. In addition, managers wanted more information than the current system provided. They wanted to be able to temper their selections with information about candidates' specific experiences and past performance.

Results of the Return-on-Investment Study

Perhaps the most positive outcome of the ROI study and program evaluation was that it strengthened the acceptance of the assessment program throughout the agency. Impressed with the promise of improved productivity, INS's top management sustained their support of the competency-based promotional assessment system.

A second outcome was the strengthening of communication lines between the R&D Branch and field personnel in the INS programs covered by the promotional assessment system. The R&D Branch intensified its up-front marketing efforts during subsequent implementation of the assessment system in the Detention and Removal, Investigations, Inspections, and Adjudications programs. Prior to implementation, managers and potential candidates in these programs received briefings that explained the changes that the new program would bring.

In addition, the R&D Branch strove to maintain the customer service that had been universally praised by survey respondents. Also, the R&D Branch expanded its already extensive involvement of subject matter experts in the design and development of the assessment instruments.

Finally, several program changes occurred. These changes enhanced implementation of the competency-based promotional assessment system in additional INS occupations. As a result of the study, the R&D Branch responded to managers' concerns by scheduling additional assessment administration sessions, thereby reducing the number of individuals who were away from their posts completing the assessments at any given time. That reduced the strain on work units that were already spread thin. Hiring managers also received longer lists of eligible candidates and information about candidates' past experience.

Another program change was the replacement of the Past Achievement Record with a new measure of job experience. The R&D Branch worked closely with subject matter experts to design a new measure that provided a more thorough and stringent assessment of job relevant experience. The new Job Experience Measure (JEM) gives credit for specific jobs, details, and collateral assignments. It assesses job knowledge indirectly through past experience.

Finally, the R&D Branch addressed candidates' desire for more information about the assessment process and about their personal performance. The R&D Branch developed new workbook-style preparation manuals. In addition, candidates received the more detailed competency-based diagnostic feedback that they had requested.

Communication of Results

Upon completing the ROI study, the R&D Branch briefed the director of the INS Office of Human Resources and Development and her staff on the results of the study. The briefing covered the procedures used to assess tangible and intangible costs and benefits, provided a brief synopsis of changes requested as a result of the analysis of qualitative data, and outlined plans for modifying the promotional assessment system. The R&D Branch focused on how the system might be changed to increase its effectiveness and its acceptance by its customers. The INS deputy commissioner, who was particularly interested in the results of the utility analysis, received a similar briefing.

Lessons Learned

The R&D Branch learned several important lessons while implementing and evaluating the competency-based promotional assessment system in the U.S. Border Patrol. Perhaps the most enlightening lesson learned was how receptive and responsive top management can be to cost data. Because the competency-based promotional assessment system produced cost savings through improved productivity, INS's senior managers willingly provided the latitude and resources needed to refine the program.

A second lesson learned was how critical it is to have support from midlevel management. Top-level management support, though necessary, may not be sufficient to ensure program success. Midlevel managers are usually responsible for implementing new programs. If their concerns are not addressed, midlevel managers can potentially foil implementation of a new system, erode top management support, and ultimately kill a promising HR program.

A third lesson was that organizational indicators of program success are highly desirable but highly dependent on the resources of organizational units outside the HR function. Unless the organization has an existing system for assessing relevant organizational indicators, it is unlikely that one can be mobilized for the purpose of program evaluation. The business of business tends to interfere.

Questions for Discussion

1. In the absence of a highly refined organizational assessment system, what low-cost indicators might be used to evaluate the effectiveness of a new selection system?
2. When implementing a new system for making potentially unpopular, "high-stakes decisions" (for example, selection, promotion, and retention), what steps should be taken to inform the target audience?
3. Discuss the role of middle management in implementing an organization-wide change? What steps should be taken to enlist their support?

4. What other human resources programs might be amenable to a utility analysis?

5. Utility is one way of demonstrating the link between individual and organizational productivity. What additional evidence might be collected?

The Author

Ilene F. Gast is a senior research psychologist at the Immigration and Naturalization Service. She specializes in developing tools for selection and development of executives, managers, and supervisors and in evaluating selection programs. Gast has more than 25 years of public sector experience in personnel assessment and related areas. During her career, she has led projects covering the full spectrum of human resources management. Her projects have included employee development and training, selection, program evaluation, workforce quality, and organizational assessment. She received her Ph.D. in industrial organizational psychology from the George Washington University in 1987. Gast can be reached at Office of Human Resources and Development, Research and Development Branch, Immigration and Naturalization Service, 800 K Street, NW, Suite 5000, Washington, DC 20536; phone: 202. 305.0590; email: ilene.f.gast@usdoj.gov.

References

Doverspike, D., J.L. Winter, M.C. Healy, and G.V. Barrett. (1996). "Simulations as a Method of Illustrating the Impact of Differential Weights on Personnel Selection Outcomes." *Human Performance,* volume 9, 259-273.

Ghiselli, E.E., J.P. Campbell, and S. Zedeck. (1981). *Measurement Theory for the Behavioral Sciences.* San Francisco, CA: W.H. Freeman and Company, 174-181.

McDaniel, M.A., F.L. Schmidt, and J.E. Hunter. (1988a). "Job Experience Correlates of Job Performance." *Journal of Applied Psychology,* volume 73, 327-330.

McDaniel, M.A., F.L. Schmidt, and J.E. Hunter. (1988b). "A Meta-Analysis of the Validity of Methods for Rating Training and Experience in Personnel Selection." *Personnel Psychology,* volume 41, 284-313.

Pollack, D.M., I.F. Gast, G.O. Beatty, K. Kimball, and L.M. Malik. (April 1997). *Development and Validation of Promotion and Diagnostic Assessments for Supervisory Border Patrol Agents at the Immigration and Naturalization Service.* Washington, DC: U.S. Immigration and Naturalization Service, Office of Human Resources and Development, Research and Development Branch.

Schmidt, F.L., and J.E. Hunter. (1998). "The Validity and Utility of Selection Methods in Personnel Psychology: Practical and Theoretical Implications of 85 Years of Research Findings." *Psychological Bulletin,* volume 124, 262-274.

Schmidt, F.L., and J.E. Hunter. (1983). "Individual Differences in Productivity: An Empirical Test of Estimates Derived from Studies of Selection Procedure Utility." *Journal of Applied Psychology,* volume 68, 407-414.

Schmidt, F.L., J.E. Hunter, and G.B. Jackson. (1982). "Meta-Analysis." *Cumulating Research Findings Across Studies.* Beverly Hills, CA: Sage Publications.

Schmidt, F.L., J.E. Hunter, R. McKenzie, and T. Muldrow. (1979). "The Impact of Valid Selection Procedures on Workforce Productivity." *Journal of Applied Psychology,* volume 64, 609-626.

Schmidt, F.L., M.J. Mack, and J.E. Hunter. (1984). "Selection Utility in the Occupation of U.S. Park Ranger for Three Models of Test Use." *Journal of Applied Psychology,* volume 69, 490-497.

Trattner, M.H. (June 1988). *The Validity of Aptitude and Ability Tests Used to Select Professional Personnel.* Washington, D.C. U.S. Office of Personnel Management, Office of Research and Development.

Further Resources

Gast. I.F. (November 1996). *Return for Investment Protocol: Competency-Based Promotional Assessments for Border Patrol.* Washington, DC: U.S. Immigration and Naturalization Service, Office of Human Resources and Development, Research and Development Branch.

Gast. I.F., G.O. Beatty, D.P. Pollack, and P. Usala. (November 1996). *Return for Investment Model.* Washington, DC: U.S. Immigration and Naturalization Service, Office of Human Resources and Development, Research and Development Branch.

Hirsch, H.R., L.C. Northrop, and F.L. Schmidt. (1986). "Validity Generalization Results for Law Enforcement Occupations." *Personnel Psychology,* (volume 39), 399-420.

Hunter, J.E. (1986). "Cognitive Ability, Cognitive Aptitudes, Job Knowledge, and Job Performance." *Journal of Vocational Behavior,* volume 29, 340-362.

Hunter, J.E., and R.F. Hunter. (1984). "Validity and Utility Analysis of Alternative Predictors of Job Performance." *Psychological Bulletin,* volume 96, 72-98.

Lyons, T.J., P.D. Usala, and I.F. Gast. (February 1999). *Development of the Job Experience Measure (JEM) Used in the Competency-Based Promotional Assessment System for Supervisory and Managerial Border Patrol Positions.* Washington, DC: U.S. Immigration and Naturalization Service, Office of Human Resources and Development, Research and Development Branch.

How a Pilot Study Launched Training ROI Evaluation

New York State Governor's Office of Employee Relations

Chandler Atkins

The case study presented reviews the initiation of a pilot study to determine how return on investment (ROI) could be used to evaluate training in state government. The pilot project was to study the "Practical Skills for Supervisors" training program currently being rolled out to as many as 2,000 New York state managers per year. It shows the development to get the project off the ground and how Kirkpatrick's Level 1 to 4 instruments were achieved. Five cohorts of participants were trained in the pilot, and the data was collected to determine Levels 1 to 4 and an ROI effectiveness rate. The program costs were determined and a cost/benefit calculation showed a 258 percent annualized return on investment. Donald Kirkpatrick critiqued the case when it was presented at a National Transportation Training Directors conference in Albany, New York.

Background
Organizational Profile and Program Background

New York state has 64 agencies that provide a range of services to New York state residents. A sample of these agencies include: Department of Transportation, Department of Motor Vehicles, Division of Budget, Office of Mental Health, Office of General Services, and the Governor's Office of Employee Relation (GOER). Many of the agencies have their own training department, and all have their own initiatives, missions, and goals. In addition to providing employee training using agency trainers or consultants, many agencies also work directly with GOER on numerous statewide labor/management-training initiatives.

This case was prepared to serve as a basis for discussion rather than to illustrate either effective or ineffective administrative and management practices.

The New York State Training Council (NYSTC) is an organization that has members and participation from many state agencies. A subgroup of the training council is the Training Director's Roundtable. Training directors from every state agency are invited to be a member of the Roundtable. After Alan Ross, then chair of the Roundtable and director of the NYS/CSEA Labor-Management Committee, heard a presentation at a 1998 ASTD training conference on ROI training evaluation, he requested that a similar presentation be made to their members. After the presentation, 11 of the 31 members present wanted their agency to begin immediately an ROI evaluation of their training.

Ross was very familiar with ROI evaluation and was most anxious to implement the process for programs administered by his unit within the Governor's Office of Employee Relations that represented 85,000 employees. The Roundtable followed his leadership, and meetings were held with staff of the Labor Management Committee to brief them on the ROI process. Dan Cunningham, then senior program associate, volunteered to spearhead the procedures that would have to be undertaken to incorporate the process into the programs they identified.

The NYS/CSEA Labor-Management Committee is involved in many training initiatives. The programs are as varied as the employees working in New York state agencies. From training programs for boiler room workers, mental health therapy aides (MHTAs), carpenters and electricians to labor-management relations, there were many training programs to examine. Agreement was reached between Cunningham and Ross to focus on three areas: labor-management relations in the Finger Lakes region, journeyman training at the SUNY Health Science Center at Brooklyn, and training for the mental health therapy aides in Buffalo.

Cunningham began a strategic plan for the evaluations. Criterions were selected to evaluate training results, and instruments were developed to measure the four levels of Kirkpatrick's evaluation. A Gantt chart of activities was developed, and pretests and posttests were designed from the content material used in the labor-management relations training program. As these activities were proceeding, the NYS budget reached an impasse and, as a result, all funds for training were stalled including the programs administered by the Labor Management Committee. In an effort to keep the ROI effort "alive," Ross contacted another GOER division, the Work Force Training and Development Unit (WFTDU), which had some funding available.

Purpose of the Evaluation

Ross held a meeting in his office with Cunningham; Onnolee Smith, director of GOER/WFTDU; and Harriet Spector, program manager for GOER/WFTDU. They talked about the budget funding issues, the need of the Training Council Roundtable to explore training ROI evaluation, the desire to find a training project to evaluate, and the need to evaluate the ROI process as a tool to be used in state government. Neither GOER nor other New York state agencies had ever used an ROI training evaluation form of analysis.

As a result, GOER did not know how to begin to implement such a tool. Smith felt that it was necessary to begin the process because "GOER was responsible for administering more than $8 million per year in training and did not have adequate information on the effectiveness of the programs they administered." Spector reported, "Agency budgets were frequently adjusted as a way to cut costs and this ultimately hurt agencies and their employees." Agencies were frequently struggling with ways to justify their human resource development expenditures. The upshot was that Smith committed GOER/WFTDU to the project, and Spector volunteered to use one of the programs she administers, The Practical Skills for Supervisors (PSFS), as the first training program to be evaluated in the state of New York.

Needs Assessment

In the summer of 1999, this recently developed three-day supervisory training program, PSFS, was launched as the pilot program to be used for the integration of Kirkpatrick's Level 1 to 4 evaluation with Phillips's Level 5 ROI analysis. The purpose of the training program was to provide new as well as seasoned supervisors with basic supervision skills. An existing five-day supervision program, Challenges in Supervision and Management, had been considered too theoretical for many new supervisors, and they therefore were having difficulty translating theory into practice. It was anticipated that the new program would correct the "transfer of learning" issue, and using Level 2, 3, 4, and 5 evaluations would provide GOER/WFTDU with confirmation that this new program was meeting its goal.

Practical Skills for Supervisors was available to entry-level supervisors in all 64 New York state agencies, making about 12,000 managers eligible for this training. The program, delivered by agency trainers or by vendors under contract with GOER, was offered either onsite or at central locations accessible to numerous agencies. GOER spends millions of dollars each year to develop the knowledge, skills, and attitudes

(KSA) of New York state's workforce and has only used Level 1 evaluations to measure the effectiveness of training. Furthermore, it was anticipated that 10 years from now, all trainers working for the state of New York would be asked to be well versed in ROI training evaluation and able to add this procedure to their training contract proposals.

Evaluation Methodology
Model

The model selected was Kirkpatrick's four levels and Phillips's ROI calculation methodology (Phillips, 1997). Kirkpatrick's model asks to what extent did the participants like the training (Level 1), to what extent did participants learn something from the training (Level 2), to what extent did the participants take what they learned back to the work site and apply it (Level 3), and to what extent have things improved on the job as a result (Level 4). Phillips wanted to know if they improved things—what is the cost/benefit ratio and return on investment (Level 5). At the beginning of the study, an assumption was made that an agency needs analysis had been completed by each state agency before a decision was made to send its employees to the Practical Skills for Supervisors training.

Data Collection Methodology

The project began by reviewing the Level 1 evaluation instrument that was currently being used in the Practical Skills for Supervisors program. A decision was made by the consultant in conjunction with management to leave the Level 1 instrument unchanged at that time and focus on the other levels of evaluation that had not been done.

To begin developing Level 2 learning goals evaluation, several program trainers and the curriculum developer were contacted. Each was asked to review the 10 content areas of the PSFS program and create 10 multiple-choice questions from each area. That would give each subject matter expert (SME) a 100 multiple-choice question test. After the SMEs developed their questions, they met as a group and collectively looked over all the questions developed for each content area. They debated the difficulty, appropriateness, and intent of each question. Spector, GOER's project manager, collaborated with the SMEs until there was agreement on 10 multiple-choice questions for each of the 10 sections. The 100-question test was then divided into four test banks of 25 questions each by selecting equivalent questions for each book of tests. They were labeled—Form A, Form B, Form C, and Form D.

The intent for developing multiple forms was that a control group would be used and participant "test learning" might be reduced with several equivalent forms. For instance Form A would be given to the training group and Form C to the control group as pretests. Then Form B would be given to the training group and Form D to the control group as posttests. Subsequently, if the control group were to enter into the training, they would not have seen Form A and B and therefore have an added advantage. Upon initiation, however, a decision was made by the consultant not to use control groups because it was difficult to form them from open enrollment at multiple state agencies. Had the participants been previously targeted for training, a matching control group could have been selected.

A content validity measurement was not conducted to see if the four forms were equivalent; however, focus groups were used to provide feedback on the meaningfulness of the questions before they were deployed. The focus groups, held in Albany and New York City, were composed of a combination of past PSFS participants and agency trainers who volunteered to assist in refining the forms. Focus group participants took the tests and provided feedback indicating which questions were giveaways, which were too difficult, and which had double meanings. After listening to the participants' comments, the four forms were modified to be as equivalent as possible in questions, style, and content.

A Level 3 evaluation form was developed to measure the extent learning was being transferred to the workplace. Fourteen competencies were identified, such as "change facilitation," "communications skills," "listening skills," and "feedback skills." Participants rated their proficiency on each of these competencies before training and three months after training on a Likert 5-point scale (excellent, very good, good, fair, poor, and not applicable).

Learners were asked to return six copies of the evaluation: one from their supervisor, two from peers, two from direct reports, and one of their own. The reason for the six copies was that the focus groups indicated that management is frequently not supportive of training and, therefore, a 360-degree feedback evaluation would show whether there was a discrepancy between participant, peer, direct report, and supervisor reports.

Furthermore, it was important to capture as much information as possible to ascertain whether respondents believed the training had been successful or new behaviors were being implemented that improved productivity. From this information it would be possible to evaluate the amount of learning being transferred to the workplace. (See table 1.)

A Level 4 evaluation criterion was then developed. Participants were asked to evaluate their level of expertise prior to the training

Table 1. Pre- and postbehavioral construct instrument.

Practical Skills for Supervisors

You or your coworker recently completed the Practical Skills for Supervisors training program. Please circle the category that best describes your relationship to the participant:

Participant   Peer   Supervisor   Direct Report

Practical Skills was designed to offer techniques, tactics, and skills that would assist participants to become more effective supervisors. The topics listed below were covered in this training program. Now we would like to know to what extent you think the skills are currently being implemented successfully in your work unit.

As you consider your workplace since you or your coworker attended the Practical Skills training, please check the box that best describes how well these skills are being applied.

	Excellent	Very Good	Good	Fair	Poor	N/A
Change facilitation	☐	☐	☐	☐	☐	☐
Communication skills	☐	☐	☐	☐	☐	☐
Listening skills	☐	☐	☐	☐	☐	☐
Giving feedback	☐	☐	☐	☐	☐	☐
Coaching	☐	☐	☐	☐	☐	☐
Counseling	☐	☐	☐	☐	☐	☐
Motivating	☐	☐	☐	☐	☐	☐
Delegating	☐	☐	☐	☐	☐	☐
Assertiveness	☐	☐	☐	☐	☐	☐
Conflict resolution	☐	☐	☐	☐	☐	☐
Problem solving	☐	☐	☐	☐	☐	☐
Supervising	☐	☐	☐	☐	☐	☐
Leadership skills	☐	☐	☐	☐	☐	☐
Embracing diversity	☐	☐	☐	☐	☐	☐

Please feel free to add any additional comments in this space.

and to evaluate it again after the training as an indication as to how much their skills had improved as a result of the training. They were also asked to provide their government salary grade or salary level. Finally, they were asked to estimate the approximate amount of time they spent doing the kinds of skills that the training highlighted. From this information it would be possible to evaluate the amount of productivity gain and convert it to a monetary value. (See table 2.)

Table 2. Level 4 instrument.

If you were the participant, please complete the following:

Grade Level: _____

Bargaining Unit: (please circle one)   CSEA-ASU   CSEA-OSU   CSEA-ISU

                                                PS&T   M/C   Other:_____

Salary Range: (please circle one)

$15-19,999	$35-39,999	$55-59,999	$75-79,999
$20-24,999	$40-44,999	$60-64,999	$80-plus
$25-29,999	$45-49,999	$65-69,999	
$30-34,999	$50-54,999	$70-74,999	

What percentage of your job uses the skills you learned in the Practical Skills program?

| 0-10% | 20-30% | 40-50% | 60-70% | 80-90% |
| 10-20% | 30-40% | 50-60% | 70-80% | 90-100% |

On a scale of 1-10 how would you rate our job performance before your training in Practical Skills?

| Poor | 1 | 2 | 3 | 4 | 5 |
| | 6 | 7 | 8 | 9 | 10 Outstanding |

On a scale of 1-10 how would you rate our job performance after your training in Practical Skills?

| Poor | 1 | 2 | 3 | 4 | 5 |
| | 6 | 7 | 8 | 9 | 10 Outstanding |

All responses will be kept strictly confidential. The data will only be used as a class total rather than on an individual participant basis. Your assistance is greatly appreciated.

NYS Governor's Office of Employee Relations

Isolation Methodology

Program participants were asked to evaluate their level of perceived effectiveness, or impact on the job, regarding learned skills prior to training and after training. Responses were recorded as a percentage of the amount of skill up to 100 percent they felt they had before training began, and then recorded as a percentage of skill up to 100 percent they felt they had after the training. For instance, if a participant believed he or she had 50 percent of the pretraining skills learned prior to training, and that after the training he or she had 70 percent of the skills learned, then there would be a 20 percent gain in knowledge, skills, and attitudes (KSAs) learned. This method did not ask for other variables that could have contributed to the increase or decrease in KSAs and assumed that the gain was due exclusively to the training as perceived by the participant. (See table 3.)

Data Conversion Methodology

For the Level 4 evaluation, respondents were asked for their salary grade and salary range so the data could be converted to learn how much a productivity gain had been achieved.

Because subjects in the pilot study had been asked for their estimate of the impact in productivity gain, this had to be calculated against their salary. The salary was then multiplied by the amount of time they estimated they spent on the tasks learned in training as a percentage. That figure yielded a percentage of their salary that was equivalent to their time spent on supervisory skills. A monetary value was then calculated by multiplying the gain in productivity by the percentage of salary spent on task. For instance, if participants were earning $60,000 and stated that 30 percent of their time was spent conducting the skills they were being trained for, then $60,000 times 30 percent, or $18,000, would be considered the costs for these KSAs to the state. Furthermore, if the productivity gain was 20 percent, then $18,000 times 20 percent, or $3,600, would be the gain realized by sending these participants to training. (See table 4.)

Costs

Costs were analyzed to prepare for an ROI evaluation. Development, material, facilitator, coordinator, ROI consultant, facilities, and travel and lodging costs were all calculated. Curriculum development costs were spread over the number of anticipated training classes. The salary costs for trainees to attend this three-day training program were calculated into the total by taking the total annualized payroll dollars

Table 3. Value added method of evaluation for ROI.

Training Skills Learned

Pre-Learner Group I	Post-Grade	% skill	skill	Gain	Learner Group II	Grade	% Pre	Post	Gain
1	G13	50%	60%	10%	1	G14	40%	60%	20%
2	G9	50%	70%	20%	2	G20	70%	70%	0%
3	G11	30%	60%	30%	3	G19	50%	60%	10%
4	G20	50%	60%	10%	4	G23	60%	80%	20%
5	G16	50%	60%	10%	5	G20	80%	90%	10%
6	G18	50%	70%	20%	6	G14	30%	50%	20%
7	G31	20%	40%	20%	7	G12	50%	70%	20%
8	G22	80%	100%	20%	8	G23	30%	50%	20%
9	G11	50%	80%	30%	9	G14	30%	50%	20%
10	G12	70%	80%	10%	10	G13	40%	60%	20%
11	G18	40%	60%	20%					
12	G13	80%	100%	20%					

Group III

Group III	Grade	% skill	skill	Gain		Grade	% Pre	Post	Gain
1	M2	60%	60%	0%	16	G27	50%	60%	10%
2	G24	50%	60%	10%	17	M2	50%	70%	20%
3	M3	60%	70%	10%	18	M2	50%	60%	10%
4	G27	50%	60%	10%	19	G27	60%	70%	10%
5	G27	40%	60%	20%	20	M3	70%	70%	0%
6	G19	50%	50%	0%	21	G31	70%	80%	10%
7	M2	60%	60%	0%	22	G24	50%	60%	10%
8	M3	70%	80%	10%	23	G23	50%	50%	0%
9	G23	80%	80%	0%	24	G27	40%	60%	20%
10	G18	70%	80%	10%	25	G27	40%	60%	20%
11	G27	80%	80%	0%	26	G27	40%	60%	20%
12	G24	50%	60%	10%					
13	M3	70%	80%	10%					
14	M2	80%	90%	10%					
15	G24	80%	90%	10%					

Table 4. Salary paid on skills learned.

Salary	% on Job	% Salary	Salary	% on Job	% Salary
$34,900	45%	$15,705	$36,871	65%	$23,966
28,000	55%	15,400	50,799	15%	7,620
31,307	85%	26,611	48,346	45%	21,756
50,799	85%	43,179	59,275	75%	44,456
41,090	75%	30,817	50,799	75%	38,099
45,887	95%	43,593	36,871	65%	23,966
85,970	25%	21,493	33,002	45%	14,850
56,325	85%	47,876	59,275	75%	44,456
31,307	95%	29,742	36,871	15%	5,530
33,002	45%	14,851	34,903	5%	1,745
45,887	35%	16,060	67,500	75%	50,625
34,903	95%	33,158	67,500	75%	50,625
75,000	85%	63,750	77,500	75%	58,125
67,500	75%	50,625	77,500	85%	65,875
80,000	95%	76,000	72,000	15%	10,800
72,500	65%	47,125	80,000	75%	60,000
67,500	65%	43,875	77,500	75%	58,125
45,000	15%	6,750	67,500	45%	30,375
77,500	65%	50,375	57,500	75%	43,125
80,000	95%	76,000	67,500	65%	43,875
62,500	95%	59,375	67,500	65%	43,875
45,000	95%	42,750	67,500	65%	43,875
77,500	25%	19,375	**$1,294,012**		**$785,744**
67,500	65%	43,875			
80,000	85%	68,000			
77,500	95%	73,625			
$1,494,377		**$1,059,985**			

Annualized Payroll:	$1,494,377
	1,294,012
	$2,788,389

Training Value:	$1,059,985
	785,744
	$1,845,729

plus benefits of 33 percent and calculating a daily cost. It was estimated that $61,886 had been spent to train the 48 responding groups in the pilot study. (See table 5.)

Results

Level 2 results from the pretests and posttests measuring the extent to which participants learned the material were calculated. It was learned that all five cohorts of learners had improved their mean scores and the number of correct answers. The overall average pretest mean was 19.99 correct answers. The overall average posttest mean was 21.85 correct answers. That was an average gain of 1.86 more correct answers after training. Furthermore it was learned that the number of correct answers between 20 and 25 had increased from 51.1 percent in the pretest to 74.6 percent in the posttest. That indicated that the number of people who were now scoring above the 80th percentile had increased by 23.5 percent. It confirmed participants were indeed learning the material. (See table 6.)

Level 3 data was then calculated to see if gains had been made. It was learned that all cohorts reported that they had improved their ability to implement and transfer the learning that they received in training to their job. For instance, one group reported a level of "change"

Table 5. Estimated costs for training 48 learners.

Training delivery	$8,945
Development costs	$1,800
Travel expenses	$900
Training room	$500
Meals, etc	$700
*Participants' time	$32,174
Payroll benefits (33%)	$10,617
ROI consultant time	$5,400
Coordinator's time	$850
Total Costs	**$61,886**

Total Annualized Payroll equals **$2,788,389**
*Payroll divided by 52 weeks equals **$53,623**
Weekly payroll divided by five days equals **$10,724**
Daily payroll times three days of training equals **$32,174**
Payroll Benefits: 33% times $32,174 equals **$10,617**

Table 6. Level 2 means and frequencies.

Level 2 Pre- and Postmeans

Group	Pre	Post
ORPS	19.2857	20.5714
ALB	19.9429	23.3750
LI	19.6818	23.1364
OGS	19.4000	20.6087
DOT	21.6800	21.5600
AVE	**19.9981**	**21.8503**

Level 2 Pre- and Postfrequency

Group	Pre 20+	Post 20+
ORPS	28.60%	53.20%
ALB	40.00%	96.90%
LI	54.50%	90.90%
OGS	52.00%	56.50%
DOT	79.70%	75.50%
AVE	**51.10%**	**74.60%**

at 23.8 percent on their pretest. On the posttest they reported a level of "change" at 33.3 percent. This was a gain of 9.5 percent in a participant's self-efficacy or perceived ability to manage change. Similar results were seen in all 14 competency areas for all five cohorts. That data was compared to the reports from supervisors, peers, and direct reports. The data indicated that in most instances there was no difference in the ranking of the groups; however, when there was a difference as with "delegation," it appeared that the participants scored themselves more harshly than did their direct reports, peers, or supervisors. (See table 7.)

Level 4 data was then calculated to see if productivity gains had been made in the workplace. Participants rated themselves on their level of expertise prior to training and after training. The difference was the amount of gain in productivity. Forty-eight respondents completed the Level 4 data inventory. The average reported gain from the training for these participants was 12.28 percent.

Participants were asked how much time they spent on their job doing the tasks being taught. The average amount of time reported being spent on task for the KSAs taught was 64.79 percent. The total

Table 7. Level 3 pre- and postbehaviors.

	Pre 1 & 2 CUM	Post 1 & 2 CUM
Change	23.80%	33.30%
Communicate	42.90%	75.00%
Listen	57.10%	66.70%
Feedback	28.60%	45.80%
Coach	19.00%	33.30%
Counsel	19.00%	50.00%
Motivate	19.00%	54.20%
Delegate	23.85%	62.50%
Assertive	14.30%	54.20%
Conflict	23.80%	41.70%
Problem	28.60%	50.00%
Supervise	9.50%	37.50%
Leader	28.60%	37.50%
Diversity	33.30%	54.20%

amount of annualized payroll dollars for these individuals was reported to be $2,788,389. A total of $1,806,597 (64.59 percent times $2,788,389) represents the amount of dollars attributable to completing tasks associated with training. Therefore, with a 12.28 percent gain realized from the self-reports of skills acquired from the training, this converts into a $221,850 gain in productivity.

ROI Calculation

From this detailed analysis of costs, and the previously calculated gains in productivity, an ROI calculation was consummated. The program benefits were $221,850 and the program costs were $61,886. The net program benefits were $159,964 divided by the program costs and multiplied by 100 yielding an ROI of 258 percent. (See table 8.)

Intangible Benefits

The administrative enthusiasm generated by the ROI evaluation process has yielded great organizational commitment and higher levels of on-the-job satisfaction from several key people in the Governor's Office of Employee Relations. Agency trainers have also become involved in the process. Train-the-trainer programs are being conducted to teach interested trainers how to creatively design

Table 8. Return-on-investment analysis.

Level 4 productivity gain	$221,850
Cost of the training	$61,886
Net gain from training	$159,964

ROI Formula = (Net gain/Costs) × 100
Hence:

$$($159,964/$61,886) \times 100$$
$$= 258\% \text{ ROI}$$

and build an evaluation process for their unique training needs and programs. As a result, trainers have now formed an ROI Network, with GOER taking the lead to schedule follow-up meetings for the members. Some members are seeing that training is considered important and meaningful, and management is interested in tracking their successes in the program. Furthermore, administrators are beginning to see the value of ROI analysis for succession planning and performance evaluation measures.

Communications Process

After about one year and the participation of five training groups, the pilot phase ended. At about the same time the pilot phase concluded, an opportunity occurred to present data to the National Transportation Training Directors Conference in Albany, New York. Donald Kirkpatrick was the keynote speaker at this event and his topic was training evaluation. Spector and this case report author were invited to give presentations on the ROI training evaluation pilot study.

Kirkpatrick critiqued the work in front of the conference attendees. He did not particularly like the use of forms A, B, C, and D. He said he preferred the use of only one form. He believed one form could be used as both a pre- and posttest instrument. Discussion ensued about the participant not being controlled for "test learning" and the trainer "teaching to the test," and not the content. Kirkpatrick asked, "Isn't the goal to get them to learn what it is we want them to learn?"

The issue was not resolved, leaving two schools of thought. Kirkpatrick was impressed with the movement past his four levels of evaluation to the ROI calculation, as were the conference participants who absorbed the material.

Since the October 2000 presentation, additional Level 3 and 4 data has been returned to GOER and are part of this case study. A presentation to the New York State Training Council's Directors Roundtable to apprise them of the findings and to look for ways to assist them in their ROI training evaluation programs will be scheduled. GOER has not decided if the results will be shared with the participants of the study; however, it is strongly recommended by Phillips, Stone, and Phillips (2001) that an organization take this step to strengthen the acceptance of future ROI projects.

Lessons Learned

One lesson learned was that more variables could be isolated in the training by asking participants to indicate how much of the gain they experienced as a result of the training as a percentage. This would be the training effect. They could then be asked the follow-up question "what is your level of confidence regarding your answer." By taking the gain in productivity, multiplying it by the training effect, and multiplying the training effect gain by the confidence level would generate a more conservative answer. For instance an initial 20 percent productivity gain with an 85 percent training effect times a 90 percent confidence level would equal ($.20 \times .85 \times .90$) or 15.3 percent productivity gain.

A second lesson learned was that while a positive ROI was calculated from 48 Level 4 respondents, slightly more than 100 participants had reported Level 2 data. The collection of Level 3 and 4 data three to four months out was more difficult. GOER is now computerizing the survey data to Websites and emails to capture the information from their very diverse and wide geographic distribution of learners and trainers. It is hoped this will increase the number of Level 3 and 4 respondents.

The third lesson learned was that ROI can work in state government as well as Level 2, 3, and 4 data collection and analysis. Each project needs to be evaluated and planned carefully, and, when done so, delivers some very reassuring information that can be used to make training decisions more effectively.

Questions for Discussion

1. Do you think having multiple forms are important in generating Level 2 data, or is Kirkpatrick's suggestion that one form is sufficient correct?
2. Should the 360-degree feedback data be coded for each participant, or can an aggregate be formulated that would be just as valuable to determine Level 3 data?
3. How would you use a control group when subjects come from diverse state agencies through an open enrollment and were not previously targeted for training?

4. What would be the best way to initiate a train-the-trainer program for hundreds of state trainers to increase their skills in ROI development and evaluation techniques?

5. What benefit does it serve to have program costs subtracted from the program gains to get a net program gain before calculating an ROI?

The Author

Chandler Atkins has been teaching and consulting for the past 21 years in upstate New York in the field of management, entrepreneurship, and organizational development. He has taught for many colleges including Adirondack Community College; Antioch University; State University of New York, Plattsburgh; The New School of Social Research; Empire State College; National University; and Santa Monica College. He has consulted for companies such as NAMIC USA, Xerox, New York State Governor's Office of Employee Relations/Work Force Training Development Unit, NYS/CSEA Labor-Management Committee, the New York State Office of General Services, Niagara Mohawk, Boston Scientific, and Verizon. Atkins is president of Atkins Training & Development, a human resource consulting company that specializes in ROI training evaluation, psychological testing for selection and appraisal, quality of work life surveys, corporate training with college credit, and organizational development interventions. Atkins holds a Ph.D. in industrial/organizational psychology. He can be reached at P.O. Box 95, Lake Luzerne, NY 12846; phone: 518.654.5452; email: chandler@atkinstraining.com; Website: www.atkinstraining.com.

Endnote

Funding for this project was jointly funded through the negotiated agreements between the state of New York and the Civil Services Employees Association, Inc., and the negotiated agreement between the state of New York and the Public Employees Federation, AFL-CIO. Program administration and additional funding were provided by the Governor's Office of Employee Relations.

References

Phillips, J. (1997). *Return on Investment.* Boston, MA.: Butterworth-Heinemann, previously published by Gulf Publishing Company.

Phillips, J., R. Stone, and P. Phillips. (2001). *The Human Resources Scorecard.* Boston, MA: Butterworth-Heinemann.

Process Mapping the Three Ps: Planning Policies, Procedures, and Programming Changes Prior to Implementing a Campus Procurement Card Initiative

The University of Arkansas

Kit Brooks, Elaine Crutchfield, David Martinson,
Jane Eaves, and Gary K. Smith

As public sector institutions grapple with the challenges associated with cost containment, streamlined processes, and value-added deliverables, performance improvement techniques commonly used in private enterprises are being implemented by top management within public institutions. This case describes how one manager's vision and commitment to ongoing professional development of his staff resulted in process mapping, a performance improvement tool rooted in business and industry, to proactively plan and analyze the redesign of the university's procurement process. Using action-learning methodology as the framework, this case illustrates the benefits of this problem-solving technique while documenting return on investment associated with using process mapping for planning.

Background

The University of Arkansas (UA) at Fayetteville is a land grant institution that was founded in 1871 and has a current enrollment of about 15,000 students. While part of a university system that includes seven separate campuses throughout the state, the Fayetteville campus is considered the flagship of the university system.

In 1994, a new chancellor was appointed to position the university for success in the 21st century. To become an internationally recognized

This case was prepared to serve as a basis for discussion rather than to illustrate either effective or ineffective administrative and management practices.

academic leader and fuel economic development within the state are two of the goals by which success will be evaluated. The goal to advance the institution's national academic standing to be among the nation's top 50 public research universities by 2010 has been the catalyst for many changes within the Fayetteville campus. In support of this goal, each department and business unit have been mandated to develop a strategic plan that outlines how the individual departments and business units support the goals of the institution and add value to the university community.

The University's Department of Finance and Administration responded to this mandate by reviewing all current processes, searching for business process improvements, and facilitating maximum performance within the UA community.

Business Affairs, a division of Finance and Administration, encompasses 10 separate business units that include purchasing, accounts payable, the university bookstore and computer store, parking and transit, printing services, risk management, scientific supplies, telephone services, travel services, and workers' compensation. As winner of numerous customer service awards and a desire to be innovators in the field, David Martinson, the vice chancellor of business affairs, was committed to providing ongoing professional development for his management staff as a response to the challenges associated with supporting the institutional goals. Hence, nine business affairs managers attended an interactive workshop to expand their knowledge of performance improvement methodologies.

This workshop was scheduled over a six-month period during 2000-2001 and included 12 four-hour sessions. The topics covered during the workshop included gap analysis, assessment and evaluation techniques, data gathering and feedback methodology, case study analysis, systems theory, and process mapping. Participants were asked to apply each of these learned principles to actual process changes that they faced within their own business units.

Context

The University of Arkansas worked closely with state regulatory agencies to obtain authority to use procurement cards (P-card). The option for the use of procurement cards became available as a result of changes in state law and state procurement regulations. Communication began between the business office staff and the staff of the state purchasing office to determine the latitude the campus would have in developing the P-card process for local use. Because procurement cards were a new process for both the university and the state, there were many details to be worked out. The university's process had to interface with the state's process as well as contain all the necessary internal accounting controls. Jane Eaves, the university's business manager, was the liaison between the university and the state purchasing office.

Eaves was also the person on the university campus to lead the discussions and planning sessions. Because she was the liaison with the state and the most knowledgeable person on campus concerning the P-card process, she was the logical person to communicate with the business office, computer programmers, and other university staff. Eaves also had the advantage of having been the driving force behind the automation of the current procurement process. That gave her credibility with the campus staff including the programmers.

The use of procurement cards will provide the following benefits to the university:
• time and monetary savings
• zero need for small dollar purchase orders
• consolidated billing
• payment cycle-time reduction
• decreased delays for purchasing departmental supplies with just-in-time purchases
• increased fraud prevention.

As a result of practicing process mapping, a group technique that produces a visual chart of the various elements involved in completing a work process, the business manager decided to process map the elements associated with implementing a new campuswide procurement process. A procurement card, an electronic credit card-type purchasing system, is radically different from the paper-based requisition system that is currently used at the university.

To identify the best practices in using the P-card system, the business manager and the business and administration strategic information system (BASIS) program specialist conducted extensive research with other institutions of higher education, industry, and governmental entities over a two-year period. That research included Internet searches, telephone and electronic communications, and on-site visits to other institutions to ascertain their historical experiences. The research did not result in a model that incorporated the level of electronic processing that the business manager wanted to implement. Most institutions researched used manually intensive types of process for reconciliation, while very few had any type of electronic reconciliation, and none imaged receipts electronically as opposed to manually photocopying them. The University of Arkansas sought to incorporate the procurement card reconciliation process into its existing process that included imaging of documents, thus relieving the departmental need for physical receipt archival.

The impact of using procurement cards forced multidimensional changes that included financial software programming, business office staff reorganization, process reengineering, and campuswide training for all campus departments.

Process Mapping as a Communication Tool

The mapping of the P-card was used to communicate the entire process to the business office staff. The map provided a visual representation of the entire process from start to finish, enabling the staff to have the same in-depth knowledge of the process and be able to discuss and evaluate the different methods to accomplish the required tasks. It also allowed them to see the flow of the process and know which section of the office would be responsible for each task in the process.

The completed map was used to communicate the process to the computer programmers. From the map, they could see the flow of the process and more easily develop the flowchart for the program. The map also improved communication of the process, allowing the programmers to visualize the process more easily and reduce the number of meetings required to clarify the steps needed to develop the program.

The map was used to communicate the process to the campus community. The map was modified for presentation to each group depending on their needs and area of responsibility. While the business office staff and the programmers were provided with copies of the entire process map including all the details, the support staff for each department was given copies containing only the information concerning their duties within the process. During the Web-based training sessions, the map of the complete process was reviewed to help the participants identify their part in the process. The support staff also received written procedures for each task required of them.

The campus administrators received a written report of the entire P-card process including the detailed process map. While most of them are not be involved in the daily operation of the process, they will need an overall knowledge of it. That report was provided to the business office staff because they needed an in-depth knowledge of the entire process to be able to communicate that information to the campus, and to answer questions about the process.

The P-card process, once implemented, would require the end-user to be more knowledgeable concerning state and university purchasing regulations because the audit process will occur after the purchase. The advantages of the P-card include the ability to purchase via the Internet and make purchases immediately from vendors without processing a requisition and waiting for a purchase order.

The P-card process mapping occurred more than a year before the rollout of the P-card program. This year was needed for developing and testing of computer programs, continued coordination with the state to finalize the rules under which the program could operate, train the business office and campus support staffs, and obtain a vendor for the procurement cards. The vendors also had to have time to develop their processes so they could provide the necessary information to the university.

Process Mapping and Action Learning

Kit Brooks and Elaine Crutchfield, external consultants from the division of continuing education, led the process mapping training sessions to develop the P-card process and train the business affairs staff in the use of process mapping. They also acted as coaches during the process mapping, an action-learning project. Using the procurement card process as a real-time business initiative to be analyzed, the consultants constantly debriefed the group about the experience of working together to solve problems. The activities entailed brainstorming and creating a visual map of the process that showed all anticipated transactions associated with issuing and managing the cards and included payment and postaudit. While this analysis technique led to the redesign of the procurement card implementation, it was labor intensive and entailed working with individuals with various learning and communication styles. While a chief benefit of action learning is the resolution of a problem, the experience of working with a diverse group of individuals is regarded as professional development.

In acting as facilitators for process mapping and action learning coaches, the external consultants developed an evaluation tool to assess the participants' perception of the benefit of the project.

The P-card process (see figures 1 and 2) is more streamlined as a result of the attention to detail that is inherent within process mapping. Because the process was refined during the planning phase, problems

Figure 1. Reconciling accounts.

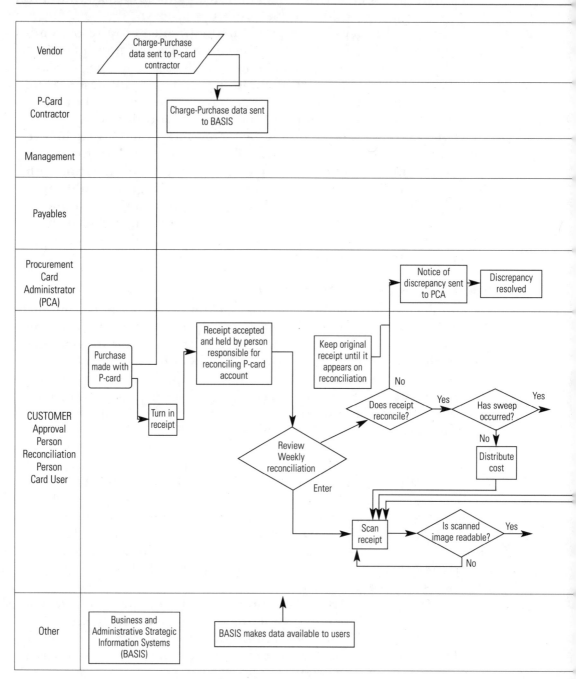

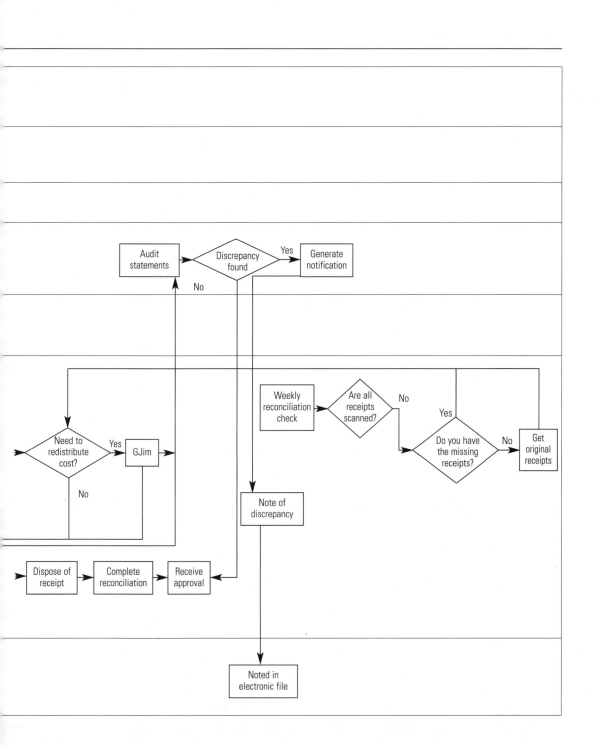

Figure 2. Issue of new P-card.

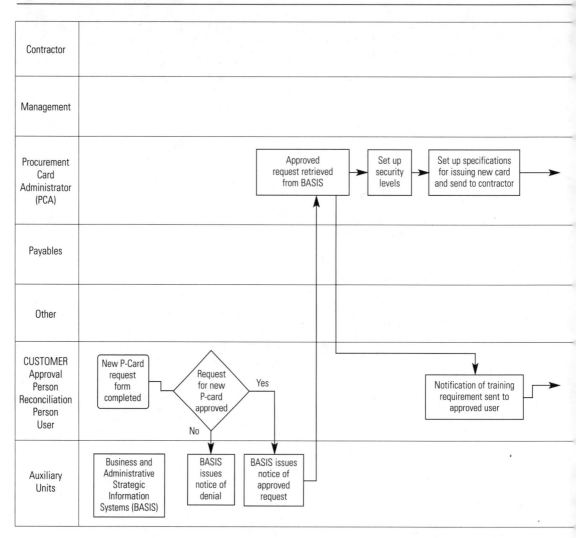

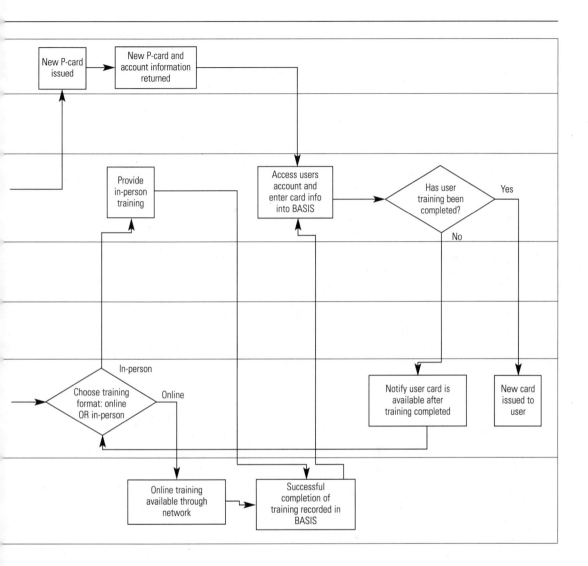

could be averted that would have negatively affected implementing the process. Transition from a lengthy centralized purchase order process for the procurement of goods to an efficient, decentralized, credit card process that allows for immediate acquisition of low- to medium-priced goods was a major change for the campus. It was vital to the success of this initiative that the planning process consider all possible variables associated with implementing the campuswide change.

During the mapping process, decisions were made, process duplications were identified, and a more efficient intervention was planned. This in turn allowed business affairs to calculate a financial return on investment (ROI) associated with using process mapping as a planning tool.

Results/ROI

The project team credited the planning process described here with several beneficial changes in how the new procurement card process would be implemented. One specific example was the decision to have procurement card receipts scanned into the financial system at the departmental level. During mapping of the process and examining resources, it became apparent that scanning at the departmental level would greatly reduce resource use. The project team defined the following efficiencies related to this decision:

- Elimination of one position in the business office that would have been dedicated to imaging receipts.
- Departments will scan their own receipts before sending them to the business office.
- Elimination of physically filing receipts within the departments saves money, time, and space.
- Auditors can access a department's procurement card purchases at any time. That eliminates the disruption of the departmental accounting technician's work and allows the auditor 24/7 accessibility of documentation.
- Payer/auditor can audit more statements by eliminating travel to departmental units, providing more timely feedback, and suggesting corrective action.
- Potential fraudulent use of the procurement card can be recognized, reported, investigated, and appropriate action taken expeditiously.

Table 1 presents the monetary value calculated for the changes in the procurement card implementation process described above. The life of the process changes were estimated to be two years, therefore annual savings due to reduction in staff positions was valued over a two-year period.

Table 1. ROI calculation for the planning process tool.

Benefits—Description and Dollar Amount	Cost—Description and Dollar Amount
All receipts imaged at the department	All receipts imaged at the department

All receipts imaged at the department

Benefits:

1. Business office scanner position eliminated (**$34,848** = $17,424/year × 2 yr)

2. Copying of receipts in departments—previous activity now eliminated (**$42,000** = 2 yr × $21,000/year = 200 depts. @ 250 receipts/mo × 12 mo @$.035/copy)

3. Filing of receipts in the departments—previous activity now eliminated (**$30,624** = 2 yr × $15,312/yr = 200 depts. @ 1/2 hr per month = 1,200 hours @ $12.76/hr)

4. Miscellaneous—non-monetary value
   - No more lost receipts
   - Retrieval time
   - 24/7 accessibility
   - Scanner used for other functions

Costs:

A. Imaging technician to:
   - Index and set p electronic file (**$592** = 16 hr @ $37/hr)
   - Install scanners in departments (**$3,700** = 100 scanners @ 1 hr each @ $37/hr)
   - Additional license costs (**$10,000**)

B. Purchase of scanners for departments (**$20,000** = 100 depts. @ $200 each)

C. Programming of electronic interface
   - System analyst (**$760** = 20 hr @ $38/hr)
   - Programmer (**$540** = 20 hr @ $27/hr)
   - Program specialist (**$540** = 20 hr @ $27/hr)

Electronically audit departmental records

1. No department person involved in audit (**$81,664** = 2 days @ $102.08 × 200 depts = $40,832/year × 2 yr)

2. Less resources required by payer/auditor (**$40,832** = 200 days @ $102.08 = 20,416/year × 2 yr)

3. No external auditor required now (**$6,400** = 80 hrs. @ $40/hr = 3,200/yr × 2 yr)

4. Miscellaneous—non-monetary value
   - Timely feedback
   - Immediate corrective action
   - Fraud prevention enhanced

Cost of training for the process mapping tool

1. Facilitators (**$1,500** = 2 facilitators @ 6 hr each × $125/hr)

2. Participants (**$732** calculated hourly at specific rates of pay for each team member with value of benefits, etc. included)

3. Technical assistance with developing final maps (**$560** = 16 hr @ $35/hr)

4. Process mapping software (**$750**)

Total Benefits = $236,368

Total Costs = $39,674

ROI = Net Benefits/Total Costs

ROI = $236,368 − $39,674 / $39,674 = 4.96 × 100 = 496%

Note: Fully loaded costs have been considered in this calculation. For example, some implementation activities were changed during the planning process that added a cost to the implementation process. While these activities improved efficiency and reduced resource expenditures, they were still counted as "costs." Another way to calculate the ROI involved viewing the costs as limited to the training and the project teams' participation in the training. This view was based on the fact that the "new costs" created by the addition of activities were not really new. Those tasks had to be completed in some manner; therefore, some related costs was expected. The planning process and tools used reduced those costs and could generate the following perception of ROI for this project. The ROI calculated based on their view of costs is

$$(\$236,368 - \$3,542) / \$3,542 = 65.73 \times 100 = 6.573\%.$$

Lessons Learned

When the consultants used a group interview to assess the perceptions of business affairs staff regarding the process mapping experience, they indicated the following lessons learned:

- Key stakeholders were educated about the complexity of the new procurement process that provided a greater appreciation for "systems thinking."
- Process mapping forced the group to consider and resolve issues in a proactive environment.
- Obstacles could be identified and options considered when mapping the entire process.
- It was easier and more cost-effective to change the process while still on paper instead of trial and error.
- Cross-unit participation in the planning provided valuable insight and affected decision making.
- Mapping was the catalyst for critical analysis that facilitated streamlining the soon-to-be-implemented procurement process.
- Performance improvement interventions can be used effectively in the public sector.

Conclusion

The business affairs team spent several hours in training learning to use process mapping. While this time was well spent even if the procurement card process had been the only process mapped, process mapping has been and will continue to be used by the business affairs department to evaluate future process changes. The procurement card process map was developed as part of this training.

The process map provided a detailed flowchart of the entire process as it had been originally envisioned. During the development of the process map, decision points were determined and the results of those decisions evaluated. Upon completion and review of the process map, several steps in the process were eliminated, simplifying the process and reducing the programming time and development costs. The completed process map, with varying levels of detail, was used to communicate with the computer programmers to develop the program; the campus administration to obtain administrative and audit approval of the process; the business office staff to allow them to understand the entire flow of the process; and as a visual aid in the training of the support staff and P-card users.

The ROI shows the projected cost savings of using process mapping over the standard development procedures used by other universities for the procurement card process. Furthermore, the ROI of the P-card process development and implementation will more than offset the development cost over the next two years. Some of the cost savings from using process mapping are difficult to calculate because the errors in the original process were determined during the planning, so the mistakes were not made and there were no costs for correcting those mistakes.

Questions for Discussion

1. Discuss how the lack of a bottom-line orientation in the public sector influences the role of ROI.
2. What cost-benefit horizon would be appropriate for analyzing a decision such as this?
3. Discuss the advantages and disadvantages of using external consultants to perform ROI analysis and interpretation, particularly in the public sector.
4. How might the decentralized organizational power structure often found in higher education affect the use and potential benefits of ROI?
5. Ongoing HRD efforts within the university's business affairs area led to the application of process mapping to process changes. What other long-term and short-term benefits might be expected from these training activities?
6. What are your reactions to, and assessment of, the organizational climate that led to the use of process mapping for designing the procurement card process?
7. What are the benefits or weaknesses of forecasting the financial benefits of process mapping in this case versus conducting a follow-up financial analysis of the outcome?

The Authors

Kit Brooks is a performance improvement specialist with the University of Arkansas Division of Continuing Education and provides organizational development expertise to a diverse client base. Through the Division of Continuing Education's Office of Service to business and industry, private and public sector enterprises, including the University of Arkansas campus at large, she has access to specialists to assess business units to implement customized performance improvement practices usually associated with the private sector use. Brooks is also assistant professor of human resource development in the college of education at the University of Arkansas. She is a senior partner of Whole Brain Assessment Group™, a consulting company that specializes in assessment and evaluation of firms in the profit and nonprofit sectors. She can be reached at the University of Arkansas; phone: 501.575.4875; email: Cabrooks@uark.edu.

Elaine Crutchfield is a senior partner of Whole Brain Assessment Group™, a consulting company that specializes in assessment and evaluation of firms in the profit and nonprofit sectors. She specializes in program evaluation and statistical analysis. Crutchfield is experienced in instructional design for the classroom and Web-based delivery and has worked extensively with various nonprofit organizations.

David Martinson has been the associate vice chancellor for business affairs at the University of Arkansas for 12 years. His responsibilities include many of the service and support activities for the campus including several auxiliary units. A native of Texas, he served in various higher education administrative roles with universities in Texas before moving to Arkansas.

Jane Eaves has been the business manager at the University of Arkansas for six years. Her areas of responsibility are purchasing, accounts payable, travel, scientific supplies, military, and surplus property. She is a native of Mississippi where she worked in the procurement field beginning in 1984 with various state agencies. Eaves has her undergraduate degree in marketing and an M.B.A. with an emphasis in management.

Gary K. Smith is the director of transit and parking at the University of Arkansas where he has been employed in various capacities for 22 years. His responsibilities include campus parking, consisting of maintenance, construction, and enforcement; and Razorback Transit, a public mass transit system serving the campus and the city of Fayetteville. Smith has a B.A. in criminal justice and an M.S. in operations management.

Calculating the Return on Investment of the Royal New Zealand Navy's Marine Engineering Retention Bonus Scheme

The Royal New Zealand Navy

Beryl Ann Oldham, Paul Toulson, Brenda Sayers,
and Graham Hart

Using the return-on-investment (ROI) process developed by Jack J. Phillips, this case study implemented impact estimation and forecasting to isolate the effects of a retention bonus scheme. Questionnaires were sent to 185 naval personnel who were either recipients of the bonus payments or managers of recipients when the payments were introduced. Forecasting methods using projections based on wastage rates before the retention bonus scheme was implemented were compared with wastage rates after its implementation. Finally, the costs associated with the implementation and the savings associated with reducing separation and replacement costs through improved retention were calculated to determine the ROI.

Background

High attrition rates among marine engineers (ME) in the Royal New Zealand Navy (RNZN) meant that by late 1995 the ME branch was thinly stretched to meet operational requirements safely, and this was creating additional pressure on remaining ME personnel. It was predicted that should this trend continue, it would soon result in the RNZN being unable to deliver its expected outputs to the New

This case was prepared to serve as a basis for discussion rather than to illustrate either effective or ineffective administrative and management practices.

Zealand government. As a result, a retention action committee was formed in early 1996, which concluded that ME personnel were dissatisfied and leaving because they believed they were not compensated adequately for the work they did and for the time they put into doing the work.

In March 1996 a paper was published with measures to address the problem of high turnover of ME personnel. The measures included initiatives to introduce later sailing times for ships, improved career management for ME personnel, better management of leave and maintenance periods, improved pay scales, time off in lieu for weekends worked, and the more contentious recommendation of retention bonus payments. It was feared that introducing any initiatives without a retention bonus would fail to provide the short-term incentives needed to keep ME personnel in the RNZN while measures to address the problems were being implemented. The paper proposed that a retention bonus directed at key personnel be phased in over three years to give the RNZN time to: 1) manage the hump of initial training for the new ANZAC class ship while running the current fleet; 2) introduce ANZACs into service and realize the expected positive morale and retention benefits; 3) review and amend the ME branch structure; and 4) establish an amended regime of pay and allowances and allow time for them to have a cumulative financial impact on the individual. (The term *ANZAC* comes from the Australian and New Zealand Army Corps 1914 to 1918 and is used to describe either an Australian or New Zealander, or joint projects between Australia and New Zealand; this class of ship is common to both countries.)

The stated aim or objective of the ME retention bonus scheme (MERBS) was to reduce attrition "in the short term while longer-term practices were developed to enhance morale and commitment." The target retention period for MERBS participants was three years, although it was scheduled to run for six years with phased start times for some personnel. Although no specific attrition target was mentioned in the MERBS proposal, another section of the document described a possible attrition rate of 15 percent over six years as "optimistic." But so far this target has been achieved. After introducing MERBS, turnover for the entire ME branch averaged 14.72 percent over the three-year target retention period ending June 30, 1999. (The annual turnover rates for years four and five of the scheduled six-year timeframe have remained under 15 percent, with average ME turnover rates of 10.12 percent for the year ending June 30, 2000, and 13.95 percent for the year ending June 30, 2001.)

The turnover rate for the actual targeted participants of MERBS was much lower—it averaged 2.8 percent over the three-year period ending June 30, 1999, while nontargeted ME personnel averaged 24.18 percent over the same period. That sharp contrast between MERBS participants and nonparticipants warranted investigation because although MERBS was considered to have been successful, it was expensive to implement and no formal evaluation or cost-benefit analysis had been conducted. In addition, some naval personnel believed that MERBS participants who remained at the end of the target period would have stayed regardless of the retention payments. The authors decided the MERBS scheme would be a good candidate for using ROI methodology to see what benefits could be attributed to the MERBS and to calculate its ROI.

Why ROI?

The importance of being able to explain the overall business value of an HR initiative and its impact on an organization's bottom line can be critical when attempting to obtain funding for future initiatives, particularly in government departments such as the New Zealand Defense Force (NZDF). MERBS was an expensive initiative; and, while it appeared to increase ME retention, no formal evaluation of its effectiveness had been undertaken.

Data Collection

The data collection and ROI analysis plans for MERBS are shown in figures 1 and 2.

Two questionnaires were developed and administered to collect Level 1 and Level 2 data. One questionnaire was sent to all MERBS participants, and one was sent to their managers. Since MERBS included initiatives other than the retention payments, the questionnaires included questions to isolate the effects of the retention payments from the other ME retention initiatives introduced at the same time—later sailing times for ships, improved career management for ME personnel, better management of leave and maintenance periods, improved pay scales, and time off in lieu for weekends worked—and to gauge participants' reaction and attitudinal change with respect to the initiatives.

Training Costs

Data for the training component of replacement costs was collected from schools at the RNZN training establishment to determine

Figure 1. Evaluation plan: Data collection.

Level	Broad Program Objectives	Data Collection Method	Timing of Data Collections	Responsibilities for Data Collection
1. Reaction, Satisfaction, and Planned Actions	• Satisfaction with retention bonus	• Questionnaire to participants and other stakeholders • Exit questionnaires	• After last bonus payments	• SOSPP/psychologists
2. Learning	• Intention to remain in RNZN • Intention to run similar schemes in future	• Climate survey • Questionnaire to stakeholders	• Mid-1998 and 1999	• Psychologists
3. Job Application	• Turnover rates reduced	• Personnel statistics • Exit surveys	• Throughout program (1996-1999)	• Strategic personnel planning cell
4. Business Impact	• Ships kept operational • Reduced HR replacement costs	• Number of days spent at sea • Collect recruiting and training data	• Ships' operations data throughout program (1996-1999) • During/after for replacement cost data	• Fleet operations • SOSPP/SOREC/heads of schools/HODS

Figure 2. Evaluation plan: ROI analysis (Level 5).

Data Items (Usually Level 4)	Methods for Isolating the Effects of the Program	Methods of Converting Data to Monetary Values	Program Cost Categories	Intangible Benefits from Programs	Other Influences/ Issues During Program Application	Communication Targets for Final Report
• ME separation rates • ME personnel replacement costs • Number of days spent at sea versus predicted	• Survey of end-user estimate of impact • Turnover rates during period • Trend analysis • NZDF annual reports/ operational data	• Cost of turnover • Program costs • Cost per day of ships' operations against ships' budgets	• Retention payments • Recruiting • Training • Uniform • Sea days • Salaries during training • Program development • Program evaluation	• Satisfaction with pay • Job satisfaction • Higher morale within ME branch • Achieving service level agreements with government	• Perceived inequity by nonME personnel • No other personnel initiatives or initiatives to reduce turnover evident at program implementation	• CNS • MC • FMEO • TBPO • DME • CFPT

training course information, including course lengths, maximum numbers of trainees per course, and the costs associated with each course. School heads, budget advisors, and the RNZN finance department were approached to obtain school budget data. Because training schemes had altered since the mid-1990s, training program schedules from 1994 onward were used to collect historical training course data. School budget data was taken from the financial year ending June 30, 1999. (Finance departmental staff members were able to confirm that school budgets had not varied greatly in the past few years.)

It was difficult to work out training costs for some specialist courses, as some of the data was not readily available. To solve this problem, the overall budget from schools responsible for specialist training was divided by the total number of training weeks for all courses run in one financial year and then multiplied by the length of each relevant ME training course. As a conservative approach was taken throughout this study, all workings were calculated assuming the maximum trainee numbers per course, which minimized unit cost savings per trainee. A common trainee salary component was used for the training courses common to all three trades and was devised by averaging the mean salary for each of the three trades at each rank level. Trainee salaries for separate trade training courses were averaged for each specific trade by rank.

Administrative and Separation Costs

Administrative set-up costs and separation costs were estimates based on conversations and correspondence via emails with relevant personnel. Monthly data captures from the NZDF human resource information database (ATLAS) were used to track recipients and non-recipients of the retention payments during the MERBS three-year period, and were the main source to obtain exit reasons from ME personnel who left the RNZN during that time. ATLAS also supplied the source data used by the RNZN workforce planning cell to produce turnover statistics and trend analysis graphs, as well as the salary information for ME personnel when MERBS began on June 30, 1996. NZDF annual reports were used to obtain forecasting and performance data pertaining to ships' operations and days spent at sea. ME career managers assisted with personnel information, and ME departmental heads supplied MERBS documentation. Files containing letters and payment data for individuals were also used to cross-check participant data.

Reaction and Learning Data

The questionnaire results are shown in figure 3. The respondents' overall reaction to MERBS was positive. Participants and their managers felt the retention initiatives (including the retention payments) had a positive influence on morale and retention, but managers thought the retention initiatives had a bigger influence on both morale and retention than did the participants. Participants who agreed the initiatives were effective on improving morale and retention chose the retention payments as the initiative that influenced them most in both morale and retention. Managers who agreed the initiatives were effective in improving morale and retention chose the retention payments as the initiative that most influenced participants to stay, but ranked retention payments second to better career management as the initiative that most influenced participants' morale. From these results, it would appear that MERBS did influence a change in attitude of participants regarding their retention and that it was the most influential of the retention initiatives.

On-the-Job Application

Turnover before, during, and after MERBS implementation was studied to determine the effect of MERBS on turnover. Turnover among recipients was lower than that of nonrecipients and, during the second and third years of the targeted period, below that of the rest of RNZN.

Retention payments participation and drop-out rates are shown in figure 4, and comparison turnover figures are shown in figure 5.

Business Impact

The business impact of MERBS can be demonstrated in tangible results as the savings in turnover costs of personnel and the continued operational deployment of ships. Prior to MERBS, it was reported that the outflow of ME personnel was proceeding at a higher rate than replacement training could occur and that all key ME personnel were at sea, with overall branch numbers so short that there was little opportunity for shore postings. That was increasing work and family pressure on a dwindling personnel resource. To proceed in that manner would have resulted in the inability of the ME branch to support any operations in the medium term.

Although ships' budgets are known and operations forecasted, the ability to keep ships operational is considered an intangible because

Figure 3. Questionnaire results.

	Participants "Yes"	Managers "Yes"
1a. Did ME retention initiatives have a positive effect on participants' morale?	85%	97%
1b. Of those who replied "yes" to last question, percentage that chose retention payments as most influential retention initiative on participants' morale.	55%	· 32%
2a. Did ME retention initiatives influence participants to stay?	53%	90%
2b. Of those who replied "yes" to last question, percentage that chose retention payments as most influential retention initiative on participants' retention.	67%	77%
3. The implementation of MERBS was successful.	67%	83%
4. Participants understood MERBS when it was introduced.	79%	90%
5. How much of participants' decision to stay was influenced by the retention payments?	41%	N/A
6. How confident were participants of the accuracy of their answer regarding their retention being influenced by retention payments (41%)?	93%	N/A
7. Retention payments schemes are an effective way of retaining people.	68%	45%
8. The ME retention payments were good value for money.	62%	79%
9. Overall, the ME retention payments were successful.	68%	86%

of the wide range of operations and the uncertainty surrounding exactly which operations would have ceased and in what order. In accordance with the NZDF Service Level Agreement with the Government of New Zealand, RNZN contributes to a range of services on behalf of the minister of defense to other government departments and the community. Each of the frigates is to be held at the level of capability and response time to deploy for the associated operational tasks as agreed between the minister and the chief of defense force. As the personnel, maintenance, preparation, and running costs of a frigate are high, it could be argued that large amounts of committed funds would have been wasted had ships been unable to fulfill their operational requirements due to ME personnel shortages. It would have been difficult to work out such complex calculations after the period concerned, and because the planning for this ROI evaluation was not built in during MERBS

Figure 4. Retention payments participation.

(Out of total ME branch numbers 206/343 eligible)

	Eligible 1996	Participated 1996/97	Participated 1997/98	Participated 1998/99	Left the Service 1996/97	Left the Service 1997/98	Left the Service 1998/99
Marine Technicians (MT)	99	84	82	103	0	2	4
Marine Mechanics (MM)	55	54	53	33	0	1	4
Marine Electricians (MEL)	52	47	46	34	0	1	3
	206	185	181	170	0	4	11

Figure 5. Turnover comparisons.

	June 1996	June 1997	June 1998	June 1999
Turnover for ME nonrecipients	N/A	43.5%	14.9%	17.3%
Turnover for all nonME personnel	19.5%	17.9%	12.9%	14.3%
Turnover for all ME personnel	27.5%	20.9%	9.9%	13.5%
Turnover of payment recipients	N/A	0.0%	2.2%	6.5%

initial planning stages, timely data collection did not occur. However, had RNZN not been able to dramatically reduce attrition in ME personnel during the MERBS period, the cost to NZDF, both fiscally and in terms of operations, would have been high and would have continued for at least another decade.

The RNZN must maintain operational readiness. To do this it invests a lot in its people, who are expensive to recruit, train, and retain. The training and experience of RNZN personnel make them highly marketable in the private and wider public sector because their skills and attributes are attractive to external employers. As the converse is seldom the case, there is little scope for lateral recruitment into RNZN from the private or public sector. Reducing turnover results in major savings when replacement costs include training.

Monetary Benefits of Program

Turnover generally results in expenses for recruitment, selection, training, and development. The monetary benefits of MERBS were based on savings in turnover costs. For the purposes of this evaluation, turnover costs were split into two categories, separation and replacement costs. Separation costs included separation pay, exit interviews, and administrative functions per leaver; and replacement costs included recruiting, training (including salaries while under training), and uniform costs. Two methods were used to calculate the monetary benefits; one method was based on the participant impact estimation, and the other was based on forecasting methods using projections based on historical turnover rates.

Participant Impact Estimation

Using the participant impact estimation, the total replacement and separation savings resulting from MERBS were $7,066,789. The calculations using the participant impact estimation are shown in figure 6.

The participant impact estimation was one of the methods used for isolating MERBS effects. Rather than crediting the retention payments with saving all of the 170 participants remaining at the end of the target period, participant impact estimates indicated that 38 percent of the remaining participants, or 64 personnel, were savings attributed to MERBS.

Forecasting Method

Figure 7 shows the turnover rates for the periods before, during, and after the retention payments. The predicted turnover for ME

Figure 6. Monetary benefits from turnover reduction using participant impact estimation.

Number of retention payment recipients at end of three-year period $= 170$
Estimated separation cost per leaver $= \$4,260$
Average replacement cost per leaver $= (\$17,872,586 / 170) = \$105,133$
Percentage of decision to stay influenced by retention payments $= 41\%$
Confidence in decision to stay influenced by retention payments percentage $= 93\%$
Participants' impact estimation of retention payments $= .41 \times .93 = .38$
Monetary benefits $= (\$4,260 + \$105,133) \times 170 \times .38 = \$7,066,789$

personnel, based on historical turnover, is shown against actual turnover for ME and nonME personnel. Actual turnover for the targeted period after the introduction of the retention payments was 73 personnel fewer than predicted.

During the MERBS period, turnover for ME personnel spread over the three years was 20.9 percent, 9.9 percent, and 13.5 percent, which can be represented in actual personnel numbers by 74, 33, and 48. Without the retention payments, historically ME turnover averaged 5.5 percent higher than nonME turnover so the expected turnover can be expressed as 23.4 percent, 18.4 percent, and 19.8 percent, which can be represented in personnel numbers by 83, 69, and 76. Therefore, the difference or improvement related to retention payments in actual personnel numbers for the three-year period can be represented as (83-74)+(69-33)+(76-48) = 73 ME personnel.

The monetary value saved in not having to replace the remaining 170 MERBS participants at the end of the three-year period on June 30, 1999, was $17,872,586. (See figure 8.) Dividing that amount by the number of participants gives a unit cost of $105,133, that when multiplied by the 73 ME personnel retained by MERBS, shows a saving in replacement costs of $7,674,709. The separation costs worked out to a unit cost of $4,260 (see figure 9); and when those costs are multiplied by the 73 ME personnel, it shows a saving in separation costs of $310,980. Therefore, total replacement and separation savings resulting from the MERBS using the forecasting method were ($7,674,709 + $310,980) = $7,985,689. (See figure 10.)

The forecasting method based on using historical turnover rates and differences to predict future turnover was another method for isolating the MERBS effects. Without such an isolating strategy, MERBS might have been credited with saving more personnel. For example, if based solely on the difference between the 27.5 percent turnover rate in the year prior to MERBS implementation and the lower turnover rates that occurred in the subsequent three years, the calculations would have indicated a huge savings of $(96-74) + (96-33) + (96-48) = 133$ ME personnel, rather than the lower and more realistic number of 73 ME personnel.

Program Costs

Figure 11 shows the program cost categories. The administrative and ROI measurement costs items were estimates taken from personnel who were closely involved in the process.

Figure 7. Turnover reduction using forecasting based on historical turnover (predicted versus actual ME turnover after retention payments).

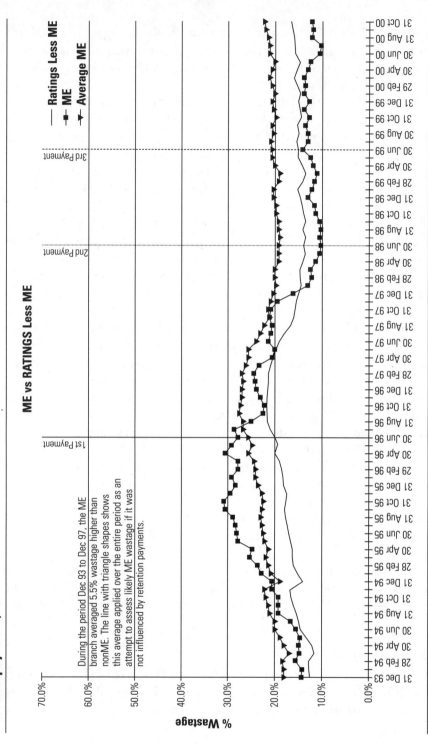

Ratings Less ME = nonME personnel turnover; ME = actual ME turnover; Average ME = predicted ME turnover..

Figure 8. Total replacement cost savings.

Personnel Category	Replacement cost per person in each category	No. of people in each category	Total cost per personnel category
AMEL	34,243	9	$308,187
LMEL	59,565	16	953,040
POMEL	90,217	7	631,519
CPOMEL	97,057	8	776,456
WOMEL	107,055	3	321,165
AMM	43,098	17	732,666
LMM	69,484	14	972,776
POMM	92,409	13	1,201,317
CPOMM	99,249	5	496,245
AMT	48,546	7	339,822
LMT	108,596	22	2,389,112
POMT	126,052	14	1,764,728
CPOMT	196,445	24	4,714,680
WOMT	206,443	11	2,270,873
Total		170	$17,872,586

Figure 9. Estimated separation cost savings per leaver.

Exit interviews		$87
Records and testimonial	1 × DO × 1 hour	24
Exit processing	1 × clerk × 30 mins	7
Terminal benefit payout	60 days — tax and superannuation	3,300
Medical examination	$200 and $3000 × 10% per leaver	500
Dental examination	Per leaver	250
Discharge routine	Leaver × 1 day	92
Total		$4,260

Figure 10. Monetary benefits from turnover reduction using forecasting based on historical turnover.

Difference or improvement related to retention payments over three-year period = 73 personnel	
Average replacement costs = $105,133 × 73 = $7,674,709	
Estimated separation costs = $4,260 × 73 = $310,980	
Monetary benefits = ($7,674,709 + $310,980) = $7,985,689	

Figure 11. Estimated ME retention bonus scheme costs.

Estimated administrative set-up costs (personnel, briefings, payments processing)	$54,756
Retention payments	$4,865,800
Estimated ROI evaluation study measurement costs (personnel; research, including questionnaire design and completion; report writing)	$5,948
Total cost	$4,926,504

ROI Calculations

Figure 12 shows the benefit-cost ratio (BCR) and ROI calculations using the forecasting method. Benefits based on savings in separation and replacement costs are used in the BCR to yield 1.62:1. Thus, for each $1 spent on the program, $1.62 was returned. The ROI calculation, which uses net benefits, shows a positive return of 62 percent.

Figure 13 shows the BCR and ROI calculations using the participant impact estimation. Benefits based on savings in separation and replacement costs are used in the BCR to yield 1.43:1. Thus, for each $1 spent on the program, $1.43 was returned. The ROI calculation shows a positive return of 43 percent.

Although the 62 percent ROI was obtained by more quantitative means than the 43 percent ROI based on participant impact estimation, there is no guarantee that the forecasting method would have yielded the expected results. Therefore, despite having confidence in the higher ROI percentage, it is recommended that the more conservative 43 percent ROI be used as the measure of effectiveness for MERBS. That is in keeping with the conservative approach that was taken throughout this study in the interests of maintaining credibility.

Figure 12. BCR and ROI calculations using forecasting based on historical turnover.

$$BCR = \frac{Benefits}{Costs} = \frac{\$7,985,689}{\$4,926,504} = 1.62{:}1$$

$$ROI = \frac{Net\ Benefits}{Costs} = \frac{\$7,985,689 - \$4,926,504}{\$4,926,504}$$
$$\times\ 100 = 62\%$$

Figure 13. BCR and ROI calculations using participant impact estimation.

$$BCR = \frac{Benefits}{Costs} = \frac{\$7,066,789}{\$4,926,504} = 1.43{:}1$$

$$ROI = \frac{Net\ Benefits}{Costs} = \frac{\$7,066,789 - \$4,926,504}{\$4,926,504}$$
$$\times\ 100 = 43\%$$

Communication Process

There were three phases to the MERBS communication process. The first phase was a publicity campaign prior to and during MERBS implementation; the second phase sought evaluation feedback from MERBS participants and their managers; and the third phase communicated MERBS evaluation results.

Before implementing MERBS, the scheme was announced via signals to the fleet, the Navy's magazine *Navy Today,* newsletter articles, meetings, and a series of briefings given by senior and midlevel managers. Participants received individual letters explaining how the scheme would operate and their entitlements under the scheme, and ME personnel were kept informed regularly on the progress of initiatives, including evaluation study results, during and following the period of implementation by representatives sitting on an ME steering group committee. In the questionnaire responses, 79 percent of the participants and 90 percent of the managers said that participants understood MERBS when it was introduced.

Prior to the evaluation study, personnel from each ship and department ashore were chosen to distribute and collect the evaluation questionnaires. These personnel were contacted by phone or email and given instructions and a list of participants and managers to be surveyed. Each of those surveyed was given background information, survey instructions, and details of whom to contact should he or she have concerns or questions. Although the survey was voluntary, 84 percent of participants and 97 percent of their managers responded.

Following the evaluation study, senior managers received personal briefs and copies of the detailed evaluation report. ME personnel were advised of the survey findings on the ROI evaluation and other ME initiatives (detailed in the Background section of this case study) at a series of briefings.

Lessons Learned

Because the planning for this ROI evaluation was not built in during the MERBS initial planning stages, timely data collection did not occur and some data collection opportunities were lost. ROI evaluation and data collection methods should always be considered during program design and development for major HR initiatives to enhance ease of data collection, data accuracy, and results credibility.

Questions for Discussion

1. Discuss the benefits of calculating the ROI of HR initiatives.
2. Critique the data collection plan.
3. What is the effect when training is included in replacement costs?
4. Discuss the isolation strategies used.
5. Were the ROI calculations realistic?
6. Which ROI calculation would you have used as the measure of effectiveness for the MERBS? Justify your answer.
7. Discuss the communication processes.
8. What were the consequences of not including ROI evaluation in the initial planning stages of the MERBS?

The Authors

Lieutenant Commander Beryl Ann Oldham is a human resources specialist in the Royal New Zealand Navy. Her interests include strategic HR planning, competency profiling, performance improvement, performance management, and measuring the results of HR initiatives. Currently a project officer involved in several HR projects, she has worked in the Navy's workforce planning cell and has held the posts of training development coordinator, and combat system maintenance training analyst on the ANZAC ship project. Oldham has recently completed a master's degree with honors in business studies, majoring in human resource management, through New Zealand's Massey University. She wishes to thank the Royal New

Zealand Navy for making this case study available for publication. She can be reached at the New Zealand Naval Base in Auckland; email: beryl.oldham@nzdf.mil.nz.

Paul Toulson is the head of the department of human resources management in the College of Business, Massey University, and is a life fellow of the Human Resources Institute of New Zealand. Toulson is a registered industrial/organizational psychologist and has been a member of the College of Business at Massey University since 1985. Prior to that, he was employed in the New Zealand Defense Force in a variety of appointments as a psychologist and personnel director. His teaching areas include HRM practices, research methods in HRM, and value-added HRM. He is interested in the whole area of valuing people in organizations and also measuring the impact of HR practices and interventions in terms of their contribution to the objectives of the organization.

Brenda Sayers is the national partner of Deloitte HR Management Solutions in New Zealand. Deloitte Solutions provides HR consulting services to a wide range of organizations in both the public and private sector. She has been accredited in the ROI process and has worked with Jack and Patricia Phillips in New Zealand for several years delivering training in HR measurement and undertaking impact studies

Graham Hart is a senior manager with Deloitte HR Management Solutions and also is accredited in the ROI process.

Evaluating the Impact of a Graduate Program in a Federal Agency

Federal Information Agency

Jack J. Phillips and Patricia Pulliam Phillips

The Federal Information Agency (FIA) provides various types of information to other government agencies and businesses as well as state and local organizations, agencies, and interested groups. Operating through a network across the United States, the work is performed by several hundred communication specialists with backgrounds in systems, computer science, electrical engineering, and information science. Almost all the specialists have bachelor's degrees in one of these fields. The headquarters and operation center is in the Washington, D.C., area, where 1,500 of these specialists are employed.

Problem and Solution

FIA has recently experienced two problems that have senior agency officials concerned. The first problem is an unacceptable rate of employee turnover for this group of specialists—averaging 38 percent in the past year alone. That has placed a strain on the agency to recruit and train replacements. An analysis of exit interviews indicated that employees leave primarily for higher salaries. Because FIA is somewhat constrained in providing competitive salaries, it has become extremely difficult to compete with private sector for salaries and benefits. Although salary increases and adjustments in pay levels will be necessary to lower turnover, FIA is exploring other options in the interim.

The second problem concerns the need to continuously update the technical skills of the staff. While the vast majority of the 1,500 specialists have degrees in various fields, only a few have master's degrees in their specialty. In this field, formal education is quickly outdated. The annual feedback survey with employees reflected a strong interest in an internal master's degree program in information science. Consequently, FIA explored implementing an in-house master's degree in information science conducted by the School of Engineering and Science at Regional State University (RSU). The master's degree program would be implemented at no cost to the participating employee and conducted on the agency's time during routine work hours. Designed to address both employee turnover and skill updates, the program would normally take three years for participants to complete.

Program Description

RSU was selected for the master's program because of its reputation and the match of its curriculum to FIA needs. The program allows participants to take one or two courses per semester. A two-course per semester schedule would take three years to complete with one course in the summer session. Both morning and afternoon classes were available, each representing three hours per week of class time. Participants were discouraged from taking more than two courses per term. Although a thesis option was normally available, FIA requested a graduate project be required for six hours of credit as a substitute for the thesis. A professor would supervise the project. Designed to add value to FIA, the project would be applied in the agency and would not be as rigorous as the thesis. Participants sign up for three hours for the project in both year two and three.

Classes were usually offered live with professors visiting the agency's center. Occasionally, classes were offered through videoconference or independent study. Participants were asked to prepare for classroom activities on their own time, but were allowed to attend classes on the agency's time. A typical three-year schedule is shown in table 1.

Senior management approved the master's curriculum, which represented a mix of courses normally offered in the program and others specially selected for FIA staff. Two new courses were designed by university faculty to be included in the curriculum. These two represented a slight modification of existing courses and were tailored to the communication requirements of the agency. Elective courses were not allowed for two reasons. First, it would complicate the offering to a certain extent, requiring additional courses, facilities, and professors—essentially adding cost to the program. Second, FIA wanted a prescribed,

Table 1. Typical three-year schedule.

M.S.—Information Science

	Year 1	Year 2	Year 3
Fall	2 Courses—6 hours	2 Courses—6 hours	2 Courses—6 hours
Spring	2 Courses—6 hours	2 Courses—6 hours	2 Courses—6 hours
Summer	1 Course—3 hours	1 Course—3 hours	Graduate Project—3 hours
		Graduate Project—3 hours	

Graduate Project—6 hours (Year 2 and 3)
Total Semester Hours—48

customized curriculum that would add value to the agency while still meeting the requirements of the university.

Selection Criteria

An important issue involved the selection of employees to attend the program. Most employees who voluntarily left the agency resigned within the first four years and were often considered to have high potential. With this in mind, the following five criteria were established for identifying and selecting the employees to enroll in the program:

1. A candidate should have at least one year of service prior to beginning classes.
2. A candidate must meet the normal requirements to be accepted into the graduate school at the university.
3. A candidate must be willing to sign a commitment to stay with the agency for two years beyond program completion.
4. A candidate's immediate manager must nominate the employee for consideration.
5. A candidate must be considered "high potential" as rated by the immediate manager.

The management team was provided initial information on the program, kept informed of its development and progress prior to actual launch, and briefed as the program was described and selection criteria was finalized. It was emphasized that the selection should be based on objective criteria, following the guidelines offered. At the same time, managers were asked to provide feedback as to the level of interest and specific issues surrounding the nomination of candidates.

A limit of 100 participants entering the program each year was established. This limit was based on two key issues:
1. The capability of the university in terms of staffing for the program—RSU could not effectively teach more than 100 participants each semester.
2. This was an experiment that, if successful, could be modified or enhanced in the future.

Program Administration

Because of the magnitude of the anticipated enrollment, FIA appointed a full-time program administrator who was responsible for organizing and coordinating the program. The duties included registration of the participants, all correspondence and communication with the university and participants, facilities and logistics (including materials and books), and resolving problems as they occur. FIA absorbed the total cost of the coordinator. The university assigned an individual to serve as liaison with the agency. This individual was not additional staff; the university absorbed the cost as part of the tuition.

The Drivers for Evaluation

This program was selected for a comprehensive evaluation to show its impact on the agency using a four-year timeframe. Four influences created the need for this detailed level of accountability:
1. Senior administrators had requested detailed evaluations for certain programs considered to be strategic, highly visible, and designed to add value to the agency.
2. This program was perceived to be very expensive, demanding a higher level of accountability, including return on investment (ROI).
3. Because retention is such a critical issue for this agency, it was important to determine if this solution was the appropriate one. A detailed measurement and evaluation should reflect the success of the program.
4. The passage of federal legislation and other initiatives in the United States, aimed at bringing more accountability for taxpayers' funds, has created a shift in increased public sector accountability.

Consequently, the implementation team planned a detailed evaluation of this program beyond the traditional program evaluation processes. Along with tracking costs, the monetary payoff would be developed, including ROI in the program. Because this is a very complex and comprehensive solution, other important measures would be monitored to present an overall, balanced approach to the measurement.

Recognizing the shift toward public sector accountability, the human resources staff had developed the necessary skills to implement the ROI process. A small group of HR staff members had been certified to implement the ROI process within the agency. The ROI is a comprehensive measurement and evaluation process that develops six types of data and always includes a method to isolate the effects of the program (Phillips, Stone, and Phillips, 2001).

The evaluation of the master's program was conducted by several of these team members with the assistance of the original developer of the ROI process, Dr. Jack J. Phillips.

Program Costs

The cost of the program was tabulated and monitored and reflected a fully loaded cost profile, which included all direct and indirect costs. One of the major costs was the tuition for the participants. The university charged the customary tuition, plus $100 per semester course per participant to offset the additional travel, faculty expense, books, and handouts. The tuition per semester hour was $200 ($600 per three-hour course).

The full-time administrator was an FIA employee, receiving a base salary of $37,000 per year, with a 45 percent employee benefits upload factor. The administrator had expenses of approximately $15,000 per year. Salaries for the participants represented another significant cost category. The average salary of the job categories of the employees involved in the program was $47,800, with a 45 percent employee benefits factor. Salaries usually increase about 4 percent per year. Participants attended class a total of 18 hours for each semester hour of credit. Thus, a three-hour course represented 54 hours of off-the-job time in the classroom. The total hours needed to complete the program for one participant was 756 hours (14×54).

Classroom facilities was another significant cost category. For the 100 participants, four different courses were offered each semester and each course was repeated at a different time slot. With a class size of 25, eight separate semester courses were presented. Each semester, half the scheduled courses were offered in the summer. Although the classrooms used for this program were those normally used for other training and education programs offered at the agency, the cost for providing the facilities was included. (Because of the unusual demand, an additional conference room was built to provide ample meeting space.) The estimate for the average cost of all meeting rooms was $40 per hour of use.

The cost for the initial assessment was also included in the cost profile. This charge, estimated to be about $5,000, included the turnover analysis and was prorated for the first three years. FIA's development costs for the program were estimated to be about $10,000 and were prorated for three years. Management time involved in the program was minimal, but estimated to be about $9,000 over the three-year period. This consisted primarily of meetings and memos regarding the program. Finally, the evaluation costs, representing the cost to actually track the success of the program and report the results to management, was estimated to be $10,000.

Table 2 represents the total costs of the initial group in the program for three years using a fully loaded cost profile. All of the cost categories described above are included. This value is necessary for the ROI calculation.

Data Collection Issues

To understand the success of the project from a balanced perspective, a variety of types of data had to be collected throughout program implementation. During the initial enrollment process, meetings

Table 2. Total fully loaded costs of master's program for 100 participants.

	Year 1	Year 2	Year 3	Total
Initial analysis (prorated)	$1,667	$1,667	$1,666	$5,000
Development (prorated)	3,333	3,333	3,334	10,000
Tuition—regular	300,000	342,000	273,000	915,000
Tuition—premium	50,000	57,000	45,500	152,500
Salaries/Benefits (participants)	899,697	888,900	708,426	2,497,023
Salaries/Benefits (program administrator)	53,650	55,796	58,028	167,474
Program coordination	15,000	15,000	15,000	45,000
Facilities	43,200	43,200	34,560	120,960
Management time	3,000	3,000	3,000	9,000
Evaluation	3,333	3,333	3,334	10,000
Total	$1,372,880	$1,413,229	$1,145,848	$3,931,957

were conducted with participants to obtain their commitment to provide data at different timeframes. The program administrator had regular access to participants who were willing to provide data about their reaction to the program, and detail the extent of knowledge and skill enhancement and the successes they achieved on the job. Measures were taken at four distinct levels:

1. reaction to individual courses and the program, including the administrative and coordination issues
2. the knowledge and skills obtained from the individual courses and learning about the program
3. application and implementation of the program as learning is applied on the job and the program is coordinated effectively
4. changes in business measures in the agency directly related to the program.

In addition to these data items, program costs were monitored so that the return on investment could be calculated.

Collecting different types of data required measures to be taken at different timeframes. It was agreed at the beginning of the program that some data categories would be collected at the end of each semester. Reaction would be measured, and learning would be monitored with individual grade point averages. At periodic intervals, follow-up data was collected to reflect the progress of the program and its application on the job. Finally, business impact data directly linked to the program was measured during the program as well as at the conclusion. While this program was perceived to have a long-term impact, data had to be collected throughout the process to reflect any early impact that developed.

Data Collection Plan

The program administrator was responsible for the initial data collection and semester feedback sections. Individual faculty members were asked to collect reaction and learning measures at the end of each course. While most of the data would come directly from the participants, the records from the agency were monitored for certain business measures, such as turnover. In addition, immediate managers of participants provided input concerning the actual use of the program on the job. Figure 1 shows the data collection plan for this program.

Reaction and Satisfaction

Reaction to the program was collected at specific time periods. A few issues involving reaction and satisfaction were collected from prospective participants at an information briefing when the program

Figure 1. Data collection plan.

Program: Federal Information Agency   Responsibility: Jack Phillips

Level	Broad Program Objective(s)	Measures	Data Collection Method/Instruments	Data Sources	Timing	Responsibilities
1	**REACTION/SATISFACTION** • Positive reaction to program, content, quality, and administration	• 4.0 on a scale from 1-5	• Reaction questionnaire	• Participants	• At the intro of the program • End of course • End of semester	• Program administrator • Faculty • Program administrator
2	**LEARNING** • Maintain above-average grades • Understand the purpose and the participant's role in the program	• 3.0 grade point average out of a possible 4.0 • 4.0 on a scale from 1-5	• Formal and informal testing in each course • Questionnaire at the end of initial meeting	• Participants • Participants	• End of each course • At the intro of the program	• Faculty • Faculty
3	**APPLICATION/ IMPLEMENTATION** • Use of the knowledge and skills on the job • Develop and apply innovative projects to add operational value • Enjoy a very high completion rate	• Various measures on a scale of 1-5 • Completion of project • Completion rate of 80%	• Questionnaires • Action plans • Monitoring records	• Participants • Participants • Agency records	• End of each year • One-year follow-up • End of program	• Program administrator • Program administrator • Program administrator

4	**BUSINESS IMPACT** • Reduce avoidable turnover • Improve job satisfaction/commitment • Career enhancement • Upgrade technology and agency capability • Improve operational results • Recruiting success	• Number of avoidable exits each month divided by the average number each month • 4.0 on a scale of 1-5 • Monetary values • Number of candidates	• Monitoring records • Questionnaires • Action plans • Monitoring records	• Agency records • Participants • Managers • Participants • Agency records	• Monthly • End of each year • End of program • One-year follow-up	• HR staff • Program administrator • Program administrator • Program administrator
5	**ROI** • Achieve a 25% return on investment	Comments: _____				

was announced. Perceived value, anticipated difficulty of the courses, and usefulness of the program on the job were captured in initial meetings. Next, reaction measures were collected for each individual course as the participants rated the course material, instructor, delivery style, and learning environment. Also, at the end of each semester, a brief reaction questionnaire was collected to provide constant feedback of perceptions and satisfaction with the program. Upon completion of the program, an overall reaction questionnaire was distributed.

Learning

The initial meeting with the participants provided an opportunity to collect information about their understanding of how the program works and their role in making the program successful. Most of the learning took place in individual courses. The faculty member assigned grades based on formal and informal testing and assessment. These grades reflected individual learning, skills, and knowledge. Professors used a variety of testing methodology such as special projects, demonstrations, discussion questions, case studies, simulations, and objective tests. The overall grade point average provided an ongoing assessment of the degree to which the participants were learning the content of the courses.

Application and Implementation

Application and implementation measures were assessed at several different time intervals. At the end of each year, a questionnaire was distributed where the participants indicated the success of the program in three areas:
1. the opportunities to use the skills and knowledge learned in the program
2. the extent to which the skills have actually been used on the job
3. the effectiveness in the use of the skills.

In addition, several questions focused on the progress with (and barriers to) the implementation of the program. At this level of analysis, it was important to determine if the program material was actually being used on the job. Program statistics were collected, including dropout and completion rates of the participants.

Business Measures

Because the program was implemented to focus on retention of specialists, the primary business measure was turnover. Turnover rates for the participants in the program were compared directly with individuals not involved in the program to determine if the rates were significantly reduced. In addition to avoidable turnover, tenure of employees was tracked, which reflected the average length of service of the target job group. It was anticipated that the program would have an impact on a variety of other business measures as well, including the following:

1. productivity (from projects)
2. quality (from projects)
3. enhanced agency capability
4. technology upgrade
5. job satisfaction
6. employee commitment
7. recruiting success
8. career enhancement.

In the planning process, it was decided that these measures would be explored to the extent feasible to identify improvements. If not, the perceived changes in these business measures would be collected directly from the participants.

Graduate Projects

An important part of the program was a graduate work-study project required to complete the master's degree. The project involved at least two semesters of work and provided six hours of credit. It was supervised by a faculty member and approved by the participants' immediate manager. The project had to add value to the agency in some way as well as improve agency capability, operations, or technology upgrade. At the same time, it had to be rigorous enough to meet the requirements of the university. In a sense, it was a master's thesis, although the participants were enrolled in a nonthesis option. Through this project, the participants were able to apply what they had learned. The project was identified during the first year, approved and implemented during the second year, and completed in the third year.

This project provided an excellent opportunity for participants to support the agency and add value to agency operations. As part of the project, participants developed an action plan detailing how their project would be used on the job. The action plan, built into the graduate project, provided the timetable and detail for application of the project. A part of the action plan is a detail of the monetary contribution to the agency (or forecast of the contribution). That was required as part of the project and, ultimately, became evidence of contribution of the project. Follow-up on the action plan provided the monetary amount of contribution from the graduate project.

Data Collection Summary

Table 3 shows a summary of the various instruments used to collect data, along with the level of evaluation data. As this table reveals, data collection was comprehensive, continuous, and necessary for a program with this much exposure and expense. Data collected at Levels 1, 2, and 3 were used to make adjustments in the program. Adjustments were made throughout the program as feedback was obtained. This action is particularly important for administrative and faculty-related issues.

ROI Analysis Plan

Figure 2 presents a completed planning document for the ROI analysis. This plan, which was completed prior to the beginning of the program, addresses key issues of isolating the influence of the program, converting the data to monetary values, and costing the program. As figure 2 reveals, avoidable turnover, the key data item, is listed along with the technology and operations improvement expected from individual graduate projects. It was anticipated that the program would pay off on turnover and improvements from projects.

Recruiting success is also listed as a measure for potential isolation and conversion. An increase in the number of applicants interested in employment with FIA was anticipated as the communication and publicity surrounding the program became known in various recruiting channels. Other business impact measures were considered to be intangible and are listed in the intangible benefits column. Intangible benefits are defined as those measures purposely not converted to monetary values. During the planning stage, it was anticipated that measures such as improved job satisfaction, enhanced agency capability, and improved organizational commitment would not be converted to monetary value. Although very important, these measures would be listed as intangible benefits—only if they were linked to the program.

The cost categories discussed earlier were detailed in this planning document. Costs are fully loaded and include both direct and indirect categories. The communication targets were comprehensive. Seven groups were identified as needing specific information from this study.

The ROI analysis and data collection plans provide all the key decisions about the project prior to the actual data collection and analysis.

Table 3. Data summary by evaluation level.

Type of Instrument	Reaction/ Satisfaction	Learning	Application/ Implementation	Business Impact
1. Questionnaire after intro to program	X	X		
2. End-of-course instructor evaluation	X			
3. End-of-semester evaluation questionnaire	X			
4 Individual course tests		X		
5. Annual evaluation questionnaire			X	
6. Action plans with follow up			X	X
7 One-year follow-up questionnaire			X	X
8. Monitoring records				X

Isolating the Effects of the Program

Several methods were used to isolate the effects of the program, depending on the specific business impact measure. For avoidable turnover, three methods were initially planned. A comparison group was identified, which would serve as the control group in a traditional control group experiment. The individuals selected for the master's program would be matched with others not in the program, using the same tenure and job status characteristics. Recognizing the difficulty of success with a control group arrangement, both the participants and managers were asked to indicate the percent of the turnover reduction they believed to be directly related to this program. A questionnaire was provided to obtain this input.

For the technology and operations improvement data, participants' estimates were used as a method for isolating the effects of the program using data from action plans for the projects. The same approach was planned for isolating the effects of the program on recruiting success.

Figure 2. ROI analysis plan.

Program: M.S. In Information Science Responsibility: _____ Date: _____

Data Items (Usually Level 4)	Methods for Isolating the Effects of the Program/ Process	Methods of Converting Data to Monetary Values	Cost Categories	Intangible Benefits	Communication Targets for Final Report	Other Influences/ Issues During Application	Comments
• Avoidable turnover	• Comparison group • Participants' estimates • Manager estimates	• External studies	• Initial analysis • Program development • Tuition • Participant salaries/ benefits • Program coordination costs • Facilities • Management time • Evaluation	• Improved job satisfaction • Improved operational commitment • Career enhancement • Enhanced agency capability • Technology upgrade	• Participants • Immediate managers of participants • Program sponsor • Senior agency administrators • Agency HR staff • RSU administrators • All agency employees	• Need to monitor external employment conditions • Need to identify other potential internal influences on turnover reductions	Payoff of program will probably rest on turnover reduction and improvements from projects
• Technology and operating improvements	• Participants' estimates	• Standard values • Historical costs • Expert input • Participants' estimates					
• Recruiting success	• Participants' estimates	• Internal expert estimates					

Converting Data to Monetary Values

The methods used to convert data to monetary values varied as well. For avoidable turnover, external studies were used to pinpoint the approximate value. From various databases, studies in similar job categories had revealed that the cost of turnover for these specialized job groups was somewhere between two and three times the average annual salary. This was considerably higher than the HR staff at FIA anticipated. As a compromise, a value of 1.75 times the annual salary was used. While this value is probably lower than the actual fully loaded cost of turnover, it is conservative to assign this value. It is much better to use a conservative estimate for this value than to calculate the fully loaded cost for turnover. Most retention specialists would agree that 175 percent of annual pay is a conservative, fully loaded cost of turnover for information specialists.

To obtain the monetary values of project improvements, participants were asked to use one of four specific methods to identify the value:
1. Standard values were available for many items throughout the agency, and their use was encouraged when placing monetary values on a specific improvement.
2. Historical costs could be used, capturing the various costs of a specific data item as it is improved, by the project. These cost savings values are taken directly from general ledger accounts and provide a very credible cost value.
3. If neither of the above methods is feasible, expert input, using internal sources, was suggested.
4. Finally, if the other methods failed to produce a value, participants were instructed to place their own estimates for the value. In those cases, the confidence of the estimate would be obtained.

For recruiting success, internal expert estimates would be used, directly from the recruiting staff. Collectively, these techniques provided an appropriate array of strategies to convert data to monetary values.

Reaction and Satisfaction Measurements

Reaction measurements, taken during the initial program introductions, were informal and confirmed that the participants recognized the value of the program and its usefulness to them as well as the agency. Also, any concerns about the difficulty of the program were addressed during that meeting.

Two opportunities to collect reaction and satisfaction data occurred at the end of each semester. For each course, the instructor obtained direct feedback using standard instrumentation. Table 4 shows the faculty evaluation selected for this program. It was a slightly modified version of what RSU normally collects for its instructors. In addition to providing feedback to various RSU department heads, this information was provided to the program administrator as well as the major sponsor for this project. This constant data flow was an attempt to make adjustments if the faculty was perceived to be unresponsive and ineffective in delivering the desired courses. As table 4 shows, on a scale from one to five, the responses were extremely effective. The only concerns expressed were with the presentation and ability to relate to agency needs. At several different times, adjustments were made in an attempt to improve these two areas. The ratings presented in table 4 were the cumulative ratings over the three-year project for the 100 participants who initially began the program.

At the end of each semester, a brief scannable questionnaire was collected to measure satisfaction with and reaction to the program. Table 5 shows the various items rated on this questionnaire. The goal was to have a composite of at least four out of five for this program, and it was achieved. The only areas of concern were the quality of the faculty, the amount of new information, and the appropriateness of the course material. Adjustments were made to improve these areas.

Learning Measurements

Learning was primarily measured through formal testing processes used by individual faculty members. As stated earlier, a variety of methods were used ranging from objective testing to simulations. The tests yielded an individual grade that translated into a grade point average. The grade objective for the overall program was to maintain a 3.0 grade

Table 4. Reaction and satisfaction with faculty.

Issue	Average Rating*
Knowledge of topic	4.35
Preparation for classes	4.25
Delivery/Presentation	3.64
Level of involvement	4.09
Learning environment	4.21
Responsiveness to participants	4.31
Ability to relate to agency needs	3.77

*On a 1-5 scale, with 5 = exceptional

Table 5. Measures of reaction to and satisfaction with the program.

Issue	Average Rating*
Value of program	4.7
Difficulty of program	4.1
Usefulness of program	4.5
Quality of faculty	3.p
Quality of program administration	4.4
Appropriateness of course material	3.9
Intent to use course material	4.2
Amount of new information	3.7
Recommendation to others	4.6

*On a 1-5 scale, with 5 = exceptional

point average out of a possible 4.0. Table 6 shows the cumulative grade point average through the three-year period ending with an average of 3.18, exceeding the target for the overall program.

Application and Implementation Measures

Application and implementation were measured with three instruments: the annual questionnaire at the end of each program year, the follow-up on the action plans, and a one-year follow-up questionnaire. The two questionnaires (annual and follow-up) provided information about overall application and use of the program and course material. Table 7 shows the categories of data for the annual questionnaire, which, for the most part, was duplicated in the follow-up

Table 6. Cumulative grade point averages.

Year	Cumulative Grade Point Average *
Year 1	3.31
Year 2	3.25
Year 3	3.18

*Out of a possible 4.0

questionnaire. As this table reveals, nine topical areas were explored with the focus on the extent to which the participants were using the program and the skills and knowledge learned. It also explored improvements and accomplishments over and above the individual project improvement. Barriers and enablers to implementation were detailed, in addition to input on the management support for the program, along with recommendations for improvement.

Several questions were devoted to each of these categories. For example, table 8 presents application data for knowledge and skills, showing four specific areas and the ratings obtained for each. While these ratings reveal success, there was some concern about the frequency of use and opportunity to use skills. The input scale for these items was adjusted to job context. For example, in the frequency of skills, the range of potential responses was adjusted to reflect anticipated responses and, consequently, in some cases it may have missed the mark. Some skills should be infrequently used because of the skills and the opportunity to use them. Thus, low marks on these two categories were not particularly disturbing considering the varied nature of program application.

Business Impact

Although business data was monitored in several ways, the annual and follow-up questionnaire obtained input on the perceived linkage with impact measures. As shown in table 7, one category of data provided the opportunity for participants to determine the extent to which this program influenced several impact measures. As

Table 7. Categories of data for annual questionnaire.

- Course sequencing/availability
- Use of skills/knowledge
- Linkage with impact measures
- Improvements/accomplishments
- Project selection and application
- Barriers to implementation
- Enablers to implementation
- Management support for program
- Recommendations for improvement

Table 8. Application data: Use of knowledge and skills.

Issue	Average Rating*
Opportunity to use skills/knowledge	3.9
Appropriateness of skills/knowledge	4.1
Frequency of use of skills/knowledge	3.2
Effectiveness of use of skills/knowledge	4.3

*On a 1-5 scale, with 5 = exceptional

far as actual business improvement value, two data items were converted to monetary values: turnover and project application.

Turnover Reduction

The primary value of the program would stem from annual turnover reduction of the target group. Table 9 shows the annualized, avoidable turnover rates for three different groups. The first is the total group of 1,500 specialists in this job category. The next group is the program participants, indicating that of the 100 initial participants, 12 left during the program (5 percent, 4 percent, 3 percent), and three left in the first year following completion, for a total of 15 in the four-year time span. For the similar comparison group, 100 individuals were identified and the numbers were replenished as turnover occurred. As the numbers revealed, essentially the entire comparison group had left the agency by the end of the third year. This comparison underscores the cumulative effect of an excessive turnover rate. Using the comparison group as the expected turnover rate yields a total expected turnover of 138 in the four-year period (34 percent, 35 percent, 33 percent, 36 percent). The actual, however, was 15 for the same period. Thus, the difference in the two groups (138 − 15) equals 123 turnover statistics prevented with this program, using the control group arrangement to isolate the results of the program.

The participants and managers provided insight into the percent of the turnover reduction attributed to the program. For their estimate, the process starts with the difference measured in the total group compared to the actual. Using a base of 100, the total group was expected to have 144 turnover statistics (39 percent, 36 percent, 35 percent, 34 percent). The difference between the total group and the actual turnover statistic is 129 (144 − 15 = 129). Because there were other contributing factors, participants were asked to indicate what percentage

Table 9. Turnover data.

Annualized Avoidable Turnover	1 Year Prior to Program	1st Year September to August	2nd Year September to August	3rd Year September to August	1 Year Post-program
Total Group 1,500	38%	39%	36%	35%	34%
Program Participants Group	N/A	5% (5 participants)	4% (4 participants)	3% (3 participants)	3% (3 participants)
Similar Group	N/A	34%	35%	33%	36%

Four-Year Expected Turnover Statistics = 138
Four-Year Actual Turnover Statistics = 15
Four-Year Total Group Turnover Statistics = 144

of this reduction they attributed to the program. The participants' and managers' estimates were combined (using a simple average to reflect equal weight) to yield a 93 percent allocation to this program. The confidence estimate for this value is 83 percent (the average of the two). Obviously, both groups realized that this program was accomplishing its major goal of reducing turnover. Thus, if 129 are adjusted by 93 percent and 83 percent, the yield is 100 turnover statistics. Given the choice of using 123 or 100, the lower number is used, although it might not be as credible as the actual control group comparisons. It is conservative to indicate that at least 100 turnover statistics were prevented in the four-year time frame for this analysis.

The value for the turnover reduction is rather straightforward, with 1.75 times the annual earnings used as a compromised value. The total value of the turnover improvement is $100 \times \$47,800 \times 1.75 = \$8,365,000$. This is a significant, yet conservative, value for the turnover reduction.

Project Values

The participants developed projects that were designed to add value to the agency by improving capability and operations. Table 10 shows the summary of the data from the projects. Eighty-eight individuals graduated from the program, and all had approved and implemented projects. Of that number, 74 actually provided data on their project completion in the one-year follow-up on their action plan. Of that number, 53 were able to convert the project to a monetary value. The participants were asked to estimate the amount of improvement that was

Table 10. Monetary values from project.

Number of Projects Approved and Implemented	88
Number of Projects Reporting Completion	74
Number of Projects Reporting Monetary Values	53
Number of Projects with Usable Monetary Values	46
Average Value of Project (Adjusted)	$ 55,480
Highest Value of Project (Adjusted)	$ 1,429,000*
Lowest Value of Project (Adjusted)	$ 1,235
Average Confidence Estimate	62%
Total Value (Adjusted Twice)	$ 1,580,000

*Discarded in the analysis

directly related to the project (percent), recognizing that other factors could have influenced the results. The values are reported as adjusted values in table 10. Only 46 of those were useable values, as unsupported claims and unrealistic values were omitted from the analysis. For example, the highest value ($1,429,000) was eliminated because of the shock value of this number and the possibility of error or exaggeration. The average confidence estimate was 62 percent. When each project value is multiplied by the individual confidence estimate, the total adjusted usable value is $1,580,000.

Intangibles

The intangible benefits were impressive with this program. Recruiting success was not converted to monetary value, but included instead as a subjective intangible value. All of the intangible measures listed in the initial data collection plan were linked to the program, according to participants or managers. A measure was listed as an intangible if at least 25 percent of either group perceived it as linked to the program. Thus, the intangibles were not included in the monetary analysis but were considered to be important and included in the final report.

BCR and ROI Calculations for Turnover Reduction

The benefits-cost ratio (BCR) is the total monetary benefits divided by the total program costs. For turnover reduction, the BCR calculation becomes:

$$\text{BCR} = \frac{\text{Monetary Benefits}}{\text{Total Program Costs}} = \frac{\$8,365,000}{\$3,931,957} = 2.13$$

The ROI calculation for the turnover reduction is the net program benefit divided by the cost. In formula form it becomes:

$$\text{ROI} = \frac{\text{Monetary Benefits} - \text{Total Program Costs}}{\text{Total Program Costs}} = \frac{\$4,433,043}{\$3,931,957} \times 100 = 113\%$$

BCR and ROI Calculations for Total Improvement

The BCR for the value obtained on turnover reduction and project completion yields the following:

$$\text{BCR} = \frac{\$8,365,000 + \$1,580,000}{\$3,931,957} = \frac{\$9,945,000}{\$3,931,957} = 2.53$$

The ROI—usable program benefits for the two improvements—is as follows:

$$ROI = \frac{\$9,945,000 - \$3,931,957}{\$3,931,957} \times 100 = 153\%$$

Communicating Results

Because these are large values, it was a challenge to communicate them convincingly to the senior team. The conservative nature of this approach helps defend the analysis and make the results more credible and believable. The step-by-step results were presented to the senior team using the following sequence:

1. a brief review of the project and its objectives
2. overview of the methodology
3. assumptions used in the analysis
4. reaction and satisfaction measures
5. learning measures
6. application and implementation measures
7. business impact measures
8. ROI
9. intangibles
10. barriers and enablers
11. interpretation and conclusions
12. recommendations.

This information was presented to the senior team in a one-hour meeting and provided an opportunity to present the methodology and results. This meeting had a three-fold purpose:

1. present the methodology and assumptions for capturing the ROI, building credibility with the process and analysis
2. using a balanced approach, show the impact of a major initiative and how it provides a payoff for the agency and taxpayers
3. show how the same type of solution can be implemented and evaluated in the future.

The project was considered a success.

Questions for Discussion

1. Can the value of this program be forecasted? If so, how?
2. Most of these costs are estimated or rounded off. It this appropriate? Explain.
3. What issues surface when developing cost data? How can they be addressed?

4. Are the ROI values realistic? Explain.
5. Is this study credible? Explain.
6. How can this type of process be used to build support for programs in the future? Explain.

The Authors

Jack J. Phillips is with the Jack Phillips Center for Research, a division of the Franklin Covey Company. Phillips developed and pioneered the use of the ROI process and has provided consulting services to some of the world's largest organizations. He has written more than 12 books on the subject.

Patricia Pulliam Phillips is chairman and CEO of The Chelsea Group, an international consulting company focused on the implementation of the ROI process. She has provided consulting services and support for the ROI process for several years and has served as author and co-author on the topic in several publications. The Phillipses can be reached at TheChelseaGroup@aol.com.

Reference

Phillips, Jack P., Ron Stone, and Patricia P. Phillips. (2001). *The Human Resources Scorecard*. Woburn, Massachusetts: Butterworth-Heinemann.

Workforce Development ROI

Silicon Valley Private Industry Council

Dennis K. Benson and Victoria P. Tran

This case study contains an actual return-on-investment (ROI) report prepared for the Silicon Valley Private Industry Council (SVPIC) in April 2000. The two authors are the independent consultant who designed the model and conducted the analysis (Benson) and the management information system (MIS) analyst for SVPIC (Tran) who dealt directly with the many data issues that needed to be resolved to make the project a success.

Background

In 1996, Silicon Valley Private Industry Council, with the personal and professional commitment and vision of Ravi Ravindran, former Job Training Partnership Act (JTPA) manager for SVPIC, approached Appropriate Solutions, Inc. (ASI) to test its ROI methodologies on SVPIC's various Title II programs. Ravindran's vision led directly to translating basic to applied research, resulting in advances in knowledge and technique in assessing the economic impact of workforce development programs.

Because ROI was a foreign concept to SVPIC, both SVPIC and ASI encountered several challenges during the first two times that data was extracted and exchanged. The initial challenges arose when SVPIC's MIS personnel had to interpret what ASI needed, query the data, and then convert the data to a format that ASI could read and analyze. The third was the most challenging, as SVPIC had to convert a file from the Unix-based system to an Excel spreadsheet, then to a database file, sometimes resulting in a file exponentially larger

This case was prepared to serve as a basis for discussion rather than to illustrate either effective or ineffective administrative or management practices.

in size than the original file. After several attempts and exchanges of correspondences between SVPIC and ASI, data was in a format that ASI could read, and the rest fell into place.

The authors considered multiple approaches to presenting the information contained in this case study with the relevance and value to the readers being seen as paramount. Consequently, the format decided on was, in medical parlance, in vivo. The actual technical report submitted to SVPIC is the core of this case study interspersed with annotations about how and why the authors made certain decisions, problems they encountered, and what lessons they learned. The authors' annotations follow each section of the actual report.

Organization Profile—Silicon Valley Private Industry Council

The Silicon Valley Private Industry Council was the entity that implemented the JTPA programs in the central and southern portions of Santa Clara County, California, which had a population of 1,096,089, based on the 1990 census. The policy board consisted of 25 representatives from community-based organizations, labor, education, rehabilitation services, public employment, economic development, and the private sector.

JTPA, enacted in 1982 and replaced by the Workforce Investment Act (WIA) in 2000, provided SVPIC with two major funding sources: Title II and Title III. While JTPA funded many different kinds of programs for targeted audiences, the major funding was devoted to economically disadvantaged adults, youth, and dislocated workers—three very disparate populations. JTPA Title II programs were geared toward assisting economically disadvantaged individuals to become self-sufficient and gain the skills and experiences needed to compete in the expanding workforce; SVPIC contracted these services with community-based organizations. Title III, also known as the Dislocated Worker Program, assisted individuals who had been laid-off or were unemployed; SVPIC delivered Title III services directly through its career center.

Needs Assessment and Evaluation

In its 17-year existence, SVPIC provided a wide range of workforce development programs to more than 56,000 people at a cost of over $178 million in taxpayer funding.

Although SVPIC consistently met, if not vastly exceeded, mandatory federal performance standards, it lacked a measure of economic accountability to the public. In 1996, having followed the different developments in ROI measurement, SVPIC approached Appropriate

Solutions to see if it was willing to apply its then untested ROI methodology to SVPIC programs. Under the guidance of SVPIC's Performance and Accountability Committee, the first application of the ASI workforce ROI model was attempted.

Over the course of the next five years, ASI worked closely with SVPIC to conduct and produce four separate ROI studies, each building on what was learned from the last. (See figure 1.)

Communication of Results

The report in this case study is one of three different reports prepared for SVPIC. In addition to the technical report, there is a color graphics executive summary (not included here) and a technical documentation

Figure 1. The concept of return on investment.

Visualize a balance scale. On the right side of the scale are stacked the costs of an activity or program. This constitutes our investment. On the left side of the scale are stacked the benefits, some of which may be financial; others, social. Is the scale balanced or does it tilt to one side or another? This scale shows your return on investment (ROI).

In authorizing the Job Training Partnership Act (JTPA) in 1992, the U.S. Congress specifically declared that these funds are to be considered not expenses, but an investment in the human capital infrastructure of the nation. Congress further declared that this investment should be measured by examining the increased economic independence of persons served and their reduced reliance on public assistance, among other things.

How this return on investment was to be measured was not specified by Congress, but left to the states and local programs to determine. The Workforce Investment Act (WIA) goes a step further—investment is its middle name.

The Government Performance and Results Act (GPRA) of 1993 holds federally funded programs to a new standard of accountability and responsibility

to the taxpayer. When taxpayer funds are used for a public expenditure, the taxpayer should expect an accounting of those funds, which goes beyond reporting whether the money was spent properly according to fiscal and accounting guidelines. The taxpayer deserves to be told what outcomes or impacts are associated with the expenditures.

The Silicon Valley Private Industry Council has acknowledged its fiscal responsibility to its citizens by adopting a recognized method of measuring the economic and financial impact and return on investment of its publicly funded employment and training programs.

Much as a corporation has different ways in which to measure different kinds of economic returns, SVPIC has choices as well. The model adopted looks at three different ways in which the citizens of Santa Clara County may potentially benefit from its workforce programs.

The Santa Clara County taxpayer is viewed as the investor in these calculations. The question: Are these investors getting their money's worth from state and federally funded workforce programs?

As this report will document, the workforce development programs of the Silicon Valley Private Industry Council operate at a net profit to the taxpayer and have a positive impact on the local economy above and beyond the operating costs of the program.

report (also not included), which provides all the computer code used to generate the numbers. The technical documentation report provides all the necessary detail that would permit an independent researcher to attempt to replicate the study. Full disclosure of methodology is an absolute requirement of any scientific ROI study.

The report is the evolution of five years of research with the Silicon Valley Private Industry Council that covered ROI studies of four separate program years and multiple federally funded workforce development programs. SVPIC was the lead investor in the development and refinement of this model, which looks at multiple returns derived from such programs.

Conducting a post hoc ROI analysis is far from painless. This is an incipient science in the human services arena. As a core investor in this development process, SVPIC clearly took a risk, as there is no guarantee with the results. SVPIC, however, felt that its investment reflected its faith in the workforce development system and its true economic impact and undertook this series of studies, culminating in this technical report, as a demonstration of its leadership in the system. In doing so, SVPIC ensured that the researcher received full cooperation at all stages of the process. Methodology and decision rules were required to be objective and unbiased.

This case study shares the public presentation of results and the inside story behind them.

The executive summary to this report is primarily photos and states the bottom line with little explanation of the technical model or how the results were derived. That brief summary addresses the information needs of most audiences.

The technical report, contained in this case study, answers those second-level detailed questions, using language that nontechnical audiences can easily understand. But even in the technical report, the contractor does not provide extreme levels of detail.

The goal of this introductory section is to provide some context for the ROI study and a brief orientation to workforce programs.

Evaluation Methodology

Objective performance accountability was established through a series of measures linked to a national regression model that examined hundreds of factors to determine the most explanatory variables in outcomes. The model included individual characteristics (for example, ethnicity), barriers (for example, disabilities), and local economic factors (for example, unemployment rate).

A national performance target was established (as much political as pragmatic) that was then adjusted up or down for the characteristics of the local population served and the local economy. But no ROI measure, despite the federal legislation, was ever designed or implemented at the federal level for JTPA, though an ROI measure was considered for the WIA.

ROI measures, to be blunt, can be dangerous. They are value-free measures. That means that X dollars invested yield Y dollars of return. In the world of IRAs and 401Ks, portfolios are most times balanced. The investor has multiple priorities, and the largest return is not always the investor's primary concern. The socially desired return may not be the highest economic return.

Model

The quest for developing valid ROI measures in the public sector must then be accompanied by a quest to attach value to the impersonal outcome of a basic ROI equation. This case study describes the challenges faced in developing a workable ROI model for publicly funded workforce development programs, and the lessons that follow describe where this process must lead in the future.

The second section of the technical report provides a brief introduction to how ROI was estimated in Silicon Valley. (See figure 2.)

This is the global summary for the technical report. It introduces three ROI measures to the reader and explains their differences. Even in finance and banking, no single number describes all aspects of ROI to an enterprise and multiple formulas are used. SVPIC wanted to use ASI's new ROI model, which had evolved to three different measures based on a decomposition of what ROI really consisted of and how it should be interpreted.

Data Collection Methodology

ROI researchers working within existing workforce development programs rarely, if ever, have the opportunity to specify data requirements in advance and receive that data. The priority for MIS systems is to meet federally mandated data requirements to which may be added state mandatory elements to which may be added locally mandated elements. The authors are aware of no MIS system in the country that was designed with ROI in mind.

Consequently, the research team must adapt the standardized ROI base model to extant data. That requires establishing a number of different assumptions so that impact variables may be estimated because

Figure 2. How we measure return on investment.

The Silicon Valley Private Industry Council has selected a model for workforce ROI developed by Appropriate Solutions, Inc., (ASI) a public policy research firm in Worthington, Ohio. The SVPIC believes that the formulas used in these estimates provide the taxpayer with an understandable, accurate, and broad view of how these programs are impacting the local and regional economies in and around Santa Clara County.

The model looks at the following related, but different, aspects of economic impact. These are summarized below and explained in detail in following sections.

ROI-T: RETURN ON INVESTMENT TO THE TAXPAYER

ROI-T estimates the amount of money that is theoretically available to be returned to the state and federal treasuries. Specifically, ROI-T estimates potential savings in the Temporary Assistance to Needy Families (TANF) program (formerly the Aid For Dependent Children program, AFDC), potential savings in food stamp expenditures, projected increased personal income taxes to California and to the federal government, and individual and company contributions to FICA.

ROI-D: RETURN ON INVESTMENT DISPOSABLE INCOME

The goal of increasing an individual's economic independence is met not just by replacing public assistance dollars with wage dollars but by increasing the net amount of dollars the individual has to spend. ROI-D looks at whether this disposable income has been increased. Increased earnings are reduced by lower welfare payments and by contributions to the tax base. If the result is a positive number, then new money has been made available to be spent in the local economy.

ROI-E: RETURN ON INVESTMENT ECONOMIC IMPACT

The best way to understand economic impact is to look at this from the opposite direction—negative impact. Hardly a community in the country has not had to face the problem of a military base closure, a major layoff by a large employer, or the closure of an important business. The economic impact of those changes ripples through the economy and has a total effect much larger than simply summing the salaries and wages lost.

The total economic impact when a new company opens or expands is also larger than just the salaries and wages added to the economy. These are well-established and accepted economic principles. The U.S. Department of Commerce developed their RIMS-II model (Regional Input-Output Modeling System) precisely to allow people to make a reasonable estimate of this ripple effect. The ASI model is the first of its kind to include these estimates as part of a return-on-investment calculation for employment and training programs.

ROI-E uses two RIMS-II multipliers in its calculation. The estimated increase in disposable income and the total cost of the workforce programs are each subjected to different multipliers. The existence of the workforce programs in the community is a valid economic stimulus and is included as an economic benefit. Also included are the increased tax contributions and the increased FICA payments. The result is an estimate of what the workforce program and its results mean to the economy financially.

ESTIMATING TOTAL RETURN

A child entering the second grade is influenced considerably by his or her experiences in the first grade. In fact, those first grade experiences stay with the individual throughout his or her lifetime, although the impact is reduced year by year as new experiences are acquired. In similar ways, an individual completing an employment and training program is considerably influenced by that experience, and that influence lasts far longer than a single year.

The Rand Corporation and California State University/Northridge have separately attempted to measure how long the impact lasts and what the economic impact might be. The economic impact is greatest in the first two years and then "depreciates" over time as new employment and educational experiences are added. Estimates from the two studies range from 12 to 20 years. For this analysis, we are using the most conservative estimate of length of time, 12 years. When all of the mathematics are worked out, the first year return-on-investment estimate is multiplied roughly by 5.25 to get to an estimated total ROI.

How Accurate Are These Estimates?

These are reasonable approximations of the true return on investment. They are based on projections, the same as you will find in any whole life insurance policy that talks about your return and cash value 30 years down the road. They are our best guess based on the best information that we have today.

They have been calculated for two purposes: First, this is part of the accounting to the citizens of Santa Clara County as to what their government has done and accomplished.

Second, these numbers provide valuable benchmarks for the professionals in workforce development to assess their programs and continuously seek to improve their efficiency and effectiveness.

The precision and accuracy of these numbers can be improved in two ways: First, improve the quality and quantity of data available. These equations do not attempt to quantify and estimate all known economic impacts. Consequently they are our lowest defensible estimates. We are confident that, given complete and accurate data, the results shown in this report would be higher, if not much higher.

Second, collect longer term impact data, reducing the number of years of projection required. Collect actual experience instead of estimating it. This requires valid postprogram data of some kind.

Each effort to improve the precision of these estimates potentially involves increased costs of data collection and delays in estimating the results, which reduces the value of the numbers for program improvement. Each increase in cost reduces the funds available for program services. The reasonable approximations reported here balance the best theory available today with a fiscally appropriate research expenditure to make the calculations.

As the nation transitions from JTPA to WIA, new systems are being designed and implemented. Careful attention to the requirements of ROI and accountability will permit these estimates in the future to be more accurate and more easily calculated.

WHAT ARE THE NUMBERS BASED ON?

The ROI measures have been computed individually on three separate populations that completed their involvement in Silicon Valley Private Industry Council's JTPA workforce development programs between July 1, 1998, and June 30, 1999 (PY98).

The programs analyzed are Title IIA for economically disadvantaged adults, Title IIC for economically disadvantaged youth, and Title III for displaced workers. The number of cases analyzed for each program are: Title IIA adult = 441; Title IIA youth = 84; Title III dislocated worker = 864. The data from which the calculations were made was provided by the Silicon Valley Private Industry Council.

Program Costs. The current data systems in place do not permit tracking of expenditures at the individual level across time. Total costs of each program operator plus the SVPIC costs for administration are summed for each program. The estimated benefits for each individual are also summed. The numbers reported could vary up or down from actual expenditures. Consequently the ROI reported is a reasonable approximation.

very few can be directly measured. That also makes the most prevalent use of ROI in workforce and human services a "reactive" model.

The quality of data available, and its many gaps, is the single most frustrating aspect of attempting an ROI analysis post hoc. Few of the data are subjected to rigorous quality control, and inconsistencies among variables undoubtedly contribute to premature aging among ROI researchers.

In theory, the data requirements are quite simple. Preprogram and postprogram estimates need to be made for earnings, tax contributions, and public assistance. The source of most of this information comes from forms that are completed when an individual enters a program and when he or she exits.

Even within a single state, however, data collection varies widely in its accuracy and completeness. Adding to the complexity is that funding and expenditures cross departmental lines; and issues of privacy, data sharing, and turf are omnipresent. And even in 2001, as this case was being written, the simple process of electronic transfer of data can be a nightmare. When data comes in from two different sources, additional work is involved.

In SVPIC, the major data used in the project came from SVPIC MIS files. An alternative to the income outcome variables would have been to use sampled data from the University of California/Berkeley follow-up study that collected status information 90 days after termination. Had that data been used and merged, the Social Security number field for merging would have had to be altered in one or the other datasets as SVPIC did not use a hyphen in the SSN field and Berkeley did. Simple things become very complex in post hoc ROI analyses.

The other major data problem encountered in ROI analysis is cost accounting. The most significant limitation to the programmatic usefulness of ROI is the inability of most programs to report individual-level costs of service. While having the ability to track individual-level investment adds an overhead burden, any manufacturer who cannot differentiate fixed from variable costs will eventually be in a precarious economic situation. Dividing the total program cost by the total number of people served is a massively inadequate measure of unit cost, but the one researchers are most often left with.

Isolation Methodology

Isolation methodologies are employed in an attempt to establish cause-and-effect relationships. The most commonly accepted method in workforce development to isolate cause and effect is use of control groups in net impact studies. Such studies have been conducted in workforce development, but are often rejected by field professionals for many pragmatic reasons, such as, studies are too expensive, studies take too long, studies provide no real-time practical value, and methodology requires denial of service.

Because it is impossible to conduct a double-blind social experiment of this kind, the denial of service then becomes a compounding effect. In fact, because of the service-orientation of field professionals, the experiment can be corrupted by staff "back-dooring" individuals who were denied service, as happened in the multimillion dollar national JTPA study.

Local programs rarely have the budget, technical personnel, or local political support to conduct net impact studies. The number of factors to be taken into account in social experimentation is so great that sampling techniques cannot be used, nor can the results from one locality safely be extrapolated to other areas regardless of the quality of the experiment. Workforce development programs are highly idiosyncratic, and the dyadic relationship between counselor and participant can play a statistically significant role.

For ROI to be effectively used by workforce development today, a gross impact approach is a practical alternative. Net impact, random assignment methodology, however, is highly appropriate for evaluating alternative approaches to service provision. That does require a competent methodology and an adequate budget, as such research increases the cost of the program.

What workforce development programs can do today is, with some limitations, measure change from time A to time B. That is gross impact analysis and what the researchers did with SVPIC in the four studies that were conducted.

The findings from the final study are found in figure 3.

Data Conversion Methodology

All intermediate calculations in the ASI model convert to dollars. These calculations, as shown in figure 3, are based on best-data-available as to changes in status over time. The objective of each ROI study is to be measurable, conservative, and defensible.

As figure 3 shows, many assumptions have to be made to move from the few pieces of data reported to a dollar estimate of impact.

Costs

Costs have already been discussed briefly. Hundreds of rules and thousands of pages of state and federal requirements govern cost

Figure 3. ROI-T: Return on investment to taxpayer.

The different calculations involved to compute ROI-T provide all of the necessary numbers for all three ROI measures. Each of these calculations and their results is explained in the following pages. When total dollars are being reported, each amount has been rounded to the nearest $1,000 to remind the reader that these are estimates.

IE: INCREASED EARNINGS
Preprogram Earnings. For each person enrolled, the Silicon Valley Private Industry Council collects information about his or her labor force status, preprogram hourly wage, and weeks unemployed during the prior 26 weeks. From the information we make an estimate of the participants' preprogram earnings.

We only know the hourly wage and do not know how many hours a week were worked on average or how many weeks of the last 52 were worked. Because we want a conservative estimate of impact, we assume a 40-hour workweek, which will overestimate weekly earnings. If the individual was not employed in the previous 26 weeks, we assume he or she was not employed in the previous 52. For all others, we add 26 weeks to the number of weeks worked in the past 26. We will likely overestimate the number of weeks worked with these assumptions.

We then compare that number to family income, when that variable is reported. If the estimated participant income is higher than a nonzero family income, then we adjust our estimate of the participant's income downward to the reported family income total. This would occur because we estimated too many hours worked or too many weeks worked.

Income reporting requirements are different, however, for dislocated workers. For these participants we disregarded family income as we did not believe it was reliable, and overestimated participant income by assuming all persons worked at least 26 weeks of 52. Where we did not have a preprogram wage provided, we substituted the median wage of dislocated workers, $14.36 per hour.

Postprogram Earnings. When the participant leaves the program, the Silicon Valley Private Industry Council records his or her hourly wage and number of scheduled hours. An estimate of postprogram income is made by multiplying the wage times the number of scheduled hours times 52 weeks.

Assumptions. Obviously both equations involve numerous assumptions. The assumptions that have been selected are intended to understate the impact.

For both individual and family income, we are assuming that the income is constant. We have no real alternative in estimating postprogram earnings but to assume that individuals employed when leaving the program remain employed at the same wage and for the scheduled number of hours. This discounts possible raises and potential overtime pay. It also assumes that persons not employed at termination never obtain a job. We have no means to estimate any changes in income from other family members and use our preprogram estimate as our postprogram estimate.

In other research conducted by Appropriate Solutions, Inc., in Ohio, aggregate earnings estimated at time of program exit increased 38% 65 weeks later for Title IIA and 72% for Title III. This research captures information from all jobs and includes wage increases as well as overtime that may have been worked. The size of the change, however, clearly reflects the added income from people who were not working at program exit, but who later became employed.

Consequently, we are comfortable that our procedures will yield a conservative estimate of income gains.

Reminder: In all the following tables, sums and differences may not appear accurate because numbers are rounded to the nearest thousand dollars.

Table 1. Change in earnings.

	Adult	Youth	Dislocated
Preprogram	$1,168,000	$29,000	$13,639,000
Postprogram	$5,618,000	$665,000	$24,120,000
Increase	$4,449,000	$636,000	$10,481,000

A Word About the Populations. With the presentation of the first data on outcomes, it is useful to make certain that the differences in the populations and goals of the different programs are recognized.

The adult and youth programs predominantly serve an economically disadvantaged population that has a higher reliance on public assistance and a lower earnings ability than do dislocated workers. In addition to employment, youth programs can also emphasize return for completion of schooling, the benefits of which are much longer term and will not be reflected in any of these equations.

For dislocated workers, program emphasis is on upgrading work skills, and success is measured by the percentage of preprogram wage that is re-placed by postprogram employment. For this program, even a breakeven result is considered excellent. Keep these distinctions in mind when reviewing the outcomes. The results in table 1 are consis-tent with performance expectations. Wage replacement for Title III is 177%, an outstanding achievement.

ITC: INCREASED TAX CONTRIBUTIONS

Projected changes in two income taxes are included in ITC: Federal personal income tax and California personal income tax. Not included are local income taxes and sales taxes. Local income taxes can vary within a single county. Sales taxes are very difficult

to estimate as they depend on variable rates and patterns of consumption.

In order to calculate ITC, it is necessary first to make estimates of increased earnings. Making tax estimates is the most challenging part of the ROI calculation process. A precise and detailed procedure would be expensive, time consuming, intrusive, and likely yield an answer no more accurate than the simplified procedure described here.

Federal income tax is graduated and based on total family earnings. Earnings brackets are in effect for one calendar year and adjusted annually for inflation. We, however, are trying to estimate tax payments for the 12 months prior to entering the program and the 12 months after leaving the program. We have used the tax tables for calendar year 1998 for estimating preprogram taxes, and the tax tables for calendar year 1999 for estimating postprogram taxes.

Assumptions. Quite clearly we are dealing with data that has a number of limitations and, consequently, have tried to use assumptions and procedures that minimize the impact. The major missing piece in this equation is having any allowance for Earned Income Credit (EIC). EIC is a negative income tax that is available to the working poor. That variable has not been included because national estimates of the percentage of eligible persons who participate is very low. If we had this information about participation, it would likely reduce the net increased tax contributions.

Table 2. State taxes paid.

	Adult	Youth	Dislocated
Preprogram	*	$0	$17,000
Postprogram	$9,000	*	$254,000
Increase	$9,000	*	$236,000

* = less than $500

(continued on page 184)

Figure 3. ROI-T: Return on investment to taxpayer (continued).

Table 3. Federal taxes paid.

	Adult	Youth	Dislocated
Preprogram	$17,000	*	$311,000
Postprogram	$333,000	$37,000	$2,460,000
Increase	$315,000	$37,000	$2,149,000

* = less than $500

FICA PAYMENTS

After the complexity of the income tax payment calculations, the computation of estimated FICA payments is very simple. Preprogram and postprogram earnings are each multiplied by the FICA rate of 15.3%. Half of this amount is contributed by the individual and half is contributed by the employer.

Table 4. FICA paid.

	Adult	Youth	Dislocated
Preprogram	$179,000	$4,000	$2,087,000
Postprogram	$860,000	$102,000	$3,690,000
Increase	$681,000	$97,000	$1,604,000

RPE: REDUCED PUBLIC EXPENDITURES

The number of different public programs in which reduced expenditures might be demonstrated is large. This particular analysis is restricted to only two programs—Temporary Assistance to Needy Families (TANF) and food stamps—because detailed information at an individual level was not available from the California Department of Social Services. Other programs that may be added in the future if adequate data is secured include Medicaid, Subsidized Housing, and Supplemental Security Income.

The rules and regulations surrounding eligibility and payment amounts are extremely complicated. The only information available to us was the welfare status of the family at time of entry into the program and household size. A table from the California Department of Social Services provided grant amounts by household size, as well as income levels. From this we generated our estimates of welfare payments.

Savings. Potential savings were calculated individually for families who were previously on TANF or on food stamps at time of enrollment, and who had unsubsidized employment at the end of their program at a wage that exceeded California income guidelines.

Assumptions. The actual establishment of benefits is much more complicated in real life than consulting a table by county and family size. Actual amounts may vary from our estimates. We have also estimated that benefits cease upon employment. Many benefits have a transition provision that gradually decreases over time or by earnings amount. Full savings may not be evident until the second postprogram year. It is assumed that persons employed do not return to welfare.

Due to lack of data, we have no valid way to estimate who may be receiving benefits at termination who were not receiving them at enrollment. Participation in these programs is voluntary, and many people, despite their eligibility, may decline to receive the benefit.

Table 5. TANF payments.

	Adult	Youth	Dislocated
Preprogram	$1,213,000	$274,000	$126,000
Postprogram	$925,000	$209,000	$59,000
Savings	$288,000	$65,000	$67,000

Table 6. Food stamps payments.

	Adult	Youth	Dislocated
Preprogram	$703,000	$115,000	$95,000
Postprogram	$522,000	$96,000	$32,000
Savings	$181,000	$19,000	$63,000

Calculating ROI-T

The difficulty and time-consuming aspects of ROI calculations are entirely in evaluating assumptions, making decisions, and performing myriad intermediate calculations. When the above numbers have been computed, all of the measures can be easily completed.

Following is the formula for estimating the first year ROI-T. RPE = Reduced Public Expenditures; ITC = Increased Tax Contributions.

$$ROI\text{-}T = RPE + ITC + FICA$$

Dividing the ROI-T by the program cost shows how many cents on the dollar are estimated to be returned in the first year.

ROI-T

	Adult	Youth	Dislocated
RPE	$470,000	$83,000	$130,000
ITC	$324,000	$37,000	$2,386,000
FICA	$681,000	$97,000	$1,604,000
Program Cost (PC)	$2,582,000	$431,000	$6,324,000
FIRST YEAR RETURN TO TAXPAYER			
ROI-T	$1,475,000	$218,000	$4,119,000
ROI-T/Dollar Cost	$0.57	$0.50	$0.65
TOTAL RETURN TO TAXPAYER			
Total ROI-T	$5,747,000	$788,000	$21,073,000
Total Per Dollar Cost	$2.23	$1.83	$3.33

(continued on page 186)

Figure 3. ROI-T: Return on investment to taxpayer (continued).

The Total ROI-T is based on the first year estimate. That formula is:

Total ROI-T = RPE + [(ITC + FICA) × 5.25]

The reader will note that RPE has not been subjected to the total ROI multiplier, described in figure 2. Only first year savings are claimed. The available data does not tell us the amount of benefits available to each individual by statute eligibility. By only using a single year, our estimate remains conservative. The true number is likely larger.

Over the benefit life of these three programs combined, an estimated $2.96 on average is returned to the taxpayer for every taxpayer dollar invested in the program. This represents a 196% return on investment.

Silicon Valley Private Industry Council employment and training programs are providing a net profit to its citizens of over $18 million.

---

allocation. Virtually none of these requirements have any possible relationship to impact assessment. Workforce development, as do many federal programs, remains rules-driven with some performance requirements, not a system that is performance-driven.

For ROI purposes, costs quite simply are all expenditures made with the intention of achieving the changes observed. Costs are of two types: 1) direct service (ideally identifiable by individual) and 2) indirect costs (administrative overhead to keep the office open and functioning).

ROI might be calculated for only some of the direct service programs offered by the organization. In SVPIC, the focus was on Title IIA (disadvantaged adults), Title IIC (disadvantaged youth), and Title III (dislocated workers). SVPIC also offered programs for groups such as veterans, older workers, summer youth, and others.

The overhead expense is simply calculated by dividing the direct service cost of the program examined by the sum of the direct service costs for all programs and then multiplying that number by the total overhead. This is the simplest process to follow and the one most likely available to the vast majority of agencies. Alternatives require more sophisticated time-keeping procedures and activity-based accounting within the administrative function. All dollars in an agency's budget must be allocated across each program.

The simplicity of that explanation evaporates when one deals with the issue of proration. Program services can deal with four specific categories of participants. The point of analysis is always those persons who exit the program in the year being examined. Some of those persons began their services in a prior fiscal year. Some of them began and exited in the current year. And some of them began this year but will not exit until the next fiscal year. A few persons may begin services in a prior year and not exit until a subsequent year.

When a system for individual cost tracking exists, proportional shares of overhead can be calculated for each person for each year of involvement. Importantly, costs can be excluded for persons who are "still in the works."

This system involves a little calculus and good logic, but is really simple when one has good data. That kind of good data, unfortunately, is not required by the rules and regulations, so fiscal systems that can report this are voluntary and purely the result of local and state initiative and creativity.

The result is that costs are generally averages that are calculated from the current year's budget and allocated across all persons who exited regardless of the volume of services received in the current fiscal year. That was the case with the cost calculation for SVPIC. (See figure 4.)

By the time one has everything together to calculate return on investment to the taxpayer (ROI-T), all the information necessary to calculate all the other measures is present as well.

Three basic steps are followed in conducting the ROI analysis.

Step 1: Input Data

Because the state of California had established most data collection requirements for JTPA, the authors had no option but to work within those boundaries. Following are the key data elements that were requested from SVPIC:

- family size
- number of dependents
- family status
- six-month family income
- TANF recipient
- food stamp recipient
- labor force status
- weeks unemployed of the past 26
- preprogram hourly wage
- hours worked at exit
- hourly wage at exit
- cmployment status at exit.

Figure 4. ROI-D: Return on investment disposable income.

A social as well as economic objective of publicly funded workforce programs is to replace welfare dollars with earned dollars. Economic growth will not occur by continued total reliance on public support. ROI-D provides an estimate as to how well this objective is being met, both in the first year and through the benefit life of the program.

Because local income and sales taxes were not included in the calculation of ITC, those funds are included in ROI-D as money that will be going into the local and regional economy.

CALCULATING ROI-D

All of the intermediate variables were calculated in order to compute ROI-T and are explained in the previous section. IE = Increased Earnings; RPE = Reduced Public Expenditures; ITC = Increased Tax Contributions; PFICA = Participant share of FICA. The formula for ROI-D is:

$$ROI\text{-}D = IE - RPE - ITC - PFICA$$

The formula for Total ROI-D is:

$$Total\ ROI\text{-}D = [(IE - ITC - PFICA) \times 5.25)] - (RPE \times 3)$$

In calculating Total ROI-T, we made the conservative assumption that only one year of welfare savings would be included. In calculating Total ROI-D, we make an equally conservative assumption by reducing increased earnings by three years of benefits.

ROI-D

	Adult	Youth	Dislocated
IE	$4,449,000	$636,000	$10,481,000
RPE	$470,000	$83,000	$130,000
ITC	$324,000	$37,000	$2,386,000
PFICA	$340,000	$49,000	$802,000
Program Cost	$2,582,000	$431,000	$6,324,000
FIRST YEAR RETURN DISPOSABLE INCOME			
ROI-D	$3,315,000	$467,000	$7,164,000
ROI-D/Dollar Cost	$1.28	$1.08	$1.13
TOTAL RETURN DISPOSABLE INCOME			
Total ROI-D	$18,460,000	$2,639,000	$37,901,000
Total Per Dollar Cost	$7.15	$6.12	$5.99

Silicon Valley Private Industry Council employment and training programs are having a positive short-term and long- term impact on local economies.

Because the data files did not contain actual welfare amounts, the California Department of Social Services provided information on average welfare grants by family size for estimation purposes.

Step 2: Consistency Checks

No matter what guarantees the MIS or database manager provides, one must always check the data. Some data, which should be verified, is rather obvious—household incomes in a healthy six figure range and family sizes in excess of 10 people. Other items are more subtle and require a knowledge of the coding conventions followed for each variable.

For instance, preprogram participant income often has to be estimated from two variables—number of weeks not employed out of the previous 26 and the hourly wage. If weeks unemployed equal 26, then the field for hourly wage is supposed to be blank. If there is any hourly wage in that case, an error has occurred, but which one? Did the coder intend to indicate 26 weeks of employment rather than unemployment, or was the hourly wage reported for a time period outside of the 26-week limit?

If the family status variable indicates a single parent family, a family size of four, and two dependents, what variable is in error? This affects the tax estimation equations.

Ideally, each potential error is verified against original data and resolved. Occasionally, original data is unavailable, in which case the researcher must establish a decision rule. Said decision rule should result in a conservative estimate of impact. For instance, when in doubt, overestimate preprogram income, which will result in a lower net change—hence, conservative.

Step 3: Calculate Variables

Calculating intermediate and final variables uses from seven to nine separate computer programs. Final runs, when all errors are removed from data, take in the range of five minutes. Believe it or not, base programming is done in dBase III+. The ASI calculation programs are under 200K bytes and fast. One client tried to replicate these programs in Access and produced a resulting code of over 4.5 million bytes. One could take a minivacation while the program ran.

The computer programs are very stripped down, and error correction routines are minimal. They are designed to be used by programmers. The important thing to remember when you are setting up your own program is that you need some computing power. You can do this in a spreadsheet, but formula calculation is more difficult than if you use a computer language with some programming "oomph."

The reader should note that reduced public expenditures is treated differently in the equations for total ROI-T and total return on investment disposable income (ROI-D). Welfare reform has been long overdue in this country, but the changes are not simple to work with. Restrictions on welfare eligibility range from two years to five years, with exceptions and transition benefits differing among the states.

With the lack of information about how many benefits remain for any individual, it is difficult to estimate savings and costs. The authors chose two different assumptions for the two equations that were intended to keep both estimates conservative. (See figure 5.)

Return on investment economic impact (ROI-E) is a composite measure that Appropriate Solutions created. The missing piece, when the first two equations were completed, was the recognition that economic multipliers do exist and that the program cost is an economic infusion into the economy. The family of equations needed to have some net aggregate measure of the total economic impact regardless of where it occurred in the economy.

The one major concern that the authors have with the output on ROI-E is the lifetime equation. This is an area that needs additional work and sophistication. A workforce program that helps people with job readiness as opposed to skills training would not have the lifetime multiplier included. It is the training and education activities that have the documented long-term impact.

Really large numbers are also hard to believe, even if they are correct. The authors feel confident about the basic ROI-E equation, however, believing it to be conservative and understating full impact. Even if better data and a more sophisticated model reduced ROI-E by half, a clear and present benefit to the taxpayer and the economy for continuing to invest in the education of its workforce is shown.

Alternatives to using Regional Input-output Modeling System (RIMS-II) do exist. The authors use RIMS-II because it is publicly available. Another system, IMPLAN, is being evaluated. The values for the two multipliers used in the ROI-E equations are different for each state, and can be provided for a price at the county level by the Department of Commerce.

Conducting an ROI analysis is an adventure. Following are some of the lessons the authors learned and what comes next in ROI development.

Figure 5. ROI-E: Return on investment economic impact.

Economic impact is about a community's economic stability and its growth. Economic growth and expansion require a well-trained and motivated workforce. When its citizens have money to spend, the merchants and the government infrastructure benefit as well. ROI-E is about why communities thrive when the economy is active, and why they shrivel when opportunities for the workforce contract.

ROI-E includes four different factors. The first is ROI-D because this is a direct financial infusion into the local and regional economy. ITC (increased tax contributions) and FICA are included because they represent new funds sent to the state and federal government. Program cost (PC) is included because these funds are largely expended in the local economy and are an economic stimulus.

The formula for ROI-E to estimate the first year economic impact is as follows.

$$\text{ROI-E} = (\text{ROI-D} \times 3.3373) + \text{ITC} + \text{FICA} + (\text{PC} \times 2.4345)$$

Two different multipliers are used. The ROI-D multiplier of 3.3373 is the U.S. Department of Commerce multiplier for retail sales plus 1.0 to include both direct and indirect effects. The assumption for using that number is that increased disposable income is going to largely appear in the retail sector.

The PC multiplier of 2.4345 is the U.S. Department of Commerce multiplier for household income plus 1.0 for the direct effect. The assumption for using that number is that program cost is largely going into staff salaries either directly or down the line. The household income multiplier is the lowest of the RIMS-II 39 multipliers.

The formula for Total ROI-E is:

$$\text{Total ROI-E} = (\text{Total ROI-D} \times 3.3373) + [(\text{ITC} + \text{FICA}) \times 5.25] + (\text{PC} \times 2.4345)$$

The total economic impact over a 12-year period from the one-year investment in employment and training programs is projected to be a substantial sum. When considering alternative uses for public funds, ROI-E provides a useful device to evaluate choices.

ROI-E

	Adult	Youth	Dislocated
ROI-D	$3,315,000	$467,000	$7,164,000
Total ROI-D	$18,460,000	$2,639,000	$37,901,000
ITC	$324,000	$37,000	$2,386,000
FICA	$681,000	$97,000	$1,604,000
Program Cost (PC)	$2,582,000	$431,000	$6,324,000
FIRST YEAR ECONOMIC IMPACT			
ROI-E	$18,354,000	$2,742,000	$43,294,000
ROI-E/Dollar Cost	$7.11	$6.36	$6.85
TOTAL ECONOMIC IMPACT			
Total ROI-E	$73,171,000	$10,561,000	$162,829,000
Total Per Dollar Cost	$28.34	$24.49	$25.75

By increasing the economic independence of its workforce, Silicon Valley Private Industry Council employment and training programs provide the foundation for continued growth and prosperity in the local area.

Lessons Learned and Plans for the Future
Intangible Benefits

A multitude of intangible benefits can be linked to these programs, but it is the authors' belief that these are classified as intangible because our theory and data are not yet capable of accurately measuring them. Most intangibles have potentially measurable economic costs and benefits.

Welfare reform has occurred under the Personal Responsibility and Work Opportunity Reconciliation Act. Is "personal responsibility" a tangible or an intangible? By federal law, "personal responsibility" for one's economic future is mandated. That can be defined and measured.

Self-esteem is a common goal of many of these programs. Does this have a measurable economic impact? What about stress reduction? Avoidance of divorce or domestic abuse? All of these have economic impacts that are difficult to impossible to measure with any acceptable level of scientific acceptance, yet from their own professional and personal experiences, the authors can aver that economic impacts do exist. Addressing this is one of the goals of the next generation ROI model.

Lesson 1. Plan Ahead

Each ROI exercise that the authors have completed to date has had to fit into a database and information system that was not designed with ROI in mind. Much of the data collected is collected because people are told to collect it. It is far easier to collect the correct data than to have to go through huge machinations in order to estimate it. Planning your data needs for an impact assessment before the program begins is infinitely easier than guessing after the fact.

Lesson 2. Check Your Data

When you have to rely totally on data you have no control over, you lose the quality assurance you would normally employ if data collection was your personal responsibility. The only safe assumption is that there are errors in the data, most of which will remain invisible to you (for example, a 1 entered instead of a 2 when both numbers are valid entries). Always look for the errors you can uncover, and be pleasantly surprised if you find none. Obviously this is also an instruction to collect accurate data in the first place, and that will involve clear instructions and training for all staff.

Lesson 3. If It Looks Too Good to Be True, It Probably Is

Even though Appropriate Solutions has done ROI analyses numerous times, the programming code must be revised each time as data fields and definitions can change within an organization over time and are always different between organizations. A simple error, such as failing to zero an array on initiation, may produce some very bizarre results. That is why it is important to calculate intermediate variables and see if they pass face validity tests before moving on to the next step. Numbers too large and numbers too small should concern you.

Lesson 4. Resist the Temptation to Say More than the Results Represent

Control your enthusiasm when you see the results. "Causal" inferences should never be made unless an experimental design was followed that allows and supports such a claim. The larger problem is to make certain clients understand the differences between gross and net impact and do not misrepresent the findings in anything they say or do.

Lesson 5. Allow Enough Time

Performing an ROI analysis for the very first time should consume about 200+ combined hours for everyone involved. That does not mean you can do this in five weeks. Appropriate Solutions budgets no fewer than 90 days, and expects usually six months. There is a lot of waiting for people to "get back to you."

Lesson 6. Get Good Fiscal Data

Fiscal data has been talked about several times. When good data is tracked by the level of investment in individuals, the analytic power of the database increases exponentially. At this level, you can begin to explore "why" questions—the key to replication—and to progress. This requires advance planning. Information is the glue that holds the Management System together—MIS.

Plans for the Future

Appropriate Solutions defines ROI in terms of four generations of models.

The Generation 1 (G1) model assumes that the client has limited data with respect to costs and impacts, but must have individual outcomes and some quantitative basis for estimating change in income and key public expenditures. Cost information is provided in an aggregate form. That is the model used for the Silicon Valley Private Industry Council and the state of Illinois analyses.

The Generation 2 (G2) model assumes that financial cost information can be estimated in some fashion for individual participants, and it is hoped that expenditures are more accurate and extensive. For instance, instead of estimating welfare benefits from a table, accurate numbers are provided. Some nonprogram expenditures, such as Pell Grants, which can be presumed to have affected the impact, are able to be included. That is the model used for the Butler County, Ohio, Private Industry Council analysis. G1 and G2 are basically reactive models that take existing client data and do the best that can be done to fit the model around the data available from the client, not unlike square pegs and round holes at times.

The Generation 3 (G3) model incorporates a broader range of impact information, both benefits and costs, and is based on a comprehensive, integrated case management system that incorporates elements included to facilitate ROI computation. Activity-based accounting is presumed for all service partners, regardless of funding source. The authors are aware of no one who has such a system. That is the goal of ongoing and future projects with the U.S. Department of Health and Human Services Office of Community Services and the Chicago Workforce Board/Illinois Department of Economic Security.

The Generation 4 (G4) model builds upon G3 by adding the capability to predict more accurately cost avoidance items—"the road not taken." It will also add the capability to create a "level playing field" adjustment that creates an ROI index relative to barriers and difficulty in achieving outcomes. G3 and G4 are prescriptive models that tell the client what data is required, which will necessitate changes in data collection and storage systems.

G3 and G4 development work is now under way and is being funded over multiple years by the U.S. Department of Health and Human Services/ Office of Community Services and by the Chicago Workforce Board in conjunction with the Illinois Department of Economic Security.

Questions for Discussion

1. Do your database systems contain the appropriate information to facilitate an ROI impact analysis? What is missing? How can you modify your data collection systems to cost-effectively add that data?

2. Do you have the financial and technical resources to do this? If not, have you considered partnerships with similar organizations, state and federal support, foundation support?

3. How confident are you that the data going into your system is accurate? How sophisticated are your error identification routines?

4. When you need data from other organizations, have you established data sharing agreements?

5. Is it possible to isolate the effects of this program from other variables? Explain.

6. Do you have a clear communications strategy for the public, stakeholders, policymakers, and your staff? This case study incorporated an actual report to a client. How would you improve on it?

7. You are subpoenaed by the U.S. Senate to testify about the performance of your program. What would you say? What could you prove?

The Authors

Dennis K. Benson is a founding partner and president of Appropriate Solutions, Inc., a public policy research and management company founded in 1978. In 1996, he published a book describing a new model for estimating ROI for workforce development programs. This was revised and expanded into a second edition in 1999. ROI clients have included the Silicon Valley Private Industry Council, the Butler County Private Industry Council, and the Illinois Department of Commerce and Community Affairs, among others. He has made numerous presentations on ROI to organizations and has numerous papers and publications in this area. He presently serves as the ROI consultant to the Office of Community Services, U.S. Department of Health and Human Services (HHS) charged with extending ROI concepts into HHS-funded programs. He has also served as a performance accountability consultant to the National Office of Job Corps, the West Virginia Bureau of Employment Programs, the Ohio Department of Education, and others. He did the conceptual design in 2000 for a Web-based performance management system for the Silicon Valley Private Industry Council. He can be reached at Appropriate Solutions, Inc., 511 Garden Drive, Worthington, OH 43085-3820; phone: 614.840.0466; email: appropsolu@aol.com.

Victoria P. Tran is presently with the Santa Clara County Social Service Administration Information Systems-GIS. She was formerly an employment and management analyst with the Silicon Valley Private Industry Council and worked closely with MIS to extrapolate and report data on various JTPA programs. She was also responsible for designing and implementing the network infrastructure, which included videoconferencing capabilities and connecting SVPIC's three One-Stop

Centers. She was also the primary operations interface of the last two ROI studies conducted by ASI for SVPIC. She designed and executed the executive summary graphic formats for both the SVPIC project and the ROI study in Butler County, Ohio.

Acknowledgment Note by Benson

I would like to thank three individuals with SCPIC whose patience and endurance directly contributed to the completion of this analysis: 1) Ruben Uribe has been unfailingly helpful in the project's administration and logistics and has provided all required financial information; 2) my co-author, Victoria P. Tran, was responsible for providing all the data requested and seeking answers to dozens of questions and assisting with the graphics and visual presentation of these findings; and 3) Srinivasan (Ravi) Ravindran, the JTPA manager for SVPIC. Ravindran commissioned the first ROI study in 1966 when this model was being initially developed and provided its first field test. He has encouraged the continuous improvement and innovation of the model and has significantly contributed to developing the performance metrics for the entire workforce development profession.

Further Resources

Benson, Dennis K. (May 2001). *Employment Risk Assessment.* Columbus, OH: Appropriate Solutions, Inc. Presented at the National Association of Workforce Development Professionals annual conference.

Benson, Dennis K. (1999). *Return on Inve$tment: Guidelines to Determine Workforce Development Impact,* second edition. Columbus, OH: Appropriate Solutions, Inc. Exclusively distributed by the National Association of Workforce Development Professionals, Washington, DC.

Benson, Dennis K. (September 2001). *Return on Investment:Progress 2001.* Columbus, OH: Appropriate Solutions, Inc. Presented at the National Association of Community Action Agencies annual conference.

Bloom, Howard S., et al. (January 1993). *The National JTPA Study: Title IIA Impact on Earnings and Employment at 18 Months.* Bethesda, MD: Abt Associates, Inc.

Doolittle, Fred, and Linda Traeger. (April 1990). *Implementing the National JTPA Study.* New York: Manpower Demonstration Research Corporation.

Lillard, Lee A., and Hong W. Tan. (March 1986). "Private Sector Training: Who Gets It and What Are Its Effects?" Santa Monica, CA: The Rand Corporation. Prepared for the U.S. Department of Labor, R-331-DOL/RC.

Moore, Richard W., Daniel R. Black, and G. Michael Phillips. (July 1995) "Accounting for Training: An Analysis of the Outcomes of California Employment Training Panel Programs." Northridge, CA: School of Business Administration and Economics, California State University. Submitted to the California Employment Training Panel.

ROMA (Results Oriented Management and Accountability) ROI Web page: http://www.ROMA1.org/committees/return.html.

Silicon Valley Private Industry Council. (2000). *SVPIC: Reflections of a Vision 1983-2000*. San Jose, CA: Silicon Valley Private Industry Council.

U.S. Department of Commerce, Bureau of Economic Analysis. (March 1997). *Regional Multipliers: A User Handbook for the Regional Input-Output Modeling System (RIMS II)*. third edition. Washington, DC: U.S. Government Printing Office.

U.S. General Accounting Office. (March 1997). "Measuring Performance: Strengths and Limitations of Research Indicators." Report GAO/RCED-97-91. Washington, DC: U.S.General Accounting Office.

Proposed Implementation of a Client Relationship Management System

Australian Capital Territory Community Care

Susan Pepper and Ronald Christie

A medium-sized Australian government agency in the health-care field identified a need for a Client Relationship Management (CRM) system that would assist them to bring some integration into their service provision. They established the overall cost for the multimillion dollar alternative and developed a business case, but had not been able to secure funding for the project. They then requested the Cyrene Group to prepare a projected return on investment on the initiative, which was to be submitted with the business case, in order to finally gain approval to proceed and be granted the investment dollars.

Background

Australian Capital Territory (ACT) Community Care is a recognized leader in the provision of community-based health and disability services in Australia. By continually developing its services to be client focused, the agency is at the vanguard of Australian community-based health and disability practice.

As a community-based service, ACT Community Care's 1,300 staff deliver services from 73 service locations, as well as client homes throughout the length and breadth of the Australian Capital Territory. The wide geographic distribution of staff and the diversity of the service offerings presents a range of organizational, logistical, and communication challenges.

At the start of the new millennium, the inability of its current systems to meet these challenges is limiting ACT Community Care's capacity to enhance and grow its services. For the first time it is threat-

This case was prepared to serve as a basis for discussion rather than to illustrate either effective or ineffective administrative and management practices.

ening the agency's ability to meet its high standards of care and client-centered innovation. ACT Community Care needs to find a solution that will reflect and enhance its recognized standing as a leading provider.

The modernization of the ACT government infrastructure in 1999 represented the first step to a resolution of these problems by providing a robust and high performance wide area network (WAN) infrastructure. Despite this, currently only one third of ACT Community Care's 1,300 staff are able to use the WAN. The majority, who do have access, are administrative rather than clinical service delivery staff.

The agency currently runs its organization on a series of program-based "stand-alone" databases. There is no single client database. This promotes fragmentation in service delivery and in capturing client and service information, and does not allow ACT Community Care to efficiently deliver coordinated services to its clients.

Organizational Need

ACT Community Care has an opportunity to provide its clients with a modern client-focused information management system, which will enhance the delivery of health services and participation in government initiatives, while fully using the WAN infrastructure investment.

The CRM system will lead to significant improvements in ACT Community Care's capability through greater visibility of client needs, services, and general information.

It is proposed that an overeaching CRM system will deliver the following benefits:
- increase service delivery productivity
- provide coordinated and efficient delivery of client services and information resulting in better client safety
- provide ability to participate in government initiatives
- promote collaboration across the various programs providing services
- provide an electronic link between centralized intake lines and service providers, while meeting legislative requirements including maintaining client privacy and appropriately managing client health records
- assist clinicians in delivering modern health care
- allow accurate collection of data including minimum data sets to meet purchaser and national reporting requirements
- assist in the monitoring of service provision, outcomes, and community needs analysis
- provide the framework for a single electronic client record

- provide better client access and convenience
- reduce exposure to litigation
- prepare workforce management
- provide ability to manage contracts and growth
- provide ability to monitor outputs and outcomes, and proactively tailor service offerings to meet identified needs.

History

Since 1996, ACT Community Care has been trying to address the above challenges through participation in a multistate consortium for developing a Community Health Information Management Enterprise (CHIME). This New South Wales-led project has been beleaguered with time delays, increasing costs, and narrowed objectives. CHIME, a clinical- rather than client-based community health information system, still as yet undelivered, no longer reflects the dynamic and client-focused environment that ACT Community Care operates within.

Fortunately, ACT Community Care has been financially prudent in relationship to this project, having contributed a total of $200,000 to what is currently a $12 million project. Having actively decided not to contribute further funds, the funds allocated previously for this application by government ($2.6 million), including a recurrent funding of $715,000, are still available and are a potential source of funding.

Since 1996, the world of information management has not stood still and, in recent years, there has been a significant development in commercial off-the-shelf CRM systems capable of rapid deployment. These systems support client-focused processes, with a single database and intelligent workflow. They are designed for easy integration with other systems, in this case, specialized clinical systems and people management information (PMI). In line with the ACT government's service delivery policy, they support multiple communication channels including call center, Web, fax, and mail, as well as face-to-face service delivery.

The chosen system must be flexible to allow for quick change and expansion, reflecting the fact that ACT Community Care exists in a dynamic marketplace.

ACT Community Care has been prompted, through the issues with CHIME, the advent of commercially available CRM software, and government initiatives around electronic service delivery and information sharing, to reevaluate its current business and specifically its IT strategy. To this end, ACT Community Care has completed a business requirements document that focused on identifying current and emerging business requirements.

Feedback received from the 2000 ACT Community care customer survey reinforced the need for "client focus" and highlighted the importance of having sufficient information available, being treated as a valued customer, working with staff who attend to requests promptly, a reasonable waiting time for appointment, and ease of contact by phone.

Rationale

The rationale for the projected return on investment (ROI) for the CRM system is based on the following:

- The data collection process will assist in ensuring that all key stakeholders' and managers' client management reporting requirements are met in the CRM system.
- Through intensive interviewing with managers and key stakeholders, the process will provide projections on costs and benefits, which can be monitored and measured when implementation begins.
- It results in the design and development of a measurement and evaluation model for implementation;
- It will assist in achieving ACT Community Care's opportunity to provide its clients with a modern client-focused information management system, which will enhance the delivery of health services and participating in government initiatives, while fully using the WAN infrastructure investment.

With the above in mind, the key stakeholders and managers were interviewed to assess needs, objectives, and outcomes for a CRM system.

Expected Outcomes

The implementation of a CRM system and supporting infrastructure will meet the previously mentioned business needs in the following ways:

- It will introduce common business processes and share common data.
- It will allow clients to interact with ACT Community Care in a number of different ways and receive consistent information through the use of a single database, such as phone, Web, fax, email, and so forth.
- It will focus on security to ensure client consent and privacy.
- It will enable ACT Community Care to gain full value for its investment in the existing infrastructure.

- It will improve information and reporting to enable better management of existing contractual requirements, specifically with respect to capturing minimum data sets. This will also provide better information to support management decision making.
- It will provide an open system that allows the agency to share information and participate in portfolio and government projects. These include the Health Information Network (HIN); PMI; integrated document management; and as part of Canberra Connect, meet the ACT government's objective to support delivery online by 2001.
- It will enable staff to respond to and deal with client needs at the first point of contact.
- It will allow common information to be shared electronically and to be accessible at all points of contact, ensuring appropriate and safe service delivery.
- It will allow ACT Community Care to understand the cost and risk associated with serving a client and proactively managing a client's care.

Evaluation Drivers

The events that precipitated this projected impact study are typical. The management and staff of the organization intuitively and instinctively knew that ACT Community Care had a series of major problems. However, in the initial cost-benefit analysis, they could only identify marginal savings over the length of the project. Consequently, the degree of savings had impacted their attempts to gain the necessary funding and, in fact, had constituted a significant delay.

Additionally, around the globe, there is more interest in measuring the impact of business strategy, including the implementation or proposed implementation of business systems and technology solutions and organizational change programs. Four major trends are driving these actions:

1. Programs are increasingly becoming more expensive to develop and deliver. The proposed CRM system is an example of this trend. Expensive programs require a comprehensive projection of benefits versus costs. An evaluation can determine the degree of success the organization could achieve and the appropriate implementation methodology, which should be followed to ensure a high return on investment.

2. Within an organization, the importance of a CRM reporting solution, which assists managers to achieve business objectives, places

the program at a level where accountability is required. Consequently, it must be subjected to an accountability review both before and after implementation.

3. Fueled in part by the success of total quality management (TQM), organizations are implementing additional measures to gauge projected success and monitor progress of the implementation against the projections. CRM systems are included in this trend, as they are measured, monitored, and evaluated.

4. Senior management, in an attempt to efficiently manage resources, have brought closer scrutiny to the distribution of resources and often require accountability for major programs.

Collectively these trends are driving the need for more accountability and evaluation in corporate programs.

Purpose of Evaluation

The proposed CRM system is an ideal candidate for a projected impact study for four reasons:

1. The CRM system targets a critical audience in ACT Community Care—management. It is imperative that current and future managers understand the challenges faced by ACT Community Care. By providing timely, relevant, consistent, and accurate information on client issues and services, managers will be in a better position to develop focused strategies, which directly align with business unit direction and service delivery.

2. The CRM system project is an expensive program to be undertaken by ACT Community Care. Expensive programs need to show their projected and real value; and a return on investment, in this instance, compares the projected benefits of the program against the projected costs of the program, which then identifies the projected rate of savings.

3. The return-on-investment analysis process identifies the commitment and ownership of senior managers for a corporate business solution. This process will also contribute to a cost-benefit strategy to shut down the legacy/renegade systems.

4. Projects, which involve key operational and strategic issues, often demand that appropriate measurements of success be developed, including return on investment.

The situation and issues surrounding the proposed CRM system made it an ideal project to explore a comprehensive evaluation. It also provides an excellent opportunity to demonstrate how to develop a projected ROI, so that the process can be transferred to ACT Community Care for use in developing future business cases and measuring and evaluating the actual CRM program development and implementation.

Objectives of the Impact Study

The study, designed to evaluate the potential success of a CRM system, has four key objectives:

1. to assess the impact of a CRM system in measurable contributions to the extent possible, up to and including the calculation of the projected ROI
2. to identify specific barriers and concerns about successful program implementation and use
3. to recommend an implementation methodology for the CRM system, based on the collective input of managers, key stakeholders, and senior managers in ACT Community Care
4. to detail the ongoing costs to ACT Community Care if no decision is made or if funding is not received.

Initial Key Issues

Several issues became apparent in the beginning of the study, which could influence the ability to develop a projected, specific, significant return on investment:

- The timeline for the projected impact study was extremely short and impeded the level of comprehensive investigation that would normally be carried out for implementing a system of this magnitude.
- There were no consistent business practices across programs, regarding client management information.
- Some business units/managers had no organizational client information reporting tool; therefore, they had developed or were developing renegade systems to support access to data in order to undertake their daily business.
- There appeared to be pockets of staff in the professional area who were reluctant to change their current practices for a number of reasons: they were frustrated, yet comfortable with their current systems and processes; they believed their roles were not administrative, therefore they should not be expected to enter data into a computerized record keeping system; they did not have access to a computer; or they were concerned about the confidentiality of clients' records.

- Perceptions of potential success are critical to the effectiveness of implementing a CRM system. Consequently, this study gauges the perceptions of the potential success of a CRM system from managers and key stakeholders. Often, perception is as important as reality.

Evaluation Methodology

The process normally uses a five-level framework; however, the levels of evaluation, as illustrated in table 1, can only be undertaken as a program is implemented or after a program has been implemented. In this instance, we have used Level 1 (reaction to the CRM system), together with the step-by-step ROI process model to ascertain the projections if a CRM system is to be implemented.

Levels of Evaluation

At Level 1, feedback was obtained to judge the reaction to the potential effectiveness and potential success of the program. While participant reaction questionnaires are typically completed at the end of the training, in this instance, reaction data was collected from key stakeholders through a series of interviews and questionnaires. We also introduced a data validation step in order to quantify data ranges and to identify any aberrations that may have occurred.

The validation method used provided an overall picture of the expected organizational savings, which were then compared to the aggregated savings that had been identified by the individual department directors and their experts. The total figures produced a mere 5 percent variance in the gross anticipated savings across the organization! The

Table 1. ROI process model: Five levels of evaluation.

Level	Measurement Focus
1. Reaction and planned action	Measures satisfaction with the program and captures planned actions.
2. Learning	Measures changes in knowledge, skills, and attitudes.
3. Application	Measures changes in on-the-job behavior.
4. Business impact (projected)	Measures projected changes in business impact variables.
5. Return on investment (projected)	Compares projected program benefits to the projected costs.

value of estimation using an agreed and rational approach had once again been vindicated.

At Level 2, measures of learning are recorded to determine the extent to which skills, knowledge, and attitudes have changed as a result of the training and program implementation. In a CRM system, learning is typically assessed in observations, exercises, simulations, and objective assessments from the project faculty. Obviously, learning cannot be evaluated until actual program implementation.

At Level 3, on-the-job behavior change is monitored and measured. At this level, the evaluation focuses on what specific on-the-job applications have been identified, which are directly linked to the project. As with Level 2, Level 3 cannot be evaluated until actual program implementation.

At Level 4, the projected business impact of a CRM was measured. Table 2 identifies the key performance measures directly linked to the program, which were considered by the key stakeholders, with a view to projecting the business impact of a CRM system.

At Level 5, *projected* return on investment—the projected monetary benefits of the program—were compared to the projected costs of the program. This is the ultimate evaluation, as the true worth of the proposed project was determined by comparing projected benefits to the projected investment.

Data Collection Strategy

A data collection strategy was designed to meet each of the objectives of this study. The number and variety of individuals contacted for input and the variety of techniques used helped to ensure that adequate, quality input was obtained for the evaluation. However, the time constraints for the projected impact study impeded the level of comprehensive data collection and validation, which would normally be applied for a project of this magnitude.

Issues

Several key issues had to be addressed when designing the data collection strategy:

- Because a CRM system had not been implemented, data could only be collected at the reaction level. Nevertheless it provided enough information to develop an assessment, which progressed through the chain of impact to business measures. Data was collected in one process in the form of an interview questionnaire with key stakeholders and managers.

Table 2. Linkage with key measures.

Indicate the extent to which you think your application of the various components of a CRM system will have a positive influence on the following measures?

	No Influence	Some Influence	Moderate Influence	Significant Influence
Productivity		22%	45%	33%
Internal customer response time		22%	33%	45%
Internal customer satisfaction		34%	33%	33%
Job satisfaction	11%	33%	34%	22%
External customer satisfaction	11%	11%	11%	67%
External customer response time		11%	44%	45%
Quality		11%	22%	67%
Cost Control		56%	11%	33%
Staffing, including: Absenteeism Staff turnover Workforce management Workforce profiling	11%	67%	22%	

There were very strong responses from all the key stakeholders, which suggests that the projected impact is very real.

- Different types of data had to be collected to provide a comprehensive view of the program. That involved qualitative and quantitative data as well as a combination of soft and hard data.
- To provide a complete assessment of the program, data had to come from a variety of different individuals so that different perspectives could be integrated throughout the overall evaluation. That strategy ensured a broad range of opinions, expertise, and contribution and enhanced stakeholder buy-in to the eventual solution.
- The data collection and subsequent analysis had to be objective. The individuals involved in the actual collection of data, that is, those from the Cyrene Group, were external to ACT Community Care. That helped ensure independence and objectivity as the data was collected, tabulated, summarized, and analyzed.
- Wherever possible, the data was reported so that the participants were not identified. That provided the respondents with an opportunity to be candid and open in their assessment and thorough and accurate

in their feedback. Interviews with key stakeholders and managers were undertaken face to face; however, confidentiality was assured prior to the start of the interview.

Data Collection Plan

An effective evaluation had to be carefully planned with appropriate timing established and responsibilities defined. The data collection plan was developed by the Cyrene Group and approved by the executive director, corporate, and business development. The volume of data collected was high and comprehensive because of a CRM system, the projected cost of a CRM system in both time and money, and the target audience involved.

Timing of Data Collection

In an ROI evaluation the timing of collection is critical and would normally be collected at the completion of each phase. However, in this instance, as previously discussed, only Level 1 reaction questionnaires were collected via an interview as this was a "projected" impact study.

Although a CRM system is designed to have a long-term impact, the specific improvements are difficult to capture if assessed years after the program is completed. In this instance, the data was required to assess the potential impact of a CRM system for ACT Community Care. Key stakeholders and managers were asked if their estimates were based on first-year-only projected results or recurrent results. If projections/results were taken over a longer period of time, additional variables would influence business measures, thus complicating the cause-and-effect relationship between program implementation and improvement.

End-of-Program Feedback

The Level 1 interview/questionnaire is an essential part of any evaluation and is usually obtained at the end of training or initial implementation. In this instance, feedback was captured by the Cyrene Group during interviews with key stakeholders and managers.

The main topics covered in the interviews are shown in table 3. As previously discussed, the questionnaires focused on Level 1 reaction data and Level 4 business impact data.

Interviews with Key Stakeholders

Interviews with the key stakeholders and managers lasted about two hours. Each interview explored projected individual application and impact including topics outlined in table 3. Additional probing

Table 3. Topics covered in the interviews for Level 1 evaluation.

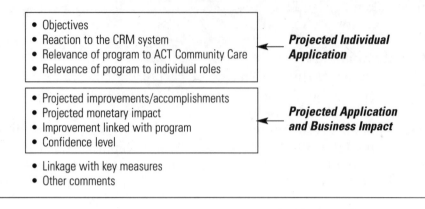

- Objectives
- Reaction to the CRM system
- Relevance of program to ACT Community Care
- Relevance of program to individual roles

◄— *Projected Individual Application*

- Projected improvements/accomplishments
- Projected monetary impact
- Improvement linked with program
- Confidence level

◄— *Projected Application and Business Impact*

- Linkage with key measures
- Other comments

was used to uncover business impact applications and to gain further insight into skill applications, barriers, concerns, and important issues surrounding the success of the proposed program. Each individual was encouraged to establish a formula on which any estimates were based. That formula was validated and the interviewee was then given the choice of owning the estimate or withdrawing. In all but one case, interviewees were very confident in their estimations, and they could see that this method had real merit.

Additionally, key stakeholders were also interviewed in relation to the ongoing costs and implications of maintaining the "status quo"—if no decision is made or a decision is made not to move to a CRM system.

Summary

Collectively, these data collection methods yielded a tremendous amount of data. The different perspectives and types of data ensured a thorough assessment of the proposed CRM system and provided a backdrop for insightful recommendations to ensure a high return on investment is received during and after implementation. We found that the estimation process was accurate and credible both in its acceptance and the results achieved.

Isolating the Effects of the Program

Normally, in this step of the process, specific strategies are explored that determine the amount of business performance directly related to the program. This is essential because there are several factors that usually influence performance data after programs have been conducted/implemented. The specific strategies used in this step will normally pinpoint the amount of improvement directly related to the program. The payoff is in increased accuracy and credibility of the ROI calculation.

While there are as many as 10 different approaches to tackle this issue, the options were limited with this evaluation because the CRM system had not been actually implemented and the various components of the solution had not been selected. The following strategies were used:

- Key stakeholders estimated the amount of improvement, which would relate to implementing a CRM system. With this approach, participants provided the total amount of projected improvement, and were asked to indicate the percent of the improvement that would be specifically related to a CRM system. In this instance, all of the projected savings were attributable to the CRM system.
- Managers estimated the impact of a CRM system on output variables. With this approach, managers were presented with the total amount of improvement and were asked to indicate the percent related to the program.
- Experts provided estimates of the impact of a CRM system on performance improvement. Because the estimates were based on experience, the internal experts were required to be familiar with CRM-type applications and how they could be applied in an ACT Community Care environment.

Collectively, these strategies provided an adequate adjustment for the critical issue of isolating the effects of the program as illustrated in the projection of savings (table 4).

The net savings are listed below by program area:

- Alcohol and Drug $110,300
- Child Youth and Women's Health $1,927,050
- Community Rehabilitation $897,860
- Dental Health $358,533
- Disability $1,633,768
- General Practice $46,298
- Integrated Health Care $2,125,200
- Corporate $371,300

Total Net Savings   **$7,470,309**

Validation Exercise

During the interview and after the above estimates were provided, we asked each program group three questions as detailed below:

1. If the CRM System is implemented as proposed, what is your projection of the savings?

Table 4. Projection of savings.

Basis for Savings	Average Value in Dollars	Average Level of Confidence in the Estimate	Average Adjusted Savings
Common business processes and data	$2,832,000	75%	$2,050,200
Clients to interact with ACT Community Care in a number of ways	$ 607,750	74%	$446,688
Ensure client consent and privacy	$1,063,100	80%	$803,210
ACT Community Care to gain full value for its infrastructure investment	$819,500	80%	$655,600
To provide information/minimum data sets to support contracts	$849,273	79%	$726,868
Open system that allows the agency to share common data	$50,200	70%	$35,140
Enable staff to deal with client needs at first point of contact	$1,725,666	79%	$1,376,383
Allow common information to be shared electronically	$105,000	80%	$84,000
Allow ACT Community Care to understand the cost and risk associated with servicing clients	$1,700,400	76%	$1,292,220
Total Savings	**$9,752,889**	**77%** Average Confidence Factor	**$7,470,309** Net Savings

Does this projection represent: First year only? First year and beyond? What is the basis for making the above projection?
2. How confident are you that the above projection will actually be achieved? (100% = Certainty and 0% = No confidence)
3. Other factors often influence improvement in performance. Please indicate the percentage of the above improvement/saving that would be directly related to the CRM system?

Results of the Validation Exercise

- The validation exercise provided for savings in excess of $16,500,000 in the first year.
- All but two of the interviewees suggested the savings were first year and beyond.

- Subsequently, the savings identified from this method equated to $44,500,000 over the projected life of the CRM system.
- That savings compares with our estimated figures from each of the programs and broken down by objectives, which came to $42,500,000, thus validating the estimate process thoroughly.
- As this figure was slightly higher than gained in previous estimates (table 4), we used the lower figure for ROI purposes.

Converting Data to Monetary Values

To calculate the return on investment, data collected in a Level 4 evaluation is converted to monetary values to compare to proposed program costs. That requires a value to be placed on each unit of data connected with the proposed program. While 10 techniques are available to convert data to monetary value, the specific strategies and techniques selected for this study were as follows:

- Projected output data were converted to projected cost savings. With this technique, projected output increases were converted to monetary values based on their unit of cost reduction.
- Where employee time is a cost, the participant's wages and benefits were used for the value of time.
- Historical costs and current records were used when available for a specific variable. In this case, organizational cost data was used to establish the specific value of a projected improvement.
- Internal experts were used to estimate a value for a projected improvement. In this situation, the credibility of the estimate hinged on the expertise and reputation of the individual.
- Key stakeholders estimated the value of the data item. For this approach to be effective, participants had to be willing and capable of providing a value for the improvement.

Converting data to monetary value is a very important step in the ROI process and is absolutely necessary to determine the monetary benefits from the implementation of programs, whether projected or actual. In this instance, we tabulated program costs through the development of all of the related costs of the proposed CRM program. Table 5 contains the cost components included in the business case documentation.

The primary program costs pertaining to implementing a CRM system are reflected in table 5. While there is often some debate as to whether salaries and benefits should be included in the cost of the program, in reality, participants are not replaced while they attend training, and so forth; therefore, the organization does not experience a replacement cost. However, the employees are compensated

Table 5. Cost components.

Cost Component	YR 0 $'000	YR 1 $'000	YR 2 $'000	YR 3 $'000	YR 4 $'000	YR $'000	YR $'000	YR $'000
CRM application software	4,065	262	262	262	262	262	262	262
InTACT Support —CRM System	630	320	320	320	320	320	320	320
Database software infrastructure	492	252	252	252	252	252	252	252
Server infrastructure	623	624	656	688	720	752	784	816
Additional WAN infrastructure	461	245	245	245	245	245	245	245
Additional desktop peripherals	404	384	384	384	384	384	384	384
Commissioning— cabling, telephony, fit-out	701	0	0	0	0	0	0	300
ACT Community Care project team—Implementation	1,172	0	0	0	0	0	0	0
ACT Community Care systems support measurement and evaluation costs	381	381	381	381	381	381	381	381
Estimated Total Yearly Outlay	**8,929**	**2,467**	**2,499**	**2,531**	**2,563**	**2,595**	**2,627**	**2,960**

for being on the job every day and they are expected to make a contribution roughly equal to their remuneration. If they are removed from the job, for say, two days, then the organization has lost their contribution for that time. To be fully loaded with costs and also to be conservative, that value should be estimated and included in the overall cost profile. Cyrene Group worked on the assumption that these costs were included in the business case costing documentation.

Cost Estimation

ACT Community Care retained the services of a professional services company to assist in the production of a business requirements document. This process reveals a total estimated cost for implementing a CRM system as $27,171,000 over seven years.

Calculating the ROI

When developing the projected ROI, two important issues had to be addressed that represented a significant challenge for the process. The first involved the methods to isolate the effects of the program, while the second was converting data to monetary values.

The role of the key stakeholders and managers was extremely critical. The key stakeholders and managers provided estimates on proposed improvements, isolated the effects of the proposed program on the improvements, and in some cases converted data to actual monetary values. While there are many other approaches to isolate the effects of the program and a variety of techniques to convert data to monetary values, several issues prevented the use of a majority of other approaches and techniques:

- As this impact study was a projection, this fact alone eliminated some of the possibilities.
- The nature of CRM systems eliminated many other techniques. The application and ultimate impact is an individual process, and the improvements must come from the key stakeholders/managers themselves. Skills can be applied in a variety of situations to drive any one of dozens of business performance measures in a business unit. Given a cross-functional group, it is feasible for each person to influence different performance improvement measures as the CRM system is applied. This situation made it difficult to project linkage of the program to any finite set of performance measures.
- The number of programs represented and the nature of their issues, challenges, and performance measures made the process difficult to project linkage to any small number of applications.

Consequently, input from key stakeholders/managers was often the most reliable way to identify the actual measure of projected performance improvement.

Challenges in Developing the Projected ROI for the Proposed CRM System

There were several challenges that were encountered as the projected return on investment was developed:

- The CRM system had not been designed and developed at this stage; therefore, the key stakeholders/managers were asked to consider the questions based on the deliverables being achieved.
- When faced with the prospect of estimations, some managers found it difficult to grasp the concept without prompting.
- In terms of estimations, ACT Community Care did not have any measures for productivity or quality, and some of the identified savings are potentially in these areas.

ROI Calculations

When developing the ROI, the conservative approach is to include only the program benefits that can be converted into monetary value and the program costs. The projected return on investment is calculated using the projected program benefits and projected costs. The projected benefit-cost ratio (BCR) is the projected program benefits divided by the projected cost. In formula form it is:

$$\text{Projected BCR} = \frac{\text{Projected Program Benefits}}{\text{Projected Program Costs}}$$

The return on investment uses the projected net benefits divided by projected program costs. The projected net benefits are the projected program benefits minus the projected costs. In formula form, the projected ROI becomes:

$$\text{Projected ROI (\%)} = \frac{\text{Projected Net Program Benefits}}{\text{Projected Program Costs}} \times 100$$

$$\text{Projected ROI} = \frac{\$42,489,555 - \$27,171,000}{\$27,171,000} \times 100 = 56\%$$

The decision to calculate a projected ROI was made to ensure that ACT Community Care implements a CRM system, which meets the needs and objectives of its key stakeholders and is funded accordingly.

Because the objectives of the proposed program reflect bottom-line contribution, the calculating of the projected ROI became a reasonably simple issue.

Intangible Benefits

Perhaps the most important results of a CRM system implementation are the intangible benefits, both short- and long-term. By definition, these benefits are not converted to monetary value for use in the ROI calculation. They would not be measured precisely and are subjective, but are still very important.

Without question, the intangible benefits of this proposed program are real and significant. Most key stakeholders were able to identify intangible benefits, some immediately applicable, while others will be long-term.

Communication and Sharing of Knowledge

One of the most obvious and significant intangible benefits is communication. Without exception, key stakeholders and managers discussed not having access to client information across programs. A CRM system should significantly enhance communication and the sharing of knowledge across programs.

Summary

There are many other long- and short-term potential intangible benefits that relate to implementing a CRM system, which include but are not restricted to:
- enhanced teamwork
- enhanced and focused alignment between client needs and business strategy
- enhanced organizational image
- quality
- increased job satisfaction
- increased productivity
- reduced unscheduled absence
- reduced labor turnover
- reduced stress/anxiety levels
- improved customer service—internal and external
- improved customer response time—internal and external
- well-informed decision making
- improved staff morale
- full value for ACT Community Care's infrastructure investment.

Lessons Learned

Because this was a projected impact study, the lessons learned will mainly be gained at our post-implementation evaluation. However, one of the shortcomings of this particular case study was that we were severely affected by a very tight timeframe (eight days), and we were compelled to use the costings that were calculated by the professional services team. Therefore, we did not have the opportunity to validate these figures, and the customer understood and accepted this handicap.

Recommendations

The proposed CRM system was approved to evaluate on the basis of assessing the impact of the deliverables with key stakeholders and managers within ACT Community Care and using their feedback as input to developing a model for implementation.

The following recommendations were offered based on the collective input from key stakeholders and managers.

Recommendation No. 1

To move quickly and efficiently to adopt a CRM system as identified, because every day that is wasted costs ACT Community Care prohibitive dollars in time, people, frustration, and effective coordination of client service delivery.

Recommendation No. 2

In this environment of change, flexible, user-friendly methods are vital when accessing customer information, as opposed to the historical approach of cumbersome processes, paperwork, and structured reports. This requires a multipronged approach to implementation, which builds a solid infrastructure to support the CRM system. This approach should include:
- change management
- business rules and processes
- education—technology and content
- data validation and integrity.

All of these components should have been included in developing the costs for the CRM system.

Recommendation No. 3

If the future agenda is to revolve around "Enhanced delivery of health services and participating in government initiatives, while fully using the WAN infrastructure investment," then ACT Community Care must get the customer data right. This means ACT Community Care must know who its customers are across programs and what services they are receiving and requiring. A CRM system provides the solution to this challenge.

Recommendation No. 4

ACT Community Care should measure all major initiatives, which affect customer service delivery and human capital within the organization. The projected return-on-investment process highlighted the vitality and need for information to be gathered and assessed prior to a project being approved and funded. This methodology will also be vital during implementing the CRM system to ensure that the project remains focused, and the benefits, which have been projected, are achieved

Summary

Collectively, these recommendations would make a potentially successful program much more effective and provide a leading edge CRM system. At the same time, it would generate tremendous power for management and staff, while enhancing customer service delivery and human capital management in ACT Community Care.

Questions for Discussion

1. Do you think a CRM system is a good target for a projected impact study?
2. What extra validation steps could you suggest to identify additional benefits?
3. Do you think that the estimation process has significant weight in this instance?
4. What other methods/strategies would you suggest for isolating the effects of the CRM solution?
5. Would you accept that the impact study provided a credible projected ROI? If not, why not?

The Authors

Susan Pepper is the managing director of the Cyrene Group, which began operations in Canberra, Australia, in 1999. The company has three major target markets: human capital, business intelligence, and return on investment consulting. Pepper's background is in human resources, gained from a career in the public sector in New South

Wales and from her diversified consulting. She has a passion for the strategic approach to people management and to the measurement and evaluation of all management initiatives. Pepper holds a business degree from Southern Cross University, Lismore, New South Wales. She has published articles on measuring ROI in the Australian Institute of Training & Development's journal and lectured business and MBA students on ROI in the Queensland and Canberra Universities. She can be reached at the Cyrene Group, 5/19 Ebenezer Street, Bonython, ACT 2905 Australia; email: susanp@cyrene.com.au.

Ronald Christie is the principal consultant for the Cyrene Group. He has extensive experience in consulting, which includes human capital, change management, and organizational development. With a degree in commerce from the University of New South Wales, Christie has developed a career through financial circles and has expanded his repertoire by working with a variety of public and private sector organizations. He has published articles on measuring ROI in the Australian Institute of Training & Development's journal and lectured business and MBA students on ROI in the Queensland and Canberra Universities.

Absenteeism Reduction Program

Metro Transit Authority*

Jack J. Phillips and Ron D. Stone

This case illustrates how changes in human resource policies and selection processes can reduce absenteeism and prevent major problems in business operations. Because of unscheduled absences, the unavailability of bus drivers caused route schedule delays and bottlenecks, which resulted in dissatisfied customers, a loss of revenue, and increased operating costs. New guidelines and disciplinary policies for unscheduled absences, as well as a change in hiring practices, were initiated to correct the situation. The ability to demonstrate the costs associated with the absenteeism problem led to the two solutions being implemented. The evaluation team was able to isolate the effects of each of the two HR initiatives and calculate the operational savings to demonstrate an impressive return on investment.

Background

The Metro Transit Authority (MTA) operates a comprehensive transportation system in a large metropolitan area. More than 1,000 buses function regularly, providing essential transportation to citizens in the metro area. Many passengers depend on the bus system for their commute to and from work, as well as other essential travel. MTA employs more than 2,900 drivers to operate the bus system around the clock.

This case was prepared to serve as a basis for discussion rather than to illustrate either effective or ineffective administrative and management practices. Names of places, organizations, or people have been disguised at the request of the author or organization.

*The original version of this case was published in Jack J. Phillips, Ron D. Stone, and Patricia P. Phillips. *The Human Resources Scorecard: Measuring Return on Investment. Boston: Butterworth-Heinemann, 2001.

As with many transit systems, MTA was experiencing excessive absenteeism with bus drivers, and the problem was growing. Just three years ago, absenteeism was 7 percent, compared with the most recent three-month period of 8.7 percent—too excessive to keep the transit system operating in a consistent manner.

To ensure that buses ran on time, a pool of substitute drivers was employed to fill in during unexpected absences. The number of drivers in the pool was a function of the absenteeism rate. At the time of this study, the pool consisted of 231 substitute drivers. When the drivers in the pool were not needed as substitutes, they performed almost no essential work for the Transit Authority although they were required to report to work. When a substitute driver was used, this usually delayed the bus schedule, making the bus late for subsequent stops.

Causes of Problems and Solutions

To determine the cause of absenteeism, an analysis was conducted using focus groups, interviews, and an analysis of human resources records. Focus groups included bus drivers and their supervisors. Interviews were conducted with supervisors and managers. HR records were examined for trends and patterns in absenteeism. The conclusions from the analysis were as follows:

- Individuals who were frequently absent had a pattern of absenteeism that dated back to the beginning of their employment and, in most cases, was present in other employment situations.
- Many of the absences could be avoided. The problem was primarily a motivation and discipline issue.
- The prevailing attitude among employees was to take advantage of the system whenever possible, up to the threshold of being terminated.

As a result of these findings, MTA initiated two solutions:

1. **A no-fault disciplinary system was implemented.** With this policy, an employee who experiences more than six unexpected (unplanned) incidences in a six-month period was terminated—no questions asked. A sickness that extends more than one day was considered one incidence. Thus, the policy would not unfairly penalize those who are absent for legitimate sickness or for scheduled surgery and other medical attention. The no-fault system was implemented after extensive negotiations with the union. When union officials realized the impact of excessive absenteeism, they agreed with the new policy.

2. **The selection process for new drivers was modified.** During the initial screening, a list of questions was developed and used to screen out applicants who had a history of absenteeism dating back to their high school days. The questions, with scoring and interpretation, were added

to the current selection process and required approximately 30 minutes of additional time during the initial employment interview.

To bring appropriate attention to the absenteeism issue and to generate results as soon as possible, both solutions were implemented at the same time.

Objectives of the Solutions

The expected outcomes were established early, in the form of implementation and impact objectives. The objectives of the two solutions were to:
- communicate the no-fault policy, including how the policy would be applied and the rationale for it
- experience little or no adverse reaction from current employees as the no-fault absenteeism policy was implemented
- maintain present level of job satisfaction as the absenteeism solutions were implemented and applied
- use the new screening process for each selection decision so that a systematic and consistent selection process would be in place
- implement and enforce the no-fault policy consistently throughout all operating units
- reduce driver absenteeism at least 2 percent during the first year of implementation of the two solutions
- improve customer service and satisfaction with a reduction in schedule delays caused by absenteeism.

Supervisors were required to conduct meetings with their employees to explain the need for the policy and how it would be applied. Supervisors completed a meeting report form after the meeting and returned it to the HR department.

The no-fault policy has the potential of influencing employment termination by essentially increasing employee turnover, which could have created problems for some supervisors. Because of this, it was important to demonstrate to the management team that these programs were effective when administered properly. Also, senior management were interested in knowing the payoff for these types of initiatives; they needed to be convinced that the company was receiving an adequate return on investment.

Data Collection

Figure 1 shows the data collection plan for the absenteeism reduction solutions at Metro Transit Authority. The objectives are defined, and the data collection methods selected are typical for these types of programs. Absenteeism, the primary business data, is

Figure 1. Data collection plan.

Program: Absenteeism Reduction   **Responsibility:** Jack Phillips   **Date** January 15

Level	Broad Program Objective(s)	Measures	Data Collection Method/Instruments	Data Sources	Timing	Responsibilities
1	**REACTION/SATISFACTION** • Positive employee reaction to the no-fault policy	• Positive reaction from employees	• Feedback questionnaire	• Employees	• At the end of the employee meetings	• Supervisors
2	**LEARNING** • Employee understanding of the policy	• Score on posttest, at least 70	• True/false test	• Employees	• At the end of the employe meetings	• Supervisors
3	**APPLICATION/ IMPLEMENTATION** 1. Effective and consistent implementation and enforcement of the programs 2. Little or no adverse reaction from current employees regarding no-fault policy 3. Use the new screening process	1. Supervisors' response on program's influence 2. Employee complaints and union cooperation	1. and 2. Follow-up questionnaire to supervisors (two sample groups) 3. Sample review of interview and selection records	1. Supervisors 2. Company records	1. Following employee meetings, sample one group at three months and another group at six months 2. Three months and six months after implementation	• HR program coordinator

4	**BUSINESS IMPACT**				• HR program coordinator
	1. Reduce driver absenteeism a least 2% during first year	1. Absenteeism	1. Company records	1. Monitor monthly and analyze one year pre- and one-year post-implementation	
	2. Maintain present level of job satisfaction as new policy is implemented	2. Employee satisfaction	2. Supervisors	2. Three months and six months after employee meetings	
	3. Improve customer service and satisfaction with reduction in schedule delays	3. Delays impact on customer service	3. Dispatch records	3. Monthly	
		1. Monitor absenteeism			
		2. Follow-up questionnaire to supervisors			
		3. Monitor bus schedule delays			
5	**ROI** Target ROI ≥ 25%	Comments: _____ _____ _____ _____			

Source: Phillips, Jack J., Stone, Ron D., and Phillips, Patricia P. (2001). *The Human Resources Scorecard: Measuring the Return on Investment*. Boston: Butterworth-Heinemann.

monitored on a postprogram basis and compared with preprogram data. Table 1 shows the absenteeism rate for the years prior to, and after, implementing both the no-fault policy and the new selection process. A complete year of data was collected to show the full impact of both solutions to capture the delayed effect in influencing the absenteeism measure. In addition, bus schedule delays of more than five minutes caused by unexpected absenteeism were monitored and are reported in table 1.

Also, for implementation and business measures, a questionnaire was developed and administered to a sample of supervisors to determine the extent to which the programs were implemented and were perceived to be operating effectively. Input was sought regarding problems and issues, as well as success stories and changes in job satisfaction.

Learning measures were taken with a simple 10-item true/false test. To ensure that employees understood the policy, the test was administered by supervisors in meetings with employees. Scores were attached with the record of the meeting, along with the time, place, agenda, and a list of the attendees. A sample of test scores revealed an average value above the minimum acceptable level of 70.

Table 1. Absenteeism and bus delays before and after implementation.

	Unscheduled Absenteeism Percent of Scheduled Days Worked		Absenteeism Related Bus Delays Percent of All Delays	
	PRE	POST	PRE	POST
July	7.2	6.3	23.3	18.3
August	7.4	5.6	24.7	18.0
September	7.1	5.0	24.9	17.5
October	7.8	5.9	26.1	18.2
November	8.1	5.3	25.4	16.7
December	8.4	5.2	26.3	15.9
January	8.7	5.4	27.1	15.4
February	8.5	4.8	26.9	14.9
March	8.6	4.9	26.8	14.7
April	8.5	4.9	27.8	14.4
May	8.8	4.0	27.0	13.6
June	8.8	4.9	26.4	13.7
Three-month average	8.7%	4.8%	27.1%	13.9%

Reaction measures were taken with a simple questionnaire using an objective format. The questionnaire was distributed at the meetings to obtain reaction to the no-fault policy.

Figure 2 shows the return-on-investment (ROI) analysis plan for evaluating the absenteeism reduction initiatives. Major elements of the plan are discussed below.

Isolating the Effects of the Solutions

Several approaches were considered for the purpose of isolating the effects of the two solutions. Initially, a control group arrangement was considered, but was quickly discarded for three important reasons:

1. To purposely withhold the policy change for a group of employees could create contractual and morale problems for the individuals in the control group.

2. Because the new policy would be known to all employees, contamination would occur in the control group, at least temporarily, as employees learned about the "crackdown" on absenteeism. The policy would have the short-term effect of reducing absenteeism in those areas where it was not implemented.

3. Because of the operational problems and customer service issues associated with absenteeism, it was not desirable to withhold a needed solution just for experimental purposes.

Trendline analysis was initially feasible because only a small amount of variance was noticeable in the preprogram trend data. Because of the possibility of this option, in the planning stage, trendline analysis was considered as a method to estimate the impact of both absenteeism initiatives. However, because multiple influences on absenteeism later developed, such as a change in economic conditions, the trendline analysis was aborted.

Finally, as a backup strategy, estimations were taken directly from supervisors as they completed the follow-up questionnaire. Supervisors were asked to identify various factors that had influenced the absenteeism rate and to allocate percentages to each of the factors, including the new screening process and no-fault policy.

Converting Data to Monetary Values

Because the primary business measure was absenteeism, a monetary value had to be developed for the cost of an unexpected absence. The value could subsequently be used to calculate the total

Figure 2. ROI analysis plan.

Program: Absenteeism Reduction   **Responsibility:** Jack Phillips   **Date:** January 15

Data Items (Usually Level 4)	Methods for Isolating the Effects of the Program/Process	Methods of Converting Data to Monetary Values	Cost Categories	Intangible Benefits	Communication Targets for Final Report	Other Influences/Issues During Application	Comments
1. Absenteeism	1. Trendline analysis and supervisor estimates	1. Wages and benefits and standard values	**Screening Process** • Development • Interviewer preparation • Administration • Materials	• Sustain employee satisfaction • Improve employee morale • Improve customer satisfaction • Fewer disruptive bottlenecks in transportation grid • Ease of implementation by supervisors	• Senior management • Managers and supervisors • Union representatives • HR staff	• Concern about supervisors' consistent administration • Partner with union reps on how to communicate results of study to employees	
2. Employee Job Satisfaction	2. Supervisor estimates	N/A					
3. Bus Schedule Delays (Influence on Customer Satisfaction)	3. Management estimates	N/A	No-Fault Policy • Development • Implementation • Materials				

Source: Phillips, Jack J., Stone, Ron D., and Phillips, Patricia P. (2001). *The Human Resources Scorecard: Measuring the Return on Investment.* Boston: Butterworth-Heinemann.

cost of the absenteeism improvement. Although several approaches to determine the cost of absenteeism were possible, the analysis at MTA was based on the cost of replacement driver staffing.

Substitute drivers, as well as the regular drivers, were expected to work an average of 240 days per year, leaving 20 days for vacation, holidays, and sick days. The average wages for the substitute drivers is $33,500 per year and the employee benefits factor is 38 percent of payroll. When a regular driver is unexpectedly absent, he or she could charge the absence either to sick leave or vacation, thus substituting a planned paid day (vacation) for the unexpected absence.

The number of substitute drivers planned was a function of expected absenteeism. Consequently, the substitute driver staffing level did not always meet the exact level needed for a specific day's unscheduled absences. Because of the service problems that could develop as a result of understaffing, the company planned for an excessive number of substitute drivers for most days.

To minimize potential delays, all substitute drivers were required to report to work each day. Substitute drivers not used in driver seats essentially performed no productive work that could be counted as added value. During the previous year, overstaffing had occurred about 75 percent of the time for weekdays and nonholidays. That overstaffing represented 4,230 days of wasted time. During the weekends and holidays, which represent 114 days, overstaffing had occurred almost half of the time, representing a total of 570 wasted days.

On some days, there was actually a shortage of substitute drivers, which caused the buses to run late, and overtime had to be used to make the adjustment. During the previous year, there had been 65 instances in which a driver was unavailable, and it was estimated that in 45 of those situations, a regular driver was paid double time to fill in the schedule. In the other 15 situations, the bus route was cancelled.

A final, and very significant, cost of absenteeism was the cost of recruiting, training, maintaining, and supervising the substitute driver pool, beyond the actual salaries paid and benefits provided. These items include recruiting and employment, training and preparation, office space, administration and coordination, and supervision. This item was estimated at 25 percent of the actual annual pay. Here is how the total direct cost of absenteeism was developed from the above information.

Average daily cost of wages and benefits for a substitute driver:

$$\$33,500 \times 1.38 \div 240 = \$192.63$$

Approximate cost of overstaffing, weekdays:

$$192.63 \times 4{,}230 = \$814{,}800$$

Approximate cost of overstaffing, weekends and holidays:

$$192.63 \times 570 = \$109{,}800$$

Approximate cost of understaffing, overtime (only one salary is used for double-time pay):

$$192.63 \times 45 = \$8{,}670$$

Approximate cost of recruiting, training, maintaining, and supervising pool of drivers:

$$33{,}500 \times 231 \times 0.25 = \$1{,}934{,}600$$

Costs for Solutions

The cost for the new screening process contains four components: development, interviewer preparation, administrative time, and materials.

The total development cost, including pilot testing, was $20,000. An additional $5,000 was charged for preparing the interviewers to administer the test. The materials and time were variable costs, depending on the number of drivers employed. About 400 drivers were hired each year. For each new driver hired, an average of three candidates are interviewed. Thus, 1,200 interviews are conducted each year, with an average time of 30 minutes each. The average hourly wage for the interviewers is $14.50 per hour. The materials are $2 per test. Table 2 shows the cost of the screening process.

Table 2. Cost of screening process.

Development cost	$20,000
Interviewer preparation	$5,000
Administrative time (1,200 × 1/2 × $14.50)	$8,700
Materials (1,200 @ $2.00)	$2,400
TOTAL	$36,100

The cost for the no-fault policy included development and implementation. The development cost was incurred internally and was estimated to be $11,000, representing the time of internal specialists. The material distributed to employees accounted for another $3,800. The costs of meetings with all supervisors and with employees were estimated at $16,500. The cost for routine administration was not included because the alternative to continue to administer the no-fault policy is to administer a progressive discipline process, and the two should take about the same amount of time. Table 3 shows the cost of the no-fault policy.

Results: Reaction, Learning, and Application

Employees expressed some concern about the new policy, but the overall reaction to the change was favorable. They perceived the new policy to be fair and equitable. In addition, employees scored an average of 78 on the true/false test about the no-fault policy. A score of 70 on the end-of-meeting test was considered acceptable.

A follow-up questionnaire, administered anonymously to a sample of supervisors, indicated that the policy had been implemented in each area and had been applied consistently. Although supervisors reported some initial resistance from the habitual absenteeism violators, the majority of employees perceived the policy to be effective and fair. The supervisors also reported that the new policy took less time to administer than the previously used progressive discipline approach.

A review of HR records indicated that 95 percent of the supervisors conducted the meeting with employees and completed a meeting report form. In addition, a review of a sample of interviews and selection records indicated that the new screening process was used in every case.

Business Impact

Absenteeism dramatically declined after implementing both processes, yielding an average absenteeism rate of 4.6 percent for the

Table 3. Cost of no-fault policy.

Development cost		$11,000
Materials		$3,800
Meeting time		$16,500
	TOTAL	$31,300

last three months of the evaluation period, compared with the pre-program rate of 8.7 percent for the same period one year earlier. In the MTA situation, a reduction in absenteeism generates a cost savings only if the substitute driver pool was reduced. Because the pool staffing was directly linked to absenteeism, a significant reduction was realized. Table 4 shows the cost savings realized, using the approach shown earlier in this case.

In addition, on the questionnaires, supervisors estimated and allocated percentages for the contribution of each factor to absenteeism reduction. The results are presented in table 5.

The bus schedule delays caused by absenteeism declined from an average of 27.1 percent for the three months prior to the initiatives to 13.9 percent for the last three months of the evaluation period.

In addition, several intangible measures were identified, including increased morale, improved customer service, and fewer bottlenecks in the entire system.

Table 4. Cost of absenteeism comparisons.

Cost Item	One Year Prior to Initiatives	One Year After Initiatives
Cost of overstaffing, weekdays	$814,000	$602,400
Cost of overstaffing, weekends and holidays	$109,800	$51,500
Cost of understaffing	$8,670	$4,340
Cost of recruiting, training, and maintaining driver pool	$1,934,600	$1,287,750
Total cost of absenteeism	$2,867,070	$1,945,990

Table 5. Supervisor estimates to isolate the effects of the solutions.

Factor	Contribution Percentage	Confidence Percentage
No-fault policy	67%	84%
Screening	22%	71%
Economic conditions	11%	65%
Other	1%	90%

Monetary Benefits

Because the total cost of absenteeism for drivers is known on a before-and-after basis (as shown in table 4), the total savings can be developed as follows:

Preprogram $2,867,070
Postprogram $1,945,990
Savings $921,080

The contribution of the no-fault policy:

$$\$921,080 \times 67\% \times 84\% = \$518,383 = \$518,000$$

The contribution of the new screening process:

$$\$921,080 \times 22\% \times 71\% = \$143,873 = \$144,000$$

Total first year benefit = $518,000 + $144,000 = $662,000

Costs

The total costs for both solutions (as shown in tables 2 and 3) are as follows:

$$\text{Total costs} = \$36,100 + \$31,300 = \$67,400$$

ROI Calculation

The benefits-cost ratio (BCR) and ROI are calculated as follows:

$$BCR = \frac{\$662,000}{\$67,400} = 9.82$$

$$ROI(\%) = \frac{\$662,000 - \$67,400}{\$67,400} = 882\%$$

Questions for Discussion

1. What are feasible ways to isolate the effects of the solutions?
2. Can the cost of absenteeism be developed for MTA? Explain.
3. Are the costs of the solutions adequate? Explain.
4. Critique the actual monetary benefits of the reduction in absenteeism.
5. Is this study methodology credible? Explain.
6. Is the ROI value realistic? Explain.
7. How should the results be communicated to various groups?

The Authors

Jack J. Phillips, a renowned expert of measurement and evaluation, is with the Jack Phillips Center for Research, a division of the Franklin Covey Company. Phillips developed and pioneered the use of the ROI process and has provided consulting services to some of the world's largest organizations. He is the author or editor of more than 30 books—12 focused on measurement and evaluation—and more than 100 articles. He can be reached at Serieseditor@aol.com.

Ron D. Stone is practice leader for the Jack Phillips Center for Research, a division of Franklin Covey. He directs the company's consulting practice in measurement and accountability and consults with clients around the globe. He has published numerous articles on ROI and has made numerous contributions to perfecting the ROI process.

About IPMA

ipma

The International Personnel Management Association (IPMA) was established in January 1973, through the consolidation of the Public Personnel Association, founded in Chicago in 1906, and the Society for Personnel Administration Foundation, founded in Washington, D.C., in 1937. IPMA is a nonprofit organization representing the interests of agencies and individuals in public sector human resources. Members are located among all levels of government—federal, state, local—across the United States and overseas. The majority of IPMA members are key executives, managers, or supervisors, who are responsible for a variety of human resource functions.

The purposes and objectives of IPMA are:

- to promote excellence in the public sector through ongoing development of professional and ethical standards and personal and career development
- to enhance the image of public sector human resource professionals by recognizing their contributions to the public service
- to foster fairness and equity by promoting application of merit principles and equal opportunity for all
- to encourage research and development in public sector human resource management
- to promote communication and sharing of information among all human resources professionals.

The association seeks to further its purposes and objectives through its many programs and projects.

International Personnel Management Association
1617 Duke Street
Alexandria, VA 22314
phone: 703.549.7100; fax: 703.684.0948
Visit our Website at: www.ipma-hr.org

ASTD PRESS

Delivering Training and Performance Knowledge
You Will Use Today and Lead With Tomorrow

- Training Basics
- Evaluation and Return-on-Investment (ROI)
- E-Learning
- Instructional Systems Development (ISD)
- Leadership
- Career Development

ASTD Press is an internationally renowned source of insightful and practical information on workplace learning and performance topics, including training basics, evaluation and return-on-investment (ROI), instructional systems development (ISD), e-learning, leadership, and career development. You can trust that the books ASTD Press acquires, develops, edits, designs, and publishes meet the highest standards and that they reflect the most current industry practices. In addition, ASTD Press books are bottom-line oriented and geared toward immediate problem-solving application in the field.

Ordering Information: Purchase books published by ASTD Press by visiting our Website at store.astd.org or by calling 800.628.2783 or 703.683.8100.

About the Editor

Patricia Pulliam Phillips is chairman and CEO of the Chelsea Group, a research and consulting company focused on accountability issues in training, HR, and performance improvement. Phillips conducts research on accountability issues and works with clients to build accountability systems and processes in their organizations. She has helped organizations implement the return-on-investment (ROI) process, developed by Jack J. Phillips, in countries around the world including South Africa, Singapore, Japan, New Zealand, Australia, Italy, Turkey, France, Germany, Canada, and the United States. She has been involved in hundreds of ROI impact studies in a variety of industries.

Phillips has more than 13 years of experience in the electrical utility industry. As manager of a market planning and research organization, she was responsible for the development of marketing programs for residential, commercial, and industrial customers. These programs included such initiatives as the residential load control program, the energy services program, and the district sales initiative. In her capacity as manager of market planning and research, Phillips also played an integral role in establishing Marketing University, a learning environment that supported the needs of new sales and marketing representatives.

Phillips has a master's of arts degree in public and private management from Birmingham-Southern College. She is certified in ROI evaluation and serves as co-author on the subject in publications including *Corporate University Review; The Journal of Lending and Credit Risk Management; Training Journal; What Smart Trainers Know,* Loraine L. Ukens, editor (Jossey-Bass/Pfeiffer, 2001); and *Evaluating Training Programs,* 2d edition, by Donald L. Kirkpatrick (Berrett-Koehler Publishers, 1998). Phillips has authored and co-authored several issues of the American Society for Training & Development *Info-line* series including *Mastering ROI* (1998) and *ROI on a Shoestring* (2001). She served as issue editor for the ASTD *In Action* casebook, *Measuring Return on Investment,* volume 3 (2001), and *Measuring Intellectual Capital* (2002). Phillips is co-author of *The Human Resources Scorecard: Measuring Return on Investment* (Butterworth-Heinemann, 2001), and author of *The Bottomline on ROI* (Center for Effective Performance, 2002). Phillips may be reached at thechelseagroup@aol.com.

About the Series Editor

Jack J. Phillips is a world-renowned expert on measurement and evaluation and developer of the ROI process, a revolutionary process that provides bottom-line figures and accountability for all types of training, performance improvement, human resources, and technology programs. He is the author or editor of more than 30 books—12 focused on measurement and evaluation—and more than 100 articles.

His expertise in measurement and evaluation is based on more than 27 years of corporate experience in five industries (aerospace, textiles, metals, construction materials, and banking). Phillips has served as training and development manager at two *Fortune* 500 firms, senior HR officer at two firms, president of a regional federal savings bank, and management professor at a major state university.

In 1992, Phillips founded Performance Resources Organization (PRO), an international consulting firm that provides comprehensive assessment, measurement, and evaluation services for organizations. In 1999, PRO was acquired by the Franklin Covey Company and is now known as the Jack Phillips Center for Research. Today the center is an independent leading provider of measurement and evaluation services to the global business community. Phillips consults with clients in manufacturing, service, and government organizations in the United States, Canada, Sweden, England, Belgium, Germany, Italy, Holland, South Africa, Mexico, Venezuela, Malaysia, Indonesia, Hong Kong, Australia, New Zealand, and Singapore. He leads the Phillips Center in research and publishing efforts that support the knowledge and development of assessment, measurement, and evaluation.

Books most recently written by Phillips include *The Human Resources Scorecard: Measuring the Return on Investment* (Boston: Butterworth-Heinemann, 2001); *The Consultant's Scorecard* (New York: McGraw-Hill, 2000); *HRD Trends Worldwide: Shared Solutions to Compete in a Global Economy* (Boston: Butterworth-Heinemann, 1999); *Return on Investment in Training and Performance Improvement Programs* (Boston: Butterworth-Heinemann, 1997); *Handbook of Training Evaluation and Measurement Methods*, 3rd edition (Boston: Butterworth-Heinemann, 1997); and

Accountability in Human Resource Management (Boston: Butterworth-Heinemann, 1996).

Phillips has undergraduate degrees in electrical engineering, physics, and mathematics from Southern Polytechnic State University and Oglethorpe University, a master's degree in decision sciences from Georgia State University, and a Ph.D. in human resource management from the University of Alabama. In 1987 he won the Yoder-Heneman Personnel Creative Application Award from the Society for Human Resource Management.

Phillips can be reached at the Jack Phillips Center for Research, P.O. Box 380637, Birmingham, AL 35238-0637; phone: 205.678.8038; fax: 205.678.0177; email: serieseditor@aol.com.

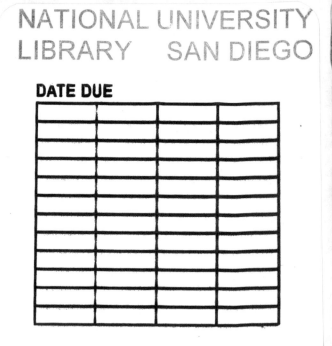